MANCHESTER UNITED ALMANAC

By:
Dean Hayes

Published by:
Yore Publications
12 The Furrows, Harefield,
Middx. UB9 6AT

© Dean Hayes

....

All rights reserved
No part of this publication may be reproduced or copied in any manner
without the prior permission in writing of the copyright holders

British Library Cataloguing-in-Publication Data
A catalogue record for this book
is available from the British Library

ISBN 1 874427 62 3

YORE PUBLICATIONS specialise in football books, normally of an historic nature...
Club histories, Who's Who books, etc. plus non-League football.
Three free Newsletters are issued per year, for your first copy,
please send a S.A.E. to:
Yore Publications, 12 The Furrows, Harefield, Middx. UB9 6AT

Printed and bound by Bookcraft, Midsomer Norton, Bath.

Author's Acknowledgements:

The Author wishes to thank the following for their help in producing this book. The members of staff at Manchester Central Library and the Lancashire Evening Post. Thanks also to Andrew Hayes and Cyril Walker. Also I would like to give special thanks to my wife Elaine who devoted time and effort in help with copy-reading, and to Dave Twydell (of Yore Publications) for publishing the first of which I hope will become a series of Football Club Almanacs.

Photographic Acknowledgements:

The majority of the modern Photographs have been supplied by the Lancashire Evening Post, for which permission to use same is greatly appreciated, plus items from the Author's personal collection. Cigarette cards have been kindly supplied by Peter Stafford. Apologies are unreservedly offered should copyright have inadvertently been infringed on any illustration(s).

The Author:

Dean Hayes is an experienced freelance sports writer specialising in football and cricket. Educated at Hayward Grammar School, Bolton, and West Midlands College, Walsall, where he graduated in Physical Education. He was a Primary School Headteacher until taking up writing full-time three years ago.

Having played football in the Lancashire Amateur League, he now concentrates solely on playing the Summer sport, and in 1996 took his 2,000th wicket in League cricket. This is Dean's second book published by Yore Publications, the first - in 1996 - was *'The Latics - The Official History of Wigan Athletic F.C.'*

YORE PUBLICATIONS

We specialise in books normally of an historic nature, especially fully detailed and well illustrated Football League club histories (over twenty to date). Also those with a diverse appeal, such as the *'Rejected F.C.'* series (compendium histories of the former Football League and Scottish League clubs, each in three volumes),, *'The Little Red Book of Chinese Football'* (A history of football in the area, plus the Author's football travels in China and Hong Kong), plus non-League football, notably the *'Gone But Not Forgotten'* series (each booklet issued every six months, covering the histories of former grounds and clubs).

Of particular interest to Manchester United followers, are *'Theatre of Dreams - The History of Old Trafford'* (R.R.P. £7-95 plus £1-00 postage), and *'Tommy Taylor of Manchester United and Barnsley'* (R.R.P. £6-95 plus £1-00 postage).

We publish a free newsletter three times per year. For your first copy please send a S.A.E. to:

YORE PUBLICATIONS, 12 The Furrows, Harefield, Middlesex, UB9 6AT

CONTENTS

	Page:
JANUARY	4
FEBRUARY	17
MARCH	30
APRIL	42
MAY	55
JUNE	66
JULY	74
AUGUST	82
SEPTEMBER	94
OCTOBER	107
NOVEMBER	120
DECEMBER	131
YEAR INDEX	142
CLUB INDEX	144

JANUARY

1

1896 Joe Cassidy who top scored for the Reds in this season with 16 goals in 19 games, scored all three goals when Grimsby Town were beaten 3-2.

1907 Jimmy Bannister, Herbert Burgess, Billy Meredith and Sandy Turnbull all made their debuts for Manchester United after being transferred from Manchester City. Each had been found guilty of offences committed while playing for the Maine Road club in 1906 and their suspensions had just expired. A crowd of 40,000 crammed into the Clayton ground for the visit of Aston Villa. It was Billy Meredith who took the ball almost to the right-hand corner flag, centred to the unmarked Sandy Turnbull and Villa were beaten 1-0.

1927 United got their biggest win of the season when they beat Sheffield United 5-0. Frank McPherson who played football in all four divisions of the Football League scored two of the goals.

1948 Burnley are beaten 5-0 with Jack Rowley netting a hat-trick. United finish the season as runners-up in the First Division and Rowley tops the scoring charts with 23 goals in 39 appearances.

1996 The Reds lose 4-1 to Tottenham Hotspur at White Hart Lane, the first time they had conceded four goals in a Premier League game. United were hit by a warm-up injury to Peter Schmeichel and with a makeshift back-four, including Frenchman William Prunier, who could speak no English, they could not cope with the pressure that Spurs applied. The writing was on the wall after just five minutes when Teddy Sheringham headed against a post and five minutes later, Armstrong's shot also hit the woodwork with Schmeichel beaten.

Sheringham eventually gave Spurs the lead they deserved but within seconds, United were level through Andy Cole. However, right on the stroke of half-time, Sol Campbell smashed home a loose ball from ten yards out. Pilkington replaced the injured Schmeichel but was picking the ball out of the net after just three minutes of the second half when Armstrong headed home Rosenthal's cross. The former Crystal Palace man scored his second and Spurs' fourth in the 66th minute to complete the scoring.

2

1905 United beat Bradford City 7-0 at home with Arkesden and Roberts scoring two goals apiece. This was the Reds last home victory in a sequence of 14 successive wins which saw them triumph 4-2 at Bolton in their following match before drawing 1-1 at Bristol City.

1915 Enoch West scores United's goal in a 1-1 draw at Manchester City in front of the season's biggest crowd of 30,000.

1933 Plymouth Argyle are beaten 4-0 in front of United's biggest crowd of the season, 30,257. Two of their goals are scored by Bill Ridding who went on to manage Bolton Wanderers from 1950 to 1968.

1954 When the Reds travelled to St James' Park, a holiday crowd of 55,780, including a large contingent of United's long-distance supporters saw United win 2-1. Their winning goal came from Bill Foulkes who shot home from fully 45 yards!

1960 The Reds lost 7-3 at St James' Park against a rampant Newcastle United side. Albert Quixall (2) and Alex Dawson scored for United as 57,200 Geordie fans roared their team on.

- January -

3 **1905** Manchester United beat Bolton Wanderers 4-2 at Burnden Park to win their 14th consecutive League game in the Second Division. This is an all-time League record, though it was later emulated by both Bristol City and Preston North End. Yet strangely, United failed to win promotion at the end of the season.

1974 A programme was printed for an FA Cup replay between Manchester United and Plymouth Argyle, yet no replay was necessary since the Reds had won the third round tie at Old Trafford 1-0 with a goal by Lou Macari. The Home Park club had printed the programme in advance as a precaution against power cuts during the three-day week.

1987 Liam O'Brien is sent off after only 85 seconds in United's 1-1 draw at Southampton. This remains the quickest-ever dismissal in the top flight.

4 **1951** Birth of Paddy Roche. He joined the Reds from League of Ireland club Shelbourne for £15,000 in October 1973, making his League debut at Oxford United in February 1975. He won seven caps for the Republic of Ireland, conceding six goals on his debut against Austria in 1971. Though he seemed to be an eternal reserve for United, first under Alex Stepney and later Gary Bailey, he did manage to appear in 53 first team games for the club before leaving to join Brentford in the summer of 1982. He made 84 appearances for the Bees before ending his career with Halifax Town.

1994 United were three goals up within the first 25 minutes of their match against Liverpool at Anfield, through Bruce, Giggs and Irwin but had to settle for a point as Liverpool fought back to draw 3-3.

5 **1932** Birth of Bill Foulkes. He joined United as an amateur from Whiston Boys' Club in St Helens in 1949, turning professional in August 1951 for a £10 signing-on fee. A strong and resilient defender, he started off at full-back, making his debut in a 2-1 win at Liverpool in December 1952. This was the position he played when he won his one and only England cap against Northern Ireland in Belfast on 2 October 1954, England winning 2-0. After surviving the Munich air crash, the St Helens-born defender was successfully converted to centre-half, a position he occupied for over ten years. He won League Championship medals in 1956, 1957, 1965 and 1967, played in three FA Cup Finals, including United's 1963 victory and was a member of the club's 1968 European Cup-winning team, having scored one of United's goals in the 3-3 draw with Real Madrid that took them into the final. Bill Foulkes played the last of his 682 first team games for the Reds 21 years after joining the club, retiring to become youth team coach before later being promoted to reserve team coach. He then went o America to coach both Chicago Sting and Tulsa Roughnecks before being appointed manager-coach of Norwegian club Lillestrom.

6 **1900** Newton Heath lost their first League fixture of the 20th century, 2-1 against Bolton Wanderers. Parkinson scored for the Heathens but Frank Barratt conceded a soft goal late in the game.

1940 Birth of Johnny Giles. Although best remembered for his days with Leeds United, for whom he played in 565 first team games, he began his League career with Manchester United. Born in Dublin, he played his early football with Dublin City, Stella Maris and Home Farm before signing for United on his 17th birthday.

He made his debut for the Reds in the 5-1 home defeat by Tottenham Hotspur in September 1959. He won an FA Cup winners' medal for United in 1963, playing at outside-right in the team that beat Leicester City 3-1. It was his last game for the club, for in August of that year, he was sold to Leeds United for £35,000. At Elland Road, he won a Second Division title medal in 1964, League Championship medals in 1969 and 1974, an FA Cup winners' medal in 1972, a League Cup winners' tankard in 1968 and Fairs Cup winners' medals in 1968 and 1971. His last match for Leeds was in the 1975 European Cup Final when they lost to Bayern Munich. He then joined West Bromwich Albion as player-manager, leading them to promotion to the First Division in his first season. After Albion, he won a Football Association of Ireland Cup winners' medal with Shamrock Rovers before playing in the NASL (USA). Giles collected a record 60 Republic of Ireland caps and was their player-manager from 1973 to 1980 before returning to the Hawthorns for a second spell as Albion manager.

1996 Denis Law was overtaken by Ian Rush as the most prolific FA Cup goalscorer since the war. Law, in second place, scored 41 goals. However, Law did net another six goals in one FA Cup match for Manchester City against Luton Town in 1961 but since the game was abandoned, these goals do not count towards his official total.

7 **1893** When Manchester United were still known as Newton Heath, they arrived at Stoke for a First Division match without goalkeeper Jack Warner who had missed the train. Three different players: Stewart, Fitzsimmons and Clements all had a turn in goal. United scored first through Coupar but lost 7-1.

1978 Brian Greenhoff was dismissed during United's third round FA Cup tie at Brunton Park. The Reds still manage to draw 1-1 with Carlisle United before going on to win the replay at Old Trafford 4-2.

8 **1916** Travis scores all four goals for Manchester United but the Reds lose 7-4 against Burnley at Turf Moor in the Lancashire Section (Principal Tournament).

1949 United play their first FA Cup tie at Old Trafford for ten years when they beat Bournemouth 6-0 with goals from Burke (2) Rowley (2) Pearson and Mitten. Their last FA Cup tie at Old Trafford had been a third round replay on 11 January 1939 when West Bromwich Albion had beaten the Reds 5-1.

9 **1902** Newton Heath were in serious trouble, owing money left, right and centre. One of its creditors, William Healey, who also happened to be the president of the club appeared before the Ashton-under-Lyne County Court where an application was made for the compulsory winding up of the Newton Heath Football Club Company Limited. The club were unable to pay their debts and the judge had little option but to initiate bankruptcy proceedings. The Football League and the official receiver closed the ground and postponed the Heathens next fixture at home to Middlesbrough. Fortunately, money began to come in, although for some months the club played from week to week not knowing whether they would survive. It was largely thanks to full-back Harry Stafford that the club did continue, sacrificing his training in order to devote his time to keeping the club going.

- January -

1954 Four goals in the first seven minutes - that was the sensational start to Manchester United's third round FA Cup tie at Turf Moor. United were two down after five minutes but two goals in the space of two minutes by Viollet and Blanchflower brought them level. Shannon hit his second and Burnley's third after 20 minutes and though Tommy Taylor scored a third goal for the Reds, they went down 5-3.

1994 It was a dazzling piece of play which saw Mark Hughes win United's third round FA Cup tie 1-0 at Bramall Lane. It came from a glorious passing movement which flowed from full-back Paul Parker through Cantona, Ince, Hughes, Ince again and then back to Hughes for the striker to score his 12th goal of the season. The Welsh international then managed to take the gloss off his game by losing his temper in the closing stages and blatantly kicking an opponent, after ignoring a great deal of provocation throughout the match.

10

1931 A Tom Reid hat-trick gives United a 3-3 draw at Stoke City in the third round of the FA Cup. The tie goes to three matches before the Reds win 4-2 at Anfield.

1948 Manchester United beat Aston Villa 6-4 at Villa Park in a memorable third round FA Cup tie. A goal down after 13 seconds, United led 5-1 at half-time. But in the second half Villa pulled back to 5-4 before Stan Pearson scored his second and United's sixth.

1954 Birth of John Gidman. An England right-back at Youth, Under 23 and full level, he joined Liverpool after leaving school but failed to impress and signed for Aston Villa. An important member of Villa's youth team, he later played a vital role in the club's promotion from the Second Division in 1974-75. He made 197 League appearances for Villa, winning a League Cup winners' tankard in 1977, the year he won his only England cap, against Luxembourg. In October 1979 he transferred to Everton for £600,000. He had two seasons at Goodison Park, playing in 64 League games before joining United in the deal which saw Mickey Thomas go to Everton in the summer of 1981. Gidman soon settled into the United defence but after his first season, a series of niggling injuries reduced his appearances. He bounced back in 1984-85 ending the season with an FA Cup winners' medal. He later moved to rivals Manchester City and after leaving to play a few games for Stoke City, he became assistant-manager at Darlington.

1987 A goal from Norman Whiteside is enough to give United victory over their neighbours and rivals Manchester City in the third round of the FA Cup in front of an Old Trafford crowd of 49,082.

1995 Manchester United manager Alex Ferguson brings off a sensational coup, signing striker Andy Cole from rivals Newcastle United for a British record fee of £7 million - £6 million plus Northern Ireland international winger Keith Gillespie.

11

1904 United's most protracted FA Cup tie against Small Heath (later Birmingham City) ends with a 3-1 win for the Reds after three replays and seven hours of football.

1919 Birth of Stan Pearson. He made his United debut in 1937-38 when the Reds won promotion to the First Division, but it wasn't until after the Second World War that he began to make an impression on the football scene, linking well with Jack Rowley. A consistent goalscorer, he hit a superb hat-trick to help defeat Derby County in the FA Cup semi-final of 1948 and followed his Cup winners' medal that year with a League Championship one in 1951-52, when he scored 22 goals in 41 games.

- January -

He won eight full England caps, represented the Football League and in 345 first team games for United, scored 149 goals. In 1954, he ended his 17 year association with the club, moving to Bury, where he scored 56 goals in 122 League outings before he ended his playing career with Chester, whom he later managed.

1957 Birth of Bryan Robson. He became Britain's costliest footballer when he left West Bromwich Albion for Manchester United in October 1981. The deal included Albion's Remi Moses but the price for Robson's signature alone was £1.5 million. During the 1976-77 season, he suffered from a broken leg three times but recovered to help the Baggies into European football when they qualified for the UEFA Cup. Capped by England at Youth, Under-21 and 'B' levels, Robson won the first of his 90 full caps against the Republic of Ireland at Wembley in 1980. Captain of both Manchester United and England, he led the Reds to three FA Cup final victories and was the scorer of two goals in their 4-0 replay win over Brighton in 1983. He skippered England in the 1982 and 1986 World Cups, although on both occasions his personal involvement was interrupted by injury and his opening goal after just 27 seconds in England's first game of the 1982 World Cup against France is still the fastest goal ever scored in the tournament. He won a League Championship medal in 1992-93 and in 1993-94 won a Premier League winners' medal as United did the 'double'. In May 1994, Robson joined Middlesbrough as player-manager and in his first season on Teesside led the club to the First Division championship. After spending heavily on bringing Juninho and Ravenelli to the Riverside Stadium, 'Boro won through to two Wembley finals but lost their place in the Premiership.

12 **1946** Playing in the Football League North, United beat Grimsby Town 5-0 with Jack Rowley scoring one of his 20 hat-tricks in United colours.

1955 Jack Rowley (again) scored the last of his 208 League and Cup goals for United in the 4-1 FA Cup win over Reading at Old Trafford. His first goal for the Reds came some 17 years and 39 days earlier, and thus is the player with the longest goalscoring span.

1957 A crowd of 44,911 witnessed the Reds' demolition of Newcastle United 6-1. David Pegg, Billy Whealan and Dennis Viollet scored two goals apiece as United ended the season as League champions.

13 **1906** United beat Staple Hill 7-2 in the first round of the FA Cup in front of distinguished politicians Winston Churchill and J.R.Clynes.

1973 Tony Dunne who had come on as substitute for Brian Kidd was given his marching orders in United's third round FA Cup tie at Wolverhampton Wanderers. Goalkeeper Alex Stepney made some brilliant saves and though the ten men put up a brave fight, they went out of the competition 1-0.

1996 Gary and Phil Neville are both booked in United's goalless draw at home to Aston Villa, making them the first pair of brothers to be cautioned in the same game playing for United.

14 **1928** United beat Brentford 7-1 in the third round of the FA Cup with four of the goals scored by James Hanson.

- January -

1954 Johnny Aston, a former Marine Commando was granted a second benefit. He was originally a forward or wing-half but did not make a success in either role, only coming into his own when tried as an emergency full-back at Grimsby Town on 28 December 1946. He went on to play in 282 League and Cup games for United.

1958 The Yugoslav side Red Star Belgrade came to Old Trafford to play United in the quarter-finals of the European Cup. United had just drawn 1-1 at Elland Road against a Leeds United side they had beaten 3-0 earlier in the season. United won 2-1 with goals from Bobby Charlton and Eddie Colman.

1961 United beat Tottenham Hotspur 2-0 at Old Trafford - the only occasion that the famous Spurs 'double' side failed to score all season. Alex Dawson replaced the injured Harry Gregg in goal and the Irish international 'keeper moved into the forward line. It was Gregg who passed the ball to Mark Pearson to score United's second goal.

1969 Sir Matt Busby announced his resignation at the end of the season as team manager of Manchester United and his change of role to that of general manager.

15

1972 A third round FA Cup tie seemed to end a fortnight of controversy at Old Trafford and sink Southampton's Cup hopes that season. Frank O'Farrell the United manager had dropped George Best from the previous week's League match for missing training. Against Southampton however, Best put on a dazzling performance, culminating in a selfless dummy that led to the equalising goal that forced a replay. Two months earlier, Best had scored a hat-trick against Southampton in a League match.

1975 Lou Macari scored both United's goals as they drew the first leg of the League Cup semi-final at Old Trafford against Norwich City in front of a 58,010 crowd. However, despite a lot of pressure in the second leg at Carrow Road a week later, it was the Canaries who scored the only goal of the game to go through to the final 3-2 on aggregate.

16

1943 Manchester United beat Blackpool 5-3 in the Football League North (Second Championship) with Buchan grabbing a hat-trick.

1954 Jimmy Berry scored United's goal in the 1-1 draw with rivals Manchester City at Old Trafford.

1957 United travelled to Spain to play Athletico Bilbao in the first leg of the European Cup quarter-final. Despite goals from Taylor, Viollet and Whealan, the Reds went down 5-3. However, three weeks later, United win the second leg at Old Trafford 3-0 to reach the semi-finals 6-5 on aggregate.

1996 United, after having escaped with a 2-2 draw in the first meeting with Sunderland at Old Trafford, travel to Roker Park where they have never won a cup-tie for this third round FA Cup replay. Goals from Paul Scholes and Andy Cole give United their first win at Roker in the competition and leaves the Wearsiders still to beat the Reds in any cup competition after twelve attempts.

17

1921 Birth of Charlie Mitten. One of the stars of Manchester United's 1948 FA Cup final win over Blackpool, Charlie Mitten was the only member of the Reds' forward line never to win a full international cap, though he did play in a Victory International against Scotland in aid of the Bolton Disaster Fund.

9

- January -

On 8 March 1950, he scored a hat-trick of penalties in a 7-0 win over Aston Villa, but at the end of the season, after a run of 113 consecutive League and Cup games for United, he was one of several players tempted to Colombian football. A year later he was back in England, but United immediately transferred him and he joined Fulham. Four years later he joined Mansfield Town where he ended his League career.

1927 United lose the third round FA Cup match against Reading after the third game against the Elm Park side. The first match saw United draw 1-1 at Reading and then held at home 2-2 after extra-time. McPherson scored for United in the second replay but The Royals won this tie at Villa Park 2-1.

1945 Birth of Ian Storey-Moore. The only professional footballer with a double-barrelled name to play for England, he was eventually forced to leave the game following an ankle injury that he aggravated in United's gymnasium. He started his career with Nottingham Forest, scoring 105 goals in 236 League matches in his ten years at the City Ground. The circumstances in which he joined United in March 1972 were a little controversial. Derby County's then assistant-manager Peter Taylor, believed that Storey-Moore was their player and introduced him to the crowd before a League match at the Baseball Ground. Though the Forest winger had signed the forms, the Forest secretary had not because he was concerned Storey-Moore would follow Terry Hennessey in doing well with their neighbours and rivals. Forest refused to let him go to Derby and instead sold him to United for £ 200,000. He scored on his United debut in a 2-0 win over Huddersfield Town and played in 43 first team games, scoring 12 goals before injury halted his career in 1974.

1948 Because of war damage to the Old Trafford ground, United's League game against Arsenal was played at Maine Road. A crowd of 81,962, the biggest ever League crowd saw Jack Rowley score United's goal in a 1-1 draw.

18

1902 During the club's last season under the title of Newton Heath, a Division Two fixture was due to be undertaken away to Bristol City, but before railway tickets could be purchased, a house-to-house collection had to be made to raise the necessary cash. During the course of the subsequent match, Caesar Augustus Llewllyn Jenkins, a Newton Heath stalwart was injured and as he was about to leave the field, a doctor called out; *'Go back Caesar and I'll stand you a fish and chips supper.'* Jenkins returned and duly received his sustenance despite a 4-0 defeat!

1958 United beat near neighbours Bolton Wanderers 7-2 at Old Trafford with Bobby Charlton hitting a hat-trick. The Reds other scorers were Viollet (2) Edwards and Scanlon.

1969 Denis Law hit a hat-trick in United's 4-1 victory over Sunderland at Old Trafford. The Reds' other scorer was George Best.

19

1957 When Wrexham were about to meet Manchester United in a fourth round FA Cup tie, a crowd of 18,069 turned up for a reserve match against Winsford United in the Cheshire League because tickets were available for the cup game. The match at the Racecourse Ground was watched by 34,445 spectators who saw United win 5-0.

1996 The most expensive transfer between Manchester United and Manchester City took place when City sold Tony Coton to United for £500,000. However, he failed to make a start in the first team and in July of the following year he joined Sunderland for £350,000.

- *January* -

20 **1900** Gillespie netted a hat-trick in the Reds 4-1 victory over Burton Swifts in a Second Division match.

1965 United played Everton at Old Trafford in the first leg of the third round Inter-Cities Fairs Cup tie. They drew 1-1 with John Connelly scoring for the Reds in front of a 50,000 crowd.

1973 The Manchester United team that drew 2-2 at home to West Ham United contained eight past and future Scottish internationals - Alex Forsyth, George Graham, Martin Buchan, Jim Holton, Denis Law, Ted MacDougall, Lou Macari and Willie Morgan. The team was managed by former Scottish boss, Tommy Docherty.

1994 Old Trafford was turned into a shrine when Sir Matt Busby died, aged 84. Supporters came from far and wide to pay silent tribute to the man who had made Old Trafford their theatre of dreams. When the first fan arrived well before dawn to lay a single bunch of flowers beneath the Munich clock memorial, it sparked a day of mourning which ended with the roped off area being a carpet of red and white as hundreds of admirers of the great man of English football lay their scarves and flowers in his memory.

21 **1975** Birth of Nicky Butt. He helped the club lift the FA Youth Cup in 1991-92 beating Crystal Palace 6-3 over two legs, scoring twice in the first leg victory at Selhurst Park. He made his first team debut for the Reds as a substitute in the 3-0 win over Oldham Athletic in November 1992. Butt was a member of the England Under-19 team that performed so well in the World Cup in Australia.

His first full start for United came in the 4-2 win over IFK Gothenburg in the European Cup competition of 1994-95, whilst his first full game in the Premier League also saw the Reds win 4-2, this time against Blackburn Rovers. Following Paul Ince's departure to Inter Milan, Nicky Butt progressed in leaps and bounds to become one of the most constructive players in the top flight. A regular in the England Under-21 side, Butt won League Championship and FA Cup winners' medals.

1977 Birth of Phil Neville. A talented all-round sportsman, he played both cricket and football for England Schoolboys and though offered a contract with Lancashire, he opted for the other Old Trafford and Manchester United. In 1994-95 he captained the Reds to the FA Youth Cup Final and won the first of six England Under-21 caps after making his first team debut for the club. In 1995-96 he established himself as a first team regular and won League and Cup medals before in May 1996, he won his first full cap against China when he and his brother Gary became the first pair of brothers to play for England since Bobby and Jack Charlton, 26 years earlier.

22 **1910** United played their last game at their Bank Street ground in front of a modest crowd of 7,000 loyal supporters. They beat Spurs 5-0 with goals from Roberts (2) Connor, Hooper and Meredith.

1938 Manchester United drew 2-2 in a fourth round FA Cup tie at Barnsley. In this match, United's Tommy Breen touched a long throw-in into his own goal, resulting in the only recorded occasion of a goal scored directly from a throw-in.

1994 Manchester United, after a moving tribute to Sir Matt Busby, beat Everton 1-0 with a goal by Ryan Giggs.

- January -

It was a scoreline that did little justice to a display Sir Matt would have been proud of and saw United go 16 points clear at the top of the Premiership.

1996 Nicky Butt is sent off in United's Premier League match against West Ham United at Upton Park, a day after his 21st birthday. However, the Reds still win 1-0, courtesy of an Eric Cantona goal.

23

1905 United played Fulham at Villa Park in the second replay of the intermediate round of the FA Cup. After drawing 2-2 at Clayton and 0-0 after extra-time at Craven Cottage, the Reds went out 1-0.

1926 United crash 6-1 at home to Manchester City with Rennox scoring the Reds' consolation goal!

1969 Birth of Andre Kanchelskis. A Soviet Union international before the disintegration of that country, he joined Manchester United as a non-contract player from Russian side Shakhtyor Donetsk in March 1991. After impressing, he was offered a contract and was an instant hit with the United fans. He scored several vital goals during his first season, many of them spectacular, and in 1992 won a League Cup winners' medal. He won a League Championship medal the following season, though only playing in 27 of the 42 matches, 13 of them as substitute. In 1994-95, Kanchelskis scored a hat-trick in the 5-0 drubbing of Manchester City but after appearing in 151 League and Cup games for the Reds he fell out of favour with Alex Ferguson and in August 1995, he joined Everton for £5 million. He scored two superb goals in the Toffees 2-1 win over Liverpool and hit a memorable hat-trick against Sheffield Wednesday before leaving Goodison Park to play for Florentina.

1991 Mark Hughes hit a hat-trick in the Football League Cup quarter-final replay against Southampton at Old Trafford as United beat the Saints 3-2.

24

1903 Alex Bell made his debut for United in the 3-1 win at Glossop. Born in Cape Town, South Africa, of Scottish parents, he joined the Reds from Ayr Parkhouse for £700. In 11 years with the club, he appeared in 306 first team games, being part of the famous United half-back line of Duckworth Roberts and Bell. In 1908 he won a League Championship medal and in 1909, an FA Cup winners' medal as the Reds beat Bristol City 1-0. Two years later, he won a second Championship medal as United finished the season one point ahead of runners-up Aston Villa. He won a full international cap for Scotland against Ireland in 1912 but during the 1912-13 season, the partnership was beginning to show its age and at the end of that campaign, Bell was allowed to join Blackburn Rovers for £1,000. He retired shortly afterwards and after the First World War had ended he became trainer at Coventry City before occupying a similar post with United's rivals, Manchester City.

1948 Drawn at home to Liverpool in the fourth round of the FA Cup the game is played at Goodison Park in front of a massive 74,000 crowd. United win 3-0 with goals from Morris, Rowley and Mitten.

1955 The longest ever FA Cup tie is finally resolved at Old Trafford when Stoke City eventually beat Bury 3-2 after 9 hours 22 minutes of football.

25

1964 Denis Law hits a hat-trick in United's 4-1 fourth round FA Cup win over Bristol Rovers in front of a 55,772 Old Trafford crowd.

- January -

1979 Gary Bailey, United's goalkeeping find, received an England call-up just nine games after making his senior debut. He was one of nine newcomers in a completely reshaped Under-21 squad to play Wales at Swansea on 6 February.

1984 United warmed up for Europe with a cool, controlled performance against the Algerian national side in Algiers. The Reds had to be satisfied with a goalless draw despite Norman Whiteside scoring what looked a perfectly good goal in the 70th minute. This was just one of a number of strange refereeing decisions by the Algerian referee!

1986 Bryan Robson making his comeback after a lengthy injury was sent off in Manchester United's fourth round FA Cup match at Sunderland which ended goalless.

1995 Eric Cantona really goes over the top. He is sent off at Selhurst Park for kicking Crystal Palace's Richard Shaw and leaps over the barrier with a two-footed attack on a spectator and then wades in with his fists before he can be dragged away.

26

1946 United beat Preston North End 1-0 in the FA Cup but the Lilywhites still went through. Because there was no League competition that season, cup-ties were played over two legs and North End won the second game 3-1.

1992 Rebel Manchester United fans stage an open meeting to protest at increased admission charges. A group called HOSTAGE (Holders of Season Tickets Against Gross Exploitation) was formed after the club's ideas for the future were revealed several months before. Fans were protesting that the club should be aiming higher than a 43,000 capacity stadium. The club believed that they had no alternative but to increase prices in order to stay competitive in the transfer market and to offset revenue lost in the re-development of the Stretford End.

1995 The 'Eric Cantona affair' takes up an extraordinary amount of media space and time as the errant Frenchman is given 14 days by the FA to answer their charges, but United have not yet spoken to him. The police receive a complaint from the Palace fan involved in the incident and will also interview United captain Paul Ince who was allegedly involved in a separate scuffle.

27

1951 Stan Pearson scores a hat-trick as United beat Leeds United 4-0 at Old Trafford in the fourth round of the FA Cup.

1968 Brian Kidd, along with Tottenham Hotspur's Joe Kinnear, is sent off in the third round FA Cup tie at Old Trafford. The match ended all-square at 2-2 but United lost 1-0 in the replay at White Hart Lane.

1994 The funeral of Sir Matt Busby at Our Lady and St Johns Church in Chorlton-cum-Hardy. The moving service was attended by around 90 former players. The funeral procession made its way towards Old Trafford with Sir Matt Busby Way lined with over 5,000 supporters. After two minutes silence, a horn blew and the hearse pulled away towards Southern Cemetery.

1995 Manchester United decide to suspend Eric Cantona for the rest of the season's first team games and fine him the maximum 2 weeks' wages (£20,000) while in France, Cantona is stripped of the national team captaincy and dropped for the season.

The Palace fan involved, 20-year-old Matthew Simmons (who, it is revealed, has a conviction for assault with intent to rob) is banned from the club for the rest of the season.

1996 United's 3-0 win over Reading in the fourth round of the FA Cup was the sixth time the two clubs had been drawn against each other in the competition, though the Reds have never met the Elm Park club in the League.

28 **1980** Granada Television's 'World in Action' accused Manchester United Football Club of corrupt and fraudulent practices. The programme alleged that United chairman Louis Edwards, who also ran a meat trading company, had won favours through questionable transactions in the meat business, as well as being involved in share dealing at the club which had thus produced substantial profits for himself. The programme also claimed that there was a special fund at Old Trafford to bribe the parents of top schoolboy players. Before all the claims could be investigated, the 65-year-old Edwards died of a heart attack. His death brought an end to any police inquiries and the story quickly disappeared from the national newspapers.

29 **1932** Birth of Tommy Taylor. Hailed as the finest English centre-forward since Tommy Lawton, he joined United from Barnsley for £29,999 in March 1953, as Matt Busby did not want him to have a £30,000 price tag around his neck! At Oakwell, he played inside-forward and in 44 League games, he scored 26 goals. On his arrival at Old Trafford, he was converted to centre-forward and made his debut against Preston North End, scoring two goals in a 5-2 win. Taylor was an opportunist type, with a powerful shot and magnificent heading ability. Within two months of him leaving Barnsley, he had won the first of his 19 caps when he played in the abandoned game against Argentina on the FA XI tour of South America. Although he played twice for England in the 1954 World Cup Finals, he did not really establish himself as an international regular until he replaced Bolton's Nat Lofthouse in 1957-58. Taylor also played and scored for the Football League XI. In his five years at Old Trafford he won two League Championship medals and an FA Cup runners-up medal, scoring United's late Wembley goal against Aston Villa. There is no doubt that the death of Tommy Taylor on the snow of a German airfield, dealt an irreparable blow to football in this country.

1949 United draw 1-1 at home to Bradford Park Avenue in the fourth round of the FA Cup at Maine Road. The crowd of 82,771 is the club's best home attendance in all competitions. The underdogs took the lead after 29 minutes before a goal by Charlie Mitten levelled things up. Mitten scored United's goal in the replay which also ended 1-1 before the Reds won the second replay 5-0.

1955 Allenby Chilton is sent off for an innocuous challenge on Manchester City's Johnny Hart in United's fourth round FA Cup tie at Maine Road. It doesn't help the Reds cause, who went down 2-0.

1996 United are found guilty by an FA Inquiry of poaching schoolboy David Brown from Oldham Athletic. The club are fined £20,000, ordered to pay costs of the Inquiry and told to agree compensation with the Boundary Park club. United refuse to comment about the decision, saying they are 'seriously thinking about making an appeal'.

30 **1892** Bob Donaldson hits a hat-trick as Newton Heath beat Crewe Alexandra 5-3 at home. The Heathens other scorers were Sneddon and R.Doughty.

14

- January -

1897 Joe Cassidy scores a hat-trick in the 5-1 first round FA Cup win against non-League Kettering Town.

1932 Tom Reid scores all three of United's goals in the Reds' 3-2 win over Nottingham Forest at Old Trafford.

1984 Italian giants Sampdoria were poised to make a £3 million bid for Bryan Robson. United manager Ron Atkinson said, *"There isn't enough money in Italy to buy Robson. I am trying to build a side - not dismantle one."* Yet chairman Martin Edwards said he would not be that sure if United received a 'silly' multi-million pound offer!

31 **1953** Non-League Walthamstow Avenue drew 1-1 with Manchester United in front of 34,748 fans at Old Trafford. The replay is held at Arsenal's nearby Highbury Stadium, where the Reds win 5-2.

1959 United and Newcastle share eight goals in an exciting Division One game at a snow covered Old Trafford. Scorers for the Reds were Charlton, Scanlon, Quixall and Viollet.

1962 A spectacular Maurice Setters goal gave Manchester United a 1-0 win over Arsenal in the fourth round of the FA Cup. It was a remarkable performance by the Reds who lost both League games to the Gunners - 3-2 at Old Trafford and 5-1 at Highbury.

5 January - The Birthday of Bill Foulkes

- January -

14 January
Tom Manley is given
a second benefit match

12 January
Jack Rowley scores
his last goal for United

22 January: A few days after the last match at Bank Street, the main stand collapsed.

16

FEBRUARY

1

1899 William Bryant scored a hat-trick for Newton Heath in the FA Cup first round replay at home to Tottenham Hotspur. However, he was still on the losing side as the visitors won 5-3.

1930 Manchester United beat West Ham United 4-1 at Old Trafford with Joe Spence scoring all four goals.

1958 United played Arsenal at Highbury and thrilled the 63,578 crowd with a display of attacking football that they had made their trademark. United stormed ahead as Duncan Edwards shot past Welsh international 'keeper Jack Kelsey after a few minutes and by half-time were 3-0 up following further goals from Tommy Taylor and Bobby Charlton. The Gunners pulled a goal back on the hour mark but within two minutes the scores were level as Jimmy Bloomfield scored twice after Herd's powerful shot had given Arsenal their first goal. United responded with goals from Viollet and Taylor before Tapscott reduced the Reds' lead to a single goal. It was a magnificent game but five days later, Edwards, Byrne, Taylor Jones and Colman died in the Munich disaster.

1961 After drawing 1-1 against Sheffield Wednesday at Hillsborough in the fourth round of the FA Cup, United crash 7-2 at home to the Owls in the replay in front of a 65,243 crowd.

2

1929 Tom Reid made his Manchester United debut and though he scored the games first goal, the Reds went down 3-2 at home to West Ham United. The Motherwell-born centre-forward began his professional career with Clydebank before joining Liverpool at the start of the 1925-26 season. In just 51 League games for the Anfield club, the robust Reid scored 31 goals. It was this scoring that persuaded the Reds to sign him and in 101 first team games, he scored 67 goals, including five hat-tricks. In March 1933, Reid left Old Trafford to play for Oldham Athletic where he continued to be a prolific goalscorer.

1935 Jack Hacking was United's oldest goalkeeper at 37 years and 42 days when he played in the Reds' 3-2 defeat against Norwich City at Carrow Road.

1957 The Manchester City groundsman had a tough battle to get the Maine Road pitch ready for the derby game following constant rain throughout the week. There were puddles lying on the surface and the City players had been banned from training on the pitch for some days. Billy Whealan scored for United after just three minutes and though Roy Clarke equalised for City ten minutes later, the Reds ran out winners 4-2 in front of a 63,872 crowd.

1966 Facing Benfica in the European Cup quarter-final first-leg United knew that they had to build up a good lead against a Portuguese side that hadn't lost at home in four years of European Cup football. Goals from Herd, Law and Foulkes gave United a 3-1 lead but just minutes from the end, the deficit was reduced to just a single goal.

1996 Manchester United announce that they have applied to the authorities for a licence to enable Old Trafford to be used as a venue for other kinds of 'matches'. If the licence is granted, the ground could even hold Civil Wedding ceremonies.

17

- February -

3 1912 Manchester United win 5-1 at Coventry City in the second round of the FA Cup with Harold Halse scoring two of the goals. United's other scorers were West, Wall and Sandy Turnbull.

1996 Eric Cantona returns to Selhurst Park for the first time since his Kung Fu attack and scores two goals as Manchester United beat Wimbledon 4-2. United's other scorers are Andy Cole and an own goal from the Dons' Chris Perry.

4 1928 Hugh McLenahan made his debut for Manchester United in a 4-1 defeat against Tottenham Hotspur at White Hart Lane. After playing wing-half for Manchester, Lancashire and England Schoolboys, he joined Stockport County as an amateur. When he signed for United in 1927, he cost the club three freezers full of ice cream - without doubt one of the strangest transfers in the history of the Football League. A versatile performer, McLenahan's career at Old Trafford was hampered by injuries and in particular a broken leg. Though he only scored 12 goals in his 116 appearances for the club, six of them came in a period of five successive matches during the 1929-30 season when he turned out at inside-forward. He left Old Trafford in December 1936, ending his career with Notts County.

1960 Goalkeeper Mike Pinner, who at one stage was the most capped post-war England amateur international with more than 50 appearances, made his United debut in the 1-1 draw at home to Aston Villa.

5 1946 Birth of David Sadler. An England amateur international centre-forward while with Maidstone United, the Reds converted him into a fine centre-half who went on to play in 333 first team games after joining the club in February 1963. He scored a hat-trick in the second leg of United's FA Youth Cup Final win over Swindon Town in 1964. Capped by England at Youth, Under-23 and full level while with United, he won a League Championship medal in 1967 and a European Cup winners' medal the following year. He was a member of England's 1970 World Cup squad in Mexico, although he did not get a game. In November 1973, he signed for Preston North End for £25,000 and stayed at Deepdale until the summer of 1977 when injury forced his retirement. He later returned to Preston to be their manager in 1981.

1952 Birth of Alex Forsyth. He was Tommy Docherty's first signing when he joined the Reds from Partick Thistle in December 1972. As a youngster, he had failed to make the grade at Arsenal and it was at Highbury that he made his debut in a United shirt. At Partick, Forsyth had won four full caps for Scotland and a Scottish League Cup medal. In six seasons at Old Trafford, the hard-tackling defender occupied both full-back positions, winning a Second Division championship medal and appearing in the 1976 FA Cup Final. Nicknamed 'Bruce' for obvious reasons, he left United in the summer of 1978 to join Rangers after a loan period with them, before ending his career with Motherwell.

1958 Matt Busby's assistant manager, Jimmy Murphy had to miss their European Cup quarter-final match against Red Star Belgrade because he was on managerial duty himself for Wales.

1968 Birth of Lee Martin. Born in Hyde, he arrived at Old Trafford as an associated schoolboy in February 1982, later joining the YTS scheme. After making his debut in the 2-1 win over Wimbledon in May 1988, he began to establish himself on the left-hand side of the Reds' defence.

- February -

He suddenly shot to fame when he scored the only goal of the 1990 FA Cup final replay against Crystal Palace. Over the next few seasons he suffered from injuries and after remaining on the fringe of the first team, he signed for Celtic in March 1994.

1992 Tremendous action and drama in the FA Cup sees favourites Manchester United become the first Division One side to go out on penalties as Southampton hero Tim Flowers saves from Ryan Giggs.

6 **1957** United had lost 5-3 to Athletico Bilbao in the European Cup quarter-final first leg in Spain, but turned things round with a superb 3-0 win in the second-leg at Old Trafford. The scorers for the Reds in front of a 70,000 crowd at Maine Road were Viollet, Taylor and Berry.

1958 The anniversary of one of the saddest events in British football, the Munich air-crash. After drawing 3-3 in their European Cup quarter-final tie in Belgrade, Manchester United were flying home from their match with Red Star. At Munich the plane refuelled but on take-off, it crashed, killing eight players (Roger Byrne, Tommy Taylor, Duncan Edwards, David Pegg, Geoffrey Bent, Eddie Colman, Mark Jones and Liam Whealan) trainer Tom Currey, coach Bert Whalley, secretary Walter Crickmer and eight sporting journalists, including the former Manchester City and England goalkeeper Frank Swift. Others travelling in the plane were seriously injured, among them Matt Busby, Bobby Charlton, Harry Gregg Jackie Blanchflower and Johnny Berry.

7 **1925** Albert Pape travelled to Old Trafford as a member of the Clapton Orient team to play Manchester United in a Second Division game. Just before the kick-off, he was transferred to United and the transfer was cleared by telephone with the Football League. Pape turned out in a United shirt much to the surprise of the 18,250 fans. Furthermore, he scored United's fourth goal in their 4-2 win. Pape went on to appear in 18 games for United, scoring five goals.

1970 Manchester United beat Northampton Town 8-2 at the County Ground in the fifth round of the FA Cup with George Best scoring six of the goals. United's other two goals were scored by Brian Kidd.

1984 Robert Maxwell made a shock £10 million bid to buy out Martin Edwards and his family. A consortium of irate Manchester businessmen was formed to match Maxwell's bid but after Edwards had said that £15 million would secure United, Maxwell let it be known that he was unwilling to pay that price.

1989 Lee Sharpe was the youngest-ever England Under-21 international when he made his debut against Greece, aged 17 years and 252 days.

8 **1890** The Reds travel to Grimsby Town for a Football Alliance match and suffer their heaviest defeat in the competition, going down 7-0.

1929 Birth of Roger Byrne. He joined United in 1948 but had to wait until November 1951 before making his debut in the goalless draw at Anfield. In the last six games of that season, he was converted to outside-left with great success and scored seven goals. United were unbeaten in that six-match spell and ended the season as First Division champions.

- February -

Reverting to full-back, Byrne succeeded Johnny Carey as captain and was no exception to the great tradition of United. He led the Reds to successive League Championship wins in the mid 1950s and to the FA Cup Final in 1957. Roger Byrne was a player with great tactical foresight that enabled him to dictate the course of play. His experience up front made him one of the great attacking full-backs and he went on to win 33 caps for England in the Number 3 shirt. His last League game for the Reds was in the classic encounter at Highbury on 1 February 1958, which United won 5-4. When he perished at Munich, this highly talented full-back had played in 277 games for United, scoring 19 goals. Roger Byrne was a classic player with a great football brain. He was experienced beyond his years - if he had survived Munich, he would no doubt have gone on to become one of England's greatest captains.

1936 Tom Manley scored four of United's goals as they beat Port Vale 7-2 at Old Trafford.

1995 United's suspended French striker Eric Cantona is involved in further controversy, allegedly completing a Caribbean family holiday instead of turning up for a police interview.

9

1957 Birth of Gordon Strachan. He began his illustrious career with Dundee before moving to Aberdeen for a fee of £50,000 in November 1977. With the Pittodrie club, he won just about every honour possible - two Premier Division Championship medals, a hat-trick of Scottish Cup winners' medals and a European Cup Winners' Cup medal. Having won the first of 50 full caps for Scotland against Northern Ireland in May 1980, he played in 183 League games, scoring 55 goals for the Dons before moving to Old Trafford. By the end of his first season with the Reds, he had won an FA Cup winners' medal, following the 1-0 extra-time win over Everton. Injuries apart, Strachan was an automatic choice in his five seasons at Old Trafford and so it was a complete surprise when he was sold to Leeds United for £300,000 just before the transfer deadline in 1989. At Elland Road, he was appointed captain and led the side to the Second Division Championship in his first season with the club. He was voted Footballer of the Year for 1991 and in 1991-92 and was a mainstay of a Leeds team that won the First Division Championship. In March 1995, he joined Coventry City on a free transfer and after a spell as Ron Atkinson's assistant, he is now manager at Highfield Road.

1965 After drawing 1-1 in the first leg, third round Inter Cities Fairs Cup match against Everton, United travelled to Goodison Park for the return meeting and won 2-1 with goals from Connelly and Herd.

1996 United strike it rich by signing a record sponsorship with Umbro, the kit manufacturers. Umbro make the move, even though there are still two years of their present deal with the club to run. They do this to prevent offers from other sports wear manufacturers such as Adidas, Nike and Reebok.

10

1906 Manchester United had beaten Bradford City 5-1 at Valley Parade but as the teams made their way to the vehicle that was to take them back to Manchester, a large section of the 8,000 crowd waited to express their disapproval. Bonthron, the United full-back was struck by one of the crowd and stones and mud were thrown at the other United players and officials. The Bradford officials and players protected Bonthron from the mob at great personal risk and some were even said to have been struck by missiles thrown by someone in the crowd.

- *February* -

1923 Ernie Goldthorpe scored United's fastest hat-trick when he scored three times between the 62nd and 66th minute in the match against Notts County. He added another to Myerscough's two goals as the Reds won 6-1 at Meadow Lane.

1948 Birth of Jimmy Rimmer. He won an FA Youth Cup winners' medal with United in 1964 and made his first team debut for the Reds in their Australian tour of 1967. He played in both legs of the 1968-69 European Cup semi-final tie with A.C. Milan but after playing in 34 games was loaned to Swansea City before joining Arsenal. After a long drawn-out dispute with Arsenal boss Terry Neill, he left for Aston Villa. Capped once by England, he won a League Championship medal in 1980-81 and a European Cup winners' medal the following years.

1951 The port of Manchester, which was trying to clear a backlog of ships caused by a strike, banned their workers from attending United's FA Cup fifth round game with Arsenal.

11

1980 The Football League and Football Association called for Manchester United's books to probe for any irregularities, including illegal payments to schoolboys. What concerned the FA was whether there were any irregularities since the amnesty was granted in 1975. The club had also featured in the World in Action television programme two weeks earlier.

1995 Eric Cantona hit the front pages of the national newspapers again. An ITN reporter who tried to film the Frenchman on the holiday island of Guadeloupe was allegedly attacked with a repeat of the 'kung-fu kick' that felled a Crystal Palace fan two weeks earlier.

12

1921 When United lost 2-1 at home to Everton, their goal was scored by Billy Meredith. In doing so, he became at the age of 48 years and 201 days, United's oldest goalscorer.

1949 Manchester United beat Yeovil Town 8-0 in the fifth round of the FA Cup at Old Trafford in front of a 81,565 crowd with Jack Rowley scoring five of the goals, including a first-half hat-trick.

1974 United hit the bottom of the First Division and five players - Holton, Kidd, Morgan, Young and Brian Greenhoff are all on the verge of an automatic two-match suspension!

1983 When thousands of supporters should have been at Old Trafford for the game against Luton Town and to remember those who had lost their lives at Munich twenty-five years previously, the ground was empty as heavy frost caused its postponement. Yet Old Trafford was the only area of Manchester affected by this weather condition!

1993 Trafford Borough Council officials changed the name of Warwick Road North to 'Sir Matt Busby Way'. The man himself unveiled one of the new road signs accompanied by Alex Ferguson and United Chairman Martin Edwards.

13

1901 Following a goalless draw at home to Burnley in the first round of the FA Cup, Newton Heath travelled to Turf Moor for the replay and lost 7-1 with Alf Schofield scoring the club's consolation goal.

1960 The fiftieth anniversary of the opening of Old Trafford was marked by a brilliant goal from Dennis Viollet in a 1-1 draw with Preston North End.

- February -

It was his 27th strike of the season which put him on his way to beating Jack Rowley's record of thirty goals in 1951-52. Viollet's final total of thirty-two still remains unbeaten at Old Trafford to this day.

1965 United's Irish internationals Harry Gregg (Northern Ireland) and Noel Cantwell (Republic of Ireland) were both sent off in a reserve match at Burnley.

1994 United won the Coca Cola Cup semi-final first-leg tie against Sheffield Wednesday 1-0. Though there were some moments when the Reds produced some brilliant football, they had to rely on a Ryan Giggs goal after 20 minutes. Taking the ball round Wednesday 'keeper Kevin Pressman, the Welsh international had gone well wide and almost to the by-line but astonishingly, he stroked the ball into the net from the narrowest of angles to give the Reds victory.

1995 As Eric Cantona's lawyer announces that he is to sue ITN over the Guadeloupe incident for 'invasion of privacy', Manchester United manager Alex Ferguson comes out strongly in support of his player.

14

1974 Bobby Charlton, legendary Manchester United forward and captain of the 1968 European Cup-winning side wrote off the Reds when he said *"You have no chance of staying in the First Division"*. United manager Tommy Docherty said *"I have the greatest respect and admiration for him as a man and a player, but on this issue I must say I am extremely surprised and disappointed at Bob"*. United drew their next match 2-2 at Derby County and ended the season in 21st place and were relegated!

15

1896 First Division giants Derby County visited Clayton for a second round FA Cup match. The Rams boasted a team full of talent. In goal was Jack Robinson, soon to become England's regular 'keeper whilst up front was John Goodall, England's centre-forward and Steve Bloomer, England's latest recruit. Bloomer of course was to lead Derby to three FA Cup Finals and appear in 23 internationals. It was Bloomer who gave the visitors the lead just before half-time but the 'Heathens' hung on and Kennedy equalised to force a replay. The Athletic News called it 'a great and glorious contribution to Manchester's football history' yet in the replay at the Baseball Ground, Derby won 5-1.

1983 The Reds produced a swashbuckling 4-2 victory over Arsenal at Highbury in the Milk Cup semi-final first leg. Norman Whiteside and Frank Stapleton gave United a 2-0 half-time lead and Steve Coppell hit two more goals before Woodcock and Nicholas pulled two late goals back for the Gunners to salvage some pride for the home side.

16

1907 Billy Meredith scored two of United's goals in a 4-2 win at Ewood Park against a strong Blackburn Rovers side. The other United scorers were Sagar and Wall.

1946 United took the lead at Liverpool in their Football League North match with a goal by Wrigglesworth direct from a corner kick and within the first minute ! Playing in blue jerseys, the Old Trafford side went on to win 5-0 with Hanlon and Rowley scoring two goals apiece.

1957 A goal from Duncan Edwards was enough to give the Reds a 1-0 FA Cup fifth round win over Everton at Old Trafford in front of 61,803 spectators.

- *February* -

1959 United beat City 4-1 in the Manchester derby at Old Trafford with goals by Bradley 2, Goodwin and Scanlon. The game which was a one-sided affair was watched by a crowd of 59,846.

17

1900 In a battle of the 'Heathens', Newton Heath beat Small Heath 3-2 at Clayton with goals from Cassidy, Godsmark and Parkinson.

1910 Two days before United played their first game at Old Trafford, a gale swept across the city and blew down the Bank Street stand at their former Clayton ground, causing extensive damage to houses in neighbouring streets.

1932 The Reds beat Burnley 5-1 at Old Trafford in front of just 11,036 spectators. Johnston 2, Ridding 2 and Gallimore were the United scorers.

18

1905 John Peddie hit a hat-trick as the Reds beat Leicester Fosse 4-1.

1939 John Hanlon scored three goals as the Reds beat Blackpool 5-3 at Bloomfield Road in an eight-goal thriller.

1953 Johnny Carey was called upon in an emergency to play the entire game at Sunderland in goal. He performed heroics as United drew 2-2 with Lewis and Pegg the goalscorers.

1957 Bobby Charlton scored the first hat-trick of his career as United beat Charlton Athletic 5-1 at the Valley.

1975 Birth of Gary Neville. Captain of United's FA Youth Cup winning side of 1992, an injury to Paul Parker in the 1994-95 season gave him the opportunity to stake his claim for a first team place.

He impressed so much, that by the end of the season, he had been included in Terry Venables' England squad. In 1995-96 he appeared in 31 League games as United won the Premier League Championship and then made an 89th minute appearance as substitute in the FA Cup Final victory over Liverpool to win medals in both competitions as the Reds completed the 'double'. He played in four Euro '96 matches for England becoming a regular for both club and country, scoring his first goal for United against Middlesbrough in May 1997.

1996 United beat Manchester City 2-1 in a fifth round FA Cup tie at Old Trafford with goals from Cantona and Sharpe. All tickets were sold and the crowd of 42,962 brought in gate receipts of almost £675,000. Television fees and advertising took the total income to £1 million which is believed to be a record for a cup-tie other than a final or semi-final.

19

1910 Manchester United leave their old ground in Clayton and play their first ever game at Old Trafford. The visitors are Liverpool and 45,000 fans turn up, but go home disappointed as United lose 4-3 after twice leading by two goals. United's team was: Moger; Stacey; Hayes; Duckworth; Roberts; Blott; Meredith; Halse; Homer; Turnbull and Wall.

1939 Birth of Pat Crerand. He cost United £56,000 from Celtic in 1963 - a record transfer fee for a wing-half at the time. His creative skills and accurate 40 and 50 yard passes were a big factor behind the club's success throughout the 1960s. During his eight and a half seasons at Old Trafford, he helped the Reds to two League titles, the FA Cup and the European Cup. He also won a Scottish FA Cup winners' medal with Celtic and was capped 16 times by Scotland. He played the last of his 392 games for United in the 4-3 win at Maine Road on the final day of the 1970-71 season before

- February -

being appointed youth team coach at Old Trafford and later assistant-manager. He left the club in July 1976 to become manager of Northampton Town.

1945 Matt Busby was appointed manager of Manchester United, a post which had been vacant since the departure of Scott Duncan in 1937.

1958 Manchester United's first match following the Munich air disaster was against Sheffield Wednesday in an FA Cup fifth round tie. There were no names printed for United's team on the programme, as its composition was in doubt right up to the kick-off. United won 3-0 with goals from Brennan 2, and Dawson before an Old Trafford crowd of 59,848.

1977 Jimmy Greenhoff scored all three goals in United's 3-1 win over Newcastle United at Old Trafford.

1995 Steve Bruce set United on their way to an FA Cup fifth round victory over Leeds United by scoring in the opening seconds. United win 3-1 with their other goals scored by McClair and Hughes.

20

1909 Manchester United beat Blackburn Rovers 6-1 in the third round of the FA Cup with both Sandy and Jimmy Turnbull each scoring a hat-trick.

1971 Alan Gowling scored four goals as United beat Southampton 5-1 at Old Trafford. The Reds other goal is scored by Scottish international winger Willie Morgan.

21

1940 Birth of Alex Dawson. A bustling, old-fashioned type of centre-forward, he scored on his debut in a 2-0 win over Burnley, a month before he turned professional. He came into prominence following the Munich disaster and was one of the reasons behind the club reaching the 1958 FA Cup Final. During that season's competition, he scored five goals in six matches, including a hat-trick in the 5-3 semi-final replay win over Fulham at Highbury. Dawson was no stranger to hat-tricks, for in 1959-60, he netted three in successive games in the Central League. After the Reds had signed David Herd in the summer of 1961, Dawson found it increasingly difficult to command a first team place and joined Preston North End for £18,000 in October of that year. At Deepdale, he became one of the club's greatest free-scoring forwards, netting 114 goals in 197 League games. He helped the Lilywhites reach the FA Cup Final of 1964 before continuing his goalscoring exploits with Bury, Brighton and Hove Albion and Brentford.

1973 A Jim Holton goal gave United a 1-1 draw at home to Florentina in the club's first ever match in the Anglo Italian Cup.

22

1958 United's best post-war Old Trafford League crowd of 66,124 saw them draw 1-1 against Nottingham Forest with Alex Dawson scoring the Reds' goal.

1986 Danish international Jesper Olsen scored all three goals in United's 3-1 win over West Bromwich Albion at Old Trafford.

23

1919 Birth of Johnny Carey. He arrived at Old Trafford in 1936 after being spotted by United's chief scout at the time, Louis Rocca. He made his first team debut as an inside-forward against Southampton early in the 1937-38 season. He helped United finish runners-up in the Second Division that season and then played in 32 First Division matches the following campaign. When he linked up with United after the war, Matt Busby was well off for forwards and converted Carey

- February -

to full-back and made him captain. Johnny Carey turned out against England in two full international matches within three days for different countries. He played for Northern Ireland in Belfast on 28 September 1946 and for the Republic of Ireland in Dublin on 30 September. Later in that same season, he played in four countries in eight days. Carey was a man so versatile that he figured in nine different positions for the Reds, ten if you include the occasion he pulled on the goalkeeper's jersey when Jack Crompton was taken ill at an away match. He led United to victory in the 1948 FA Cup Final over Blackpool and was voted Footballer of the Year in 1949. The following year, he was voted Sportsman of the Year and in 1951-52, led the Reds to the League title. When he retired, the United directors took the unusual step of inviting him to their boardroom to express their appreciation of his long and loyal service to the club. United were keen to keep him on the staff and offered him the position of coach. However, Blackburn Rovers made him a better offer as coach with more prospects of becoming manager. He took the Ewood Park club into the First Division before managing Everton, Leyton Orient and Nottingham Forest. One of the most highly respected men in the game - a superb footballer and inspiring captain - he was undoubtedly one of the all-time Greats!

1983 A crowd of 56,635 watched United beat Arsenal 2-1 in the League Cup semi-final second leg with goals from Coppell and Moran to win 6-3 on aggregate.

1994 Former Manchester United player George Graham, then manager of Arsenal, was chosen to pick a squad of 21 players (one from each Premiership club) to play in a memorial match for Bobby Moore. From Manchester United's squad, he chose Eric Cantona.

24

1906 United achieved one of their greatest results in their early history when they beat Aston Villa 5-1 in the third round of the FA Cup, with John Picken scoring a hat-trick and Charlie Sagar hitting the other two. Villa were the previous season's FA Cup winners.

1940 Birth of Denis Law. One of the great strikers and characters in the modern game, yet when he arrived at Huddersfield Town from Aberdeen in 1956, he was a thin, bespectacled 16-year-old who looked nothing like a footballer. He stayed with the Yorkshire club until March 1960 when Manchester City paid £55,000 for his services. It was a League record fee, surpassing the previous British transfer record by £10,000. On 28 January 1961, Law produced a display of a lifetime to score six goals in a fourth round FA Cup tie at Luton Town, only for the referee to abandon the game with 21 minutes still to play. On 13 July 1961, Italian giants Torino paid £100,000 for Law's skills. It was the first time that a British club had been involved in a six-figure transfer. Twelve months later, he joined Manchester United when they became the first British club to pay over £100,000 for a player. Law was unselfish in setting up goals for team-mates yet he had a killer instinct himself and in the six-yard box he was electric. He could score goals from impossible situations. His blond hair and one arm raised to salute a goal helped establish the Law legend. On 3 November 1962 he scored four goals against Ipswich Town and four days later scored a further four goals for Scotland against Norway. He rounded off a superb first season by scoring at Wembley as United beat Leicester City 3-1. Though his disciplinary record stopped him from being voted 'Footballer of the Year', the English soccer writers' counterparts on the continent voted him European Footballer of the Year in 1964. He returned to Maine Road in 1973 and scored his last League goal on 27 April 1974, consigning United to the Second Division!

- February -

1969 Manchester United defeat Birmingham City 6-2 in an FA Cup fifth round replay with Denis Law scoring a hat-trick.

1991 Lee Sharpe scored the only goal of the game as United beat Leeds United 1-0 at Elland Road in the Football League Cup semi-final second leg to win through to the final 3-1 on aggregate.

25

1901 Goalkeeper Jimmy Whitehouse, who made 64 first team appearances, played at inside-left in Newton Heath's match at Walsall and laid on the goal for Morgan in the Heathens 1-1 draw.

1960 The Munich Memorial was unveiled above the main entrance to the ground, the last simple act of a sad chapter in the club's history.

1980 The death of United chairman Louis Edwards from a heart attack just a month after 'World In Action' accused the club of corrupt and fraudulent practices

1996 In United's first visit to Burnden Park for sixteen years, the Reds beat Bolton Wanderers 6-0 to establish their biggest Premier League away victory. United's scorers were Scholes 2, Beckham, Bruce, Cole and Butt.

26

1898 After losing 5-1 at Woolwich Arsenal the previous month, Newton Heath beat them by the same scoreline at home.

1910 In a season in which United finish fifth in the First Division, they travelled to Aston Villa, where they suffered their worst defeat of the season, going down 7-1.

1964 United beat Sporting Lisbon of Portugal 4-1 in the first leg of the European Cup Winners' Cup quarter-final at Old Trafford with Denis Law hitting a hat-trick.

1966 David Herd scored a hat-trick in United's 4-2 win over Burnley at Old Trafford.

1973 Birth of Ole Gunnar Solskjaer. After playing part-time football for Norwegian Third Division side FK Cklausengen, he joined Manchester United for £1.5 million in the summer of 1996. Practically unheard of outside his own country, he scored on his debut as substitute for David May against Blackburn Rovers and ended the season with 19 goals in 46 appearances.

27

1901 As attendances for Newton Heath's Second Division games had dropped off, the club needed cash and so organised a grand bazaar in St James' Hall, Oxford Street - it was one of the most important events in the history of Manchester United Football Club. One of the attractions of the show was a St Bernard dog. It broke loose and knocked over a stall in the centre of the room. A fireman on duty in the hall went in to search and saw two eyes staring at him in the darkness. He failed to realise it was the dog and left by the side entrance as did the St Bernard. The dog owned by Sir Harry Stafford, the club's right-back and captain, strayed to find its way to J.H.Davis, who took immediate fancy to the animal. Stafford asked Mr Davis for a contribution to the club's funds and this led to the club changing hands, with Davis becoming the first chairman of Manchester United.

1960 Manchester United won 6-0 at Blackpool with Bobby Charlton scoring a hat-trick. The other goals were scored by Dennis Viollet 2 and Albert Scanlon.

1971 A knife was thrown on to the Old Trafford pitch during the match with Newcastle United, leading to the club being called before the FA Disciplinary Committee under a charge of crowd misbehaviour.

- February -

28 **1932** Birth of Noel Cantwell. Born in Cork, he joined West Ham United in 1952 and played in 245 League games for the Hammers before joining Manchester United for £30,000 on 21 November 1960. That same day, he pulled on a United shirt for the first time as the Reds played Bayern Munich in a friendly. Cantwell was captain when United won the FA Cup in 1963 and went on to appear in 144 League and Cup games for United before leaving to join Coventry City, where he replaced Jimmy Hill as manager. He was also the Republic of Ireland manager until September 1968. He then became manager of Peterborough United before becoming disillusioned with the English game and left to work in the NASL. He later returned to Peterborough as General Manager but parted company with the club again in 1989. A former PFA Chairman, the genial Irishman was also a double international, playing cricket for his country as well as appearing in 36 full internationals for the Republic of Ireland.

1956 Birth of Jimmy Nicholl. Born in Hamilton, Canada of Irish parents, Jimmy Nicholl was only a baby when his family moved to Belfast. He joined United as an apprentice in 1972, turning professional two years later. He made his League debut in April 1975, coming on as a substitute for Martin Buchan in a 1-0 win at Southampton.

Eventually replacing Alex Forsyth at right-back, he went on to appear in 247 first team games for the Reds and played in the 1977 and 1979 FA Cup Finals. Captain of the Northern Ireland youth team, he appeared in 73 full internationals for his country and was one of their stars in the 1982 World Cup. He left Old Trafford for Sunderland that year and after spending the summers of 1983 and 1984 playing in the NASL with Toronto Blizzards, he returned to England to play for West Bromwich Albion. He later managed Raith Rovers before taking charge at Millwall.

1968 After Brian Kidd had given United the lead against Polish side Gornik Zabrze in the European Cup quarter-final first leg, they were indebted to Polish defender Florenski, who put through his own goal to give the Reds a 2-0 lead to take to Poland.

29 **1912** After drawing 1-1 at Reading in the third round of the FA Cup, Sandy Turnbull scored two goals and Harold Halse the other as United won the replay at Old Trafford 3-0.

1964 United entertained Sunderland in the sixth round of the FA Cup. In an entertaining game, the Reds had to rely on an own goal from Sunderland's Republic of Ireland international centre-half Charlie Hurley to get a 3-3 draw.

19 February
Harry Moger played in the first match at Old Trafford

- *February* -

BARDSLEY & Co., | Sausage Skin, Seasoning, & Machinery, Butchers' Outfitters, Meat, Brine, & Milk Preservatives, | Liverpool Road, Manchester.

THE OFFICIAL PROGRAMME

The ONLY OFFICIAL ORGAN of Manchester City, Newton Heath, Broughton Rangers, & Salford Clubs

No. 31. SATURDAY, FEBRUARY 18th, 1899. ONE PENNY.

ENTERED AT STATIONERS HALL.

TO FOOTBALL PATRONS!

The Official Football Programme

Is the **ONLY** LIST ALLOWED TO BE SOLD ON THE GROUNDS OF THE
MANCHESTER CITY, NEWTON HEATH, SALFORD, and BROUGHTON RANGERS,

The "PROGRAMME" is also sold in the approaches to the Grounds, and contains the **ONLY TEAMS** Officially supplied by the Clubs.

Be sure and ask for the **Official Programme.**

Amusements.

COMEDY THEATRE.   TO-NIGHT at 7,
Last Night of
Mr J. PITT HARDACRE'S Tenth Annual Grand Pantomime,
LITTLE RED RIDING HOOD.
Monday next, February 20th,—
THE SLEEPING BEAUTY AND THE YELLOW DWARF.

THEATRE ROYAL.   TO-NIGHT at 7,
Grand Annual Pantomime,
THE BABES IN THE WOOD.
Last Night, Saturday, February 25th.

PRINCE'S THEATRE.   TO-NIGHT at 7,
Mr. ROBERT COURTNEIDGE'S
Third Annual Pantomime,
SINBAD THE SAILOR.

BEFORE BUYING
WATCHES, CLOCKS, JEWELLERY, ORNAMENTS, &c.,
SEE THE GREAT DISPLAY AT

HARDON'S
41 and 43 OGDEN STREET,
Fairfield Street, ARDWICK.

UNEQUALLED VALUE in Ladies' and Gents' Silver Watches, **8/11**
CENTRE SECONDS CHRONOGRAPH, **5/6**
ALL WEIGHTS IN SILVER ALBERTS.
A ONE-OUNCE ALBERT FOR **3/11**
LADIES' GOLD DRESS OR ENGAGEMENT RINGS FROM **3/6**
DOMINOS, ACCORDIANS, PLAYING CARDS.   FOOTBALL BAGS at **1/11 and 2/6**

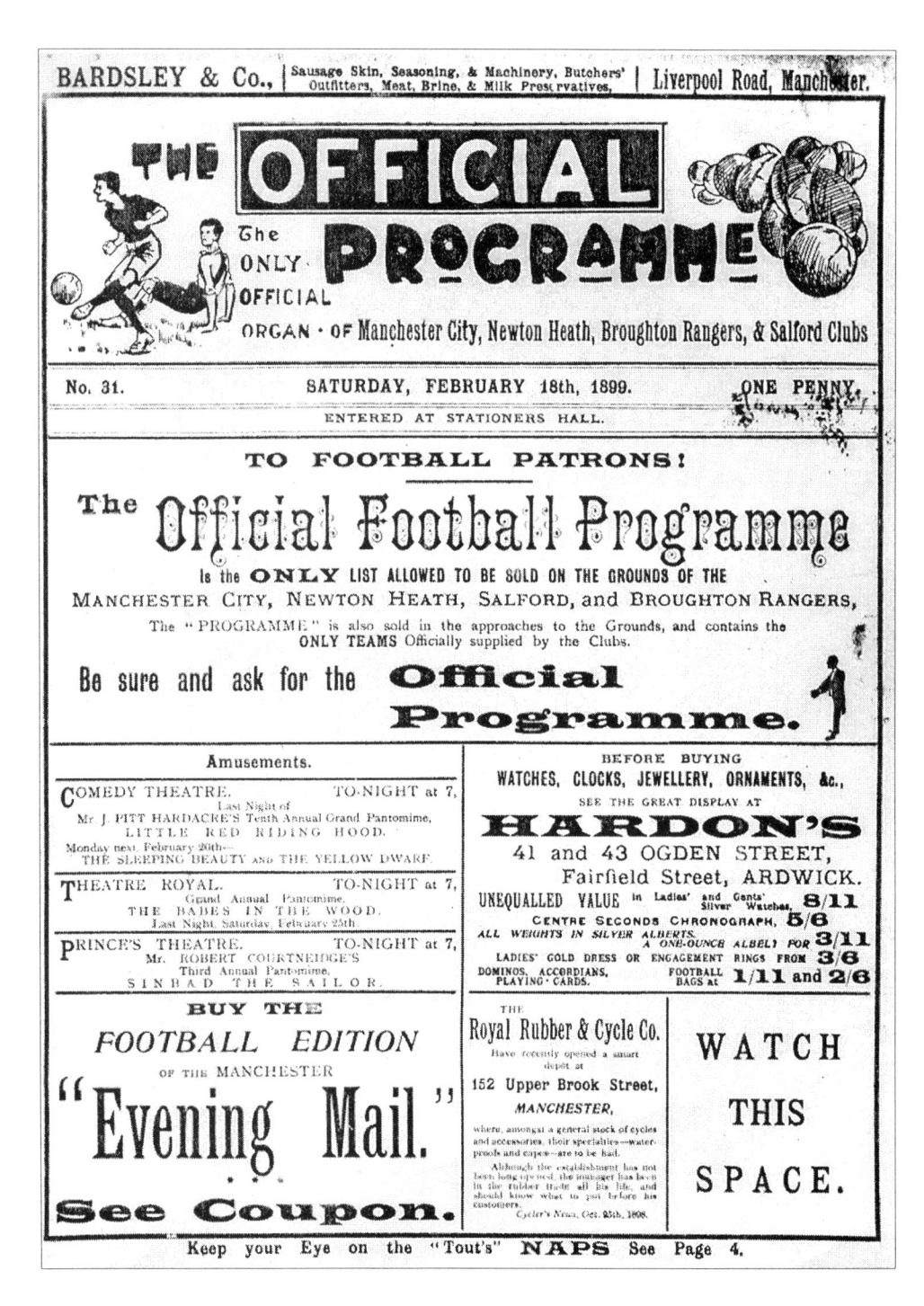

BUY THE
FOOTBALL EDITION
OF THE MANCHESTER
"Evening Mail."
See Coupon.

THE
Royal Rubber & Cycle Co.
Have recently opened a smart depot at
152 Upper Brook Street,
MANCHESTER,
where, amongst a general stock of cycles and accessories, their specialties—waterproofs and capes—are to be had.
Although the establishment has not been long opened, the manager has had to put before his customers.
Cycler's News, Oct. 25th, 1898.

WATCH

THIS

SPACE.

Keep your Eye on the "Tout's" **NAPS** See Page 4.

1 February: No doubt a similar programme would have been produced for the match

- February -

(Above) 18 February
Bobby Charlton scores his first hat-trick

(Right) Also 18 February (different year!)
John Carey has to play in goal.

MARCH

1

1913 John Mew made his debut for United at home to Middlesbrough but despite his good handling and positional play, the Reds lose 3-2. One of the smallest goalkeepers ever to play for the Reds, it was during the First World War when he finally won a regular first team place. He appeared in 126 wartime matches, including being an ever-present in three of the four seasons. In 1920, he won an England cap, keeping a clean sheet in a 2-0 win over Ireland at Roker Park. He played in 199 League and Cup games for United before joining Barrow in 1926. A year later, the former Reds' keeper went abroad to coach in Belgium and South America.

1924 United won 2-0 at Nelson in a Second Division game with Kennedy and Spence scoring the goals. The attendance of 2,750 is United's lowest gate in a competitive match since the First World War.

1980 Though the First Division Championship seemed to be a battle between United and Liverpool, the Reds ran into a nightmare at Portman Road when they lost 6-0 to Ipswich Town. Only goalkeeper Gary Bailey with two penalty saves saved them from an even more embarrassing defeat. Bolton-born centre-forward Paul Mariner scored a hat-trick for the home side, his final goal coming in the 85th minute when Gates crossed into the United penalty area that was empty of red shirts for the Ipswich striker to complete the scoring.

2

1953 United boss Matt Busby signed Tommy Taylor from Barnsley for 29,999. He had asked the Oakwell club to knock a pound off the original asking price as he feared the high figure might go to Taylor's head!

1957 Two goals from United winger Johnny Berry are enough to defeat Third Division giantkillers Bournemouth in the sixth round of the FA Cup at Dean Court.

1994 Even an injury to Eric Cantona failed to disturb United as they won the second leg of the Coca Cola semi-final at Hillsborough 4-1. The Reds' lead from the first leg was slender but after a devastating run from Roy Keane early in the game and a fine cross struck home by Brian McClair, United were always in control. Giggs added a second after 12 minutes and though Hirst pulled one back for the Owls, two goals from Mark Hughes crowned a magnificent game.

3

1927 Manchester United signed a player from Stockport County, Hugh McLenahan, for a fee of three freezers full of ice cream!

1967 United's League match at Highbury against Arsenal, which ended 1-1, was watched by 28,423 spectators on closed-circuit television screens at Old Trafford. It was the first time that pictures of a game had been relayed in this way. The match was projected onto seven screens measuring 40 feet wide by 30 feet high and though the camerawork was acceptable, one of the screens blew down!

4

1963 Manchester United beat Huddersfield Town 5-0 in the third round of the FA Cup with Denis Law, who was once on the Terriers books, scoring a hat-trick for the Reds.

1995 United recorded the biggest ever win in the Premiership - 9-0 over Ipswich Town at Old Trafford. It was the Reds biggest win of the century.

- March -

Andy Cole set a new Premiership scoring record by scoring five goals in the game. United's other scorers in a game watched by a crowd of 43,804 were Roy Keane, Mark Hughes 2, and Paul Ince.

1996 Eric Cantona scored the winner at St James' Park as the Reds beat Newcastle United 1-0 in front of a crowd of 36,584 Peter Schmeichel gave a stunning display in goal to keep the Magpies at bay.

5 **1949** John Downie made his debut for United, scoring the winning goal in a 3-2 win for the Reds at Charlton Athletic. United paid a club record outgoing transfer fee of £18,000 to secure his services. The Falkirk-born forward helped United win the League Championship in 1951-52, scoring 11 goals in 31 games, but midway through the following season, he lost his first team place. Having scored 36 goals in 115 appearances, he left Old Trafford in the summer of 1953 to play for Luton Town. Later moves took him to Hull City, Mansfield Town and Darlington before he hung up his boots.

1994 Chelsea's Gavin Peacock scored the only goal of the game at Old Trafford to end United's amazing 34 game unbeaten run.

1996 The Stock Market reacted to the Reds' 1-0 win at St James' Park the previous evening by marking up their share prices by 13p which then added £7.9 million to the club's value as the shares reached their highest point of the season at 280p each. The Reds' share issue is 60.8 million which at 280p a share, values Manchester United Football Club at £170 million, although twenty days later, the Stock Market marked the club's shares up to a massive 286p.

1997 United produced one of their most emphatic results in Europe with a 4-0 European Cup quarter-final first leg win over Porto at Old Trafford. It was a display full of breathtaking counter-attacking football. Goals from David May, Eric Cantona, Ryan Giggs and Andy Cole had the United fans poking a bit of good-natured fun at their Maine Road counterparts by singing 'Are you City in disguise?' It was a marvellous result for United and English football.

6 **1909** In the FA Cup quarter-final tie, United were losing 1-0 to Burnley with just 18 minutes to go. But then the match was abandoned because of a sudden heavy snowstorm. United went on to win the replay 3-2 and then the Cup itself. The referee who abandoned the game at Turf Moor was Herbert Bamlett who, in 1927, became United's manager!

1949 Birth of Martin Buchan. Made captain of Aberdeen when he was only 20 years old, he led the Dons to the Scottish FA Cup in 1970 and the following year, was voted Scotland's Player of the Year. He was lured down from north of the border by the then United manager, Frank O'Farrell, for a fee of £125,000. He gained a Second Division championship medal in 1974-75 and captained the Reds to victory in the 1977 FA Cup final against Liverpool. He also lined up for United against Southampton and Arsenal in the 1976 and 1979 finals. He collected 34 caps for Scotland, all but two of them being whilst he was with the club. He left Old Trafford in the summer of 1983, moving to Oldham Athletic, but after just 28 League appearances for the Latics, he retired from playing. He later had a short spell as manager of Burnley.

7 **1933** Birth of Jackie Blanchflower. Brother to the great Tottenham Hotspur and Northern Ireland captain, Danny Blanchflower, he made his League debut for United at right-half in the goalless draw at Liverpool

- March -

in November 1951. Though he later played the majority of his games at inside-forward, he moved to centre-half during the 1955-56 season and it was in this position that he is best remembered. He showed his versatility when he took over in goal when Ray Wood was injured during the FA Cup Final of 1957. The winner of two League Championship medals, he also won 12 caps for Northern Ireland. Reliable in everything he did, the injuries he received in the Munich air disaster meant that he never played again.

1995 The police charged United's Paul Ince with common assault over an incident alleged to have occurred at Selhurst Park after the infamous Cantona foray into the front stalls.

8

1941 Old Trafford housed its last game before it was bombed by the Luftwaffe. United beat Bury 7-3 with Johnny Carey and Jack Rowley both scoring hat-tricks.

1950 The most penalties converted by one player in a Football League game is three, which has happened on several occasions, but only three times in the top flight. One of them occurred at Old Trafford when Charlie Mitten scored a hat-trick of penalties and also got one other goal in United's 7-0 win over Aston Villa. United then went 55 games before next scoring from the spot!

9

1895 Walsall came to Clayton, Newton Heath's ground, and were trounced 14-0 in a match in which Joe Cassidy, the club's latest signing from Glasgow Celtic, made his debut, scoring four of the goals. However, Walsall's protests against the ground conditions was upheld and the match replayed 25 days later. To make their point, Newton Heath won the rearranged game 9-0 but ended the season third in the League. They then lost their Test Match for promotion 3-0 to Stoke.

1946 Three goals in nine minutes by Jack Rowley helped United beat Blackburn Rovers 6-2 in a Football League North match. A crowd of 31,000 saw United's new forward formation in irresistible mood with Delaney outstanding. Following Rowley's first half hat-trick, United added another three goals in the second half through Hanlon 2, and Delaney. In the closing minutes, Hanlon had the ball in the net again only to be judged offside.

1964 A full strength United side beat Sunderland in a sixth round FA Cup second replay game at Leeds Road, Huddersfield. The Reds who got up off the floor to force replays with the Wearsiders, even went a goal behind in this third meeting. On a mud bath of a pitch, Denis Law hit his seventh hat-trick of the season to make it a triumphant return to the club who launched him into League football. Chisnall and Herd grabbed United's other goals in a 5-1 win.

1966 The night George Best dazzled Benfica's Stadium of Light in United's second leg European Cup quarter-final match against the Portuguese side. United had won the first leg at Old Trafford 3-2 and took the second 5-1. Best scored twice in the opening 12 minutes and ran rings round the Benfica defence whenever he had the ball. He was not fully fit after an injury when the first leg of the European Cup semi-final was played away against Partisan Belgrade and went straight into hospital for a cartilage operation after the game. United lost that tie 2-1 and Best was out of action for the rest of the season.

10

1899 Newton Heath placed two players on the transfer list and suspended a third following an investigation into their activities off the field. These activities were never explained but it was assumed that the three had been drinking.

- March -

The two players who were suspended and placed on the transfer list were Boyd, a prolific goalscorer who hit 35 goals in 62 appearances for the club, and Cunningham, the club's regular inside-forward. The other player involved was Gillespie, although he later apologised after serving his suspension and was reinstated.

1909 Two goals from Jimmy Turnbull and another from Harold Halse were enough to help United beat Burnley 3-2 in the quarter-finals of the FA Cup at Turf Moor after the original match played four days earlier had been abandoned after 72 minutes, with Burnley leading 1-0.

11

1941 Old Trafford was blitzed as Hitler's bombs targeted the area to halt engineering production for the country's war effort. The main stand was destroyed along with the dressing rooms and offices. By the end of the hostilities there was a small tree growing on the terraces. The club made a claim to the War Damage Commission for reconstruction but it was not until August 1949 that they were able to play football again at Old Trafford.

1992 United beat Middlesbrough 2-1 after extra-time at Old Trafford in the Football League Cup semi-final second leg to win through to the final at Wembley. On a night when it rained throughout the game, a goal from Lee Sharpe and another in extra-time from Ryan Giggs saw United home.

12

1894 A Bob Donaldson hat-trick helps Newton Heath defeat Blackburn Rovers 5-1.

1994 A moment of madness from Peter Schmeichel saw the Manchester United goalkeeper sensationally sent off just before half-time to collect a one match suspension which put him out of the Coca Cola Cup Final a fortnight later.

The Danish 'keeper came charging out of his area to block a shot with his arms. United pulled off Paul Parker and replaced him with Les Sealey. Just seconds into the second half, ten men United took the lead through Mark Hughes and Andre Kanchelskis added two more before the visitors pulled a goal back.

1996 During the night Old Trafford was visited by burglars, who in an attempt to break into the office of United Chairman Martin Edwards, caused around £10,000 worth of damage. After climbing a 50ft wall, they smashed a hole in the stadium roof before crawling along a heating duct to gain entry into the office block. Once they were inside the chairman's second floor office, they located the safe and threw it out of the window onto the concourse below. However, after the burglars had made their escape from the ground, they failed to remove the safe! Unbelievably, throughout this escapade the alarm system did not go off.

13

1948 Thousands of people were still outside the Hillsborough ground just before the kick-off in the FA Cup semi-final tie between Manchester United and Derby County, many making last minute efforts to obtain tickets. A Stan Pearson hat-trick, including two goals in the space of three minutes, helped United to a 3-1 win.

1958 Stretford's ex-serviceman's Association held a concert in aid of the Manchester United fund at which Bert Trautmann, Manchester City's German-born goalkeeper presented a memorial to United. which was expected to be hung in the club's boardroom.

1971 A dinner was held to commemorate 25 years of service to Manchester United Football Club by Sir Matt Busby CBE.

- March -

He became the club's manager in 1946 after a successful playing career with Manchester City and Liverpool. He later became director and then president of the club.

1974 During the goalless draw at Maine Road, Lou Macari and City's Mike Doyle were dismissed together. Both players refused to leave the pitch and to try and resolve the matter, referee Clive Thomas decided to take both teams off the pitch for five minutes. The game watched by 51,331 eventually resumed with both sides down to ten men.

14 **1958** Just twenty-four hours before United's Football League game against Burnley at Turf Moor, Bobby Charlton played in the Army Cup Final at Didcot, Berkshire. Travelling from his unit in Shrewsbury, Charlton starred in a win for his side before catching a fast train north Friday evening, and getting a night's sleep before travelling with the Reds to Burnley where they lost 3-0.

1994 Manchester United protested against the decision that both FA Cup semi-finals were to take place at Wembley. The club were simply reflecting the views of their supporters who felt that a suitable venue in the north could have been found.

15 **1920** United's Billy Meredith was the oldest man ever to play for a British international side. He was 45 years and 229 days old when he played for Wales in their 2-1 win against England at Highbury.

1947 The Scottish international centre-half, Neil McBain, who played in 43 League and Cup games for Manchester United in the 1920s became the oldest player in Football League history, when as manager of New Brighton, he turned out as emergency goalkeeper for his side at the age of 51 years and 120 days.

1958 United lost 3-0 to Burnley at Turf Moor, the Reds completely going to pieces after the sending off of young Mark Pearson. Before he was dismissed, United played attractive football and honours were about even. The referee had cautioned a number of players on both sides in a sudden five minute spell of bad tempered incidents and lost patience with the next offender who just happened to be Pearson.

16 **1949** Birth of Alan Gowling. He arrived at Old Trafford after playing for England schoolboys, Great Britain Amateurs and Manchester University, where he took a degree in Economics. While at University he played for the Reds' junior teams and in one game for the 'B' team he scored seven goals ! He made his debut for the first team in a 4-2 win at Stoke City, scoring United's third goal. He went on to play in 87 League and Cup games for the Old Trafford club, scoring 21 goals, including four in a 5-1 win over Southampton in February 1971. In the summer of 1972, he joined Huddersfield Town and scored 58 goals in 128 League games for the Terriers, before signing for Newcastle United. Forming a good understanding with Malcolm Macdonald, he netted 30 goals in 92 League games and was then transferred to Bolton Wanderers for £120,000 in March 1978. In 1982, he resigned the Chairmanship of the PFA and ended his playing days with Preston North End.

17 **1906** John Picken scored a hat-trick as United beat Chesterfield 4-1. Scottish-born Picken began his League career with Bolton Wanderers and in his first season at Burnden Park helped the Trotters win promotion to the First Division. After four seasons with Bolton, he moved to join Southern League side, Plymouth Argyle. A prolific scorer over his two seasons with the Devon club, he joined United in 1905 and scored on

- *March* -

his debut in a 5-1 win over Bristol City. He ended that season as United's top scorer with 25 goals in 37 League and Cup games, including another hat-trick in a 5-1 FA Cup victory over Aston Villa. After helping the Reds to promotion to the First Division, he lost his place to Sandy Turnbull and so missed out on a League Championship and FA Cup winners' medal. However, he regained his place and in 1911 collected a League Championship medal.

18

1899 After Newton Heath had lost 2-1 to New Brighton Tower in front of 20,000 spectators, thus denting their promotion hopes, a section of the crowd took action against the referee. By all accounts, the official had ignored his linesmen and made a number of questionable decisions. He was jostled and jeered by a group of hot-headed youths but the police prevented anything further from developing.

1939 Birth of Ron Atkinson. Unable to make the first team at Aston Villa, he was given a free transfer and joined Headington United in 1959. They changed their name to Oxford United and wing-half Atkinson captained them to two Southern League championships before they were admitted to the Football League. He helped win promotion from the Fourth Division in 1965 and then climb into the Second Division three years later. He served Oxford for 15 years, playing in 560 matches, 383 of them in the Football League. After a short spell in charge at Kettering, he joined Cambridge United and led them to the Fourth Division championship. They were on course for a second promotion when he joined West Bromwich Albion. After the Baggies had finished third in the First Division, he moved to Manchester United and immediately went back to his former club to sign Bryan Robson for 1.5 million. United won the FA Cup in 1983 and 1985 but in 1986, Big Ron was sacked, receiving £100,000 in compensation.

He joined Spanish club Atletico Madrid, but after just 96 days he was sacked, despite taking the club to third position. He returned to England to manage Sheffield Wednesday but after leading the Owls to success in the League Cup, he joined Aston Villa. He took the Villans to runners-up in the first-ever Premier League and beat Manchester United in the League Cup Final. He later managed Coventry City before handing over the reins to former United favourite Gordon Strachan.

1964 United suffered their worst European defeat 5-0 at the hands of Sporting Lisbon in the quarter-final second leg of the Cup Winners' Cup.

19

1946 United players and officials travelling to Germany for the Reds' match with BAOR, failed to arrive at Fuhlshuttel Airport on time. A reception committee comprising of an Army major and two captains waited for three hours to welcome the party. Plans to entertain the players were cancelled and instead a visit to the Garrison Theatre to see Nellie Wallace was arranged for the night.

1969 Manchester United crushed Queen's Park Rangers 8-1 in front of a 36,638 Old Trafford crowd. Willie Morgan scored the only hat-trick of his career, whilst Best 2, Aston, Kidd and Stiles scored United's other goals.

20

1942 Birth of Wyn Davies. He entered League football with Wrexham for whom he scored 22 goals in 55 games. This then prompted Bolton Wanderers to sign the Welsh centre-forward in March 1962. A regular for four and a half years with the Burnden Park club, he scored 74 goals in 170 League and Cup games before moving to Newcastle United for 80,000 in October 1966. He was a member of the Magpies 1969 Fairs Cup winning team but in 1971 returned to the

- March -

north-west with Manchester City. He moved to Old Trafford, where he scored four goals in 16 games before later playing for Blackpool, Crystal Palace, Stockport County and Crewe Alexandra. Capped 34 times by Wales, he is now a baker in Bolton.

1946 United lose 2-1 to a BAOR side in Germany before a crowd of 25,000 British servicemen and a few Germans who ignored orders not to attend the game by climbing up some nearby trees.

1958 Ernie Taylor, United's diminutive inside-forward, had a size 4 pair of socks made for him for the Reds FA Cup semi-final against Fulham at Villa Park.

1961 Birth of Jesper Olsen. A Danish international, Olsen was a cultured midfield player, signed from Ajax of Amsterdam in July 1984. A self-confessed United fan since boyhood, he made his debut for the Reds in a 1-1 draw against Watford on the opening day of the 1984-85 season. In his first season at Old Trafford, he played in 51 games, scoring six goals and won an FA Cup winners' medal. Despite scoring 13 goals in 36 League and Cup games the following season, including all three in a 3-0 win over West Brom., there were those who questioned his contribution to the club's cause when things were not going United's way. He scored 24 goals in 175 appearances before leaving to join French club Bordeaux for £400,000.

1985 United travelled to Videoton for the second leg of the UEFA Cup quarter-final. After losing 1-0 after extra-time, the match is tied over two legs at 1-1. United then went out of the competition, losing 5-4 on penalties.

1996 United beat Arsenal 1-0 at Old Trafford with Eric Cantona's goal worthy of winning any game. The crowd of 50,028 was the first time a Premier League attendance had passed the 50,000 mark.

21

1959 A Dennis Viollet hat-trick helped the Reds beat Leeds United at Old Trafford 4-0.

1968 Birth of Gary Walsh. Due to the form of Gary Bailey and Chris Turner, Wigan-born Walsh had to wait until December 1986 before making his League debut for United in a 3-3 draw at Aston Villa. By the end of the 1986-87 season, he was first choice 'keeper but in December 1987 he lost his place to Turner. During this spell of 26 matches, he was capped twice for the England Under-21 side. Over the next few seasons his opportunities were limited due to the fine form of Jim Leighton, Les Sealey and finally Peter Schmeichel. He was rescued from obscurity by former United colleague Bryan Robson just before the start of the 1995-96 season, when he joined Middlesbrough for £500,000.

1984 Manchester United beat Barcelona 3-0 in the second leg of the third round of the European Cup Winners' Cup. They had lost the first leg in Spain 2-0 and few gave the Reds much chance. Yet United gave one of their finest displays in European football with Robson 2, and Stapleton getting the goals.

22

1884 Newton Heath's first representative recognition came when four of the team - the redoubtable and enthusiastic Sam Black, Blears, Fulton and Moran - were selected to play for Manchester and District against Liverpool and District on the Bootle Cricket Ground at Old Hullard Lane.

1949 Manchester United's FA Cup semi-final plans were kept a closely guarded secret as the players had their weekly practice behind closed doors at Old Trafford. The public and press were not allowed access or to approach the field of play and stewards on special duty at the gates, turned away all-comers.

- March -

The ban was imposed because of the club's problem at inside-right with Downie the new inside-forward from Bradford being cup-tied. Manager Matt Busby took part but Jack Rowley who was recovering from a head injury did not. However, he was due soon to have the plaster removed from his head and was regarded as a certain starter for the semi-final which United drew 1-1 with Wolves before losing the replay 1-0.

1958 United drew 2-2 with Fulham in the FA Cup semi-final at Villa Park. Both the Reds goals were scored by Bobby Charlton.

1980 The 100th derby match with Manchester City took place at Old Trafford. A crowd of 56,387 saw a Mickey Thomas goal give the Reds victory.

1994 Eric Cantona is sent off in United's 2-2 draw at Highbury. It is his second red card in successive games but even the Arsenal players protest his innocence to the referee.

23

1985 A hat-trick by Mark Hughes and a goal by Norman Whiteside help United beat Aston Villa 4-0 in front of a 40,941 Old Trafford crowd.

1995 Eric Cantona is bailed pending appeal after being sentenced by Croydon magistrates to two weeks' jail for his assault on a spectator at Selhurst Park on 25 January. United team-mate Paul Ince who pleaded 'not guilty' to an assault charge at the same game, is bailed to his trial on 25 May.

24

1917 United's Woodcock scored a hat-trick in a 6-3 win over Bolton Wanderers in a Lancashire Section (Principal Tournament) wartime match.

1961 Birth of Peter Davenport. He began his footballing career as an amateur with Everton but in 1980 he was released and joined Nottingham Forest, where he made a sensational start scoring four goals in his first five appearances, including a hat-trick against Ipswich Town. He soon became Forest's top striker and won an England cap against the Republic of Ireland. He had scored 54 goals in 118 League appearances before, in March 1986, he joined Manchester United for £570,000. Though he topped the club's goalscoring charts in 1986-87, the move didn't particularly work out for him and after scoring 26 goals in 106 matches, he joined Middlesbrough. In 1990-91, he was back in the top flight with Sunderland, later playing for Airdrie, St Johnstone and Stockport County.

1962 Hereford referee Jim Finney lost his £46 gold watch on the Old Trafford pitch but still found time to give a split-second offside ruling that gave Manchester United a point against Sheffield Wednesday in a 1-1 draw. Referee Finney's watch was found by a player and given to Matt Busby before being returned to Mr Finney.

1979 Andy Ritchie scored a hat-trick in United's 4-1 win against Leeds United at Old Trafford. At the age of 18 years and 118 days, he becomes the club's youngest scorer of a post-war League hat-trick.

1990 When United beat Southampton 2-0 at the Dell, full-back Colin Gibson scored with his 'last' kick of the game before being substituted, and then Mark Robins scored with his first kick after coming on as a substitute, though it was not as Gibson's replacement.

25

1908 United lost 7-4 in an eleven goal thriller at Anfield, although they then went on to win the First Division championship.

37

- March -

1939 Old Trafford's record attendance of 76,962 is set when the ground stages the FA Cup semi-final between Grimsby Town and Portsmouth. The Mariners lose their goalkeeper during the early stages of the match and Portsmouth go on to win 5-0.

1940 Birth of Nobby Lawton. Though his best days were spent with Preston North End, Lawton joined United as a youngster in 1956, moving up to the professional ranks in April 1958. He made his debut in a 3-2 win at Luton Town two years later and went on to appear in 44 first team games before signing for North End in March 1963 for £11,500. He became the Deepdale club's best post-war captain, his inspirational qualities leading the club to the FA Cup Final in 1964. He was one of the club's bargain buys of the decade, playing in 164 League and Cup games, scoring 23 goals.

1957 United played their first ever game at Old Trafford under floodlights but failed to celebrate as they went down 2-0 to Bolton Wanderers in a First Division match.

26

1932 Tom Reid scored a hat-trick against Oldham Athletic, a club he was later to join, as the Reds defeated the team from Boundary Park, 5-1.

1949 A Charlie Mitten goal helped United to secure a 1-1 draw in the FA Cup semi-final match against Wolverhampton Wanderers at Hillsborough.

1955 Billy Whealan made his debut in a 2-0 win at Preston North End. Signed from Dublin's Home Farm club, he was a prolific goalscorer, netting 52 goals in just 96 games for United. He won League Championship medals in 1955-56 and 1956-57, when he scored 26 goals in 39 League games, including all three goals in a 3-1 win at Burnley.

In that 1956-57 season, he also scored four FA Cup goals and three in the European Cup. Capped four times by the Republic of Ireland, he did not play in the game against Red Star Belgrade, but made the trip and lost his life at Munich.

1958 United won through to the FA Cup Final at Wembley after beating Fulham 5-3 in a thrill-packed semi-final replay at Highbury. The man who took them through to the final against Bolton Wanderers was burly Alex Dawson who scored a superb hat-trick. At the age of 18 years 33 days he became United's youngest scorer of a post-war hat-trick. Twice United took the lead through Dawson but twice Fulham equalised. Then just on the stroke of half-time, Shay Brennan, a shock choice for the outside-left position put United in front. Dawson scored his third goal just after half-time to put United 4-2 up and though Dwight pulled one back for the Londoners, Bobby Charlton scored a fifth for the Reds in injury time.

1983 United met Liverpool in the Milk Cup Final at Wembley. Norman Whiteside scored a superb goal after only 12 minutes but then Kevin Moran was injured and had to leave the field and Gordon McQueen tore a hamstring. Inevitably, the Anfield side equalised but United held out until the final whistle to force extra-time. Unfortunately with their crippled resources they fell behind to a spectacular Ronnie Whealan goal and Liverpool took the trophy 2-1.

27

1909 A Harold Halse goal gave United victory over Newcastle United in the FA Cup semi-final at Bramall Lane in front of a 40,118 crowd.

- *March* -

1965 United's fourth consecutive appearance in an FA Cup semi-final against Leeds United at Hillsborough was one of the most ill-tempered of matches. Denis Law and Jack Charlton wrestled before they were torn apart, with Law's shirt almost ripped off his back. In a game which did both clubs little credit, only two players were booked when at least five should have been sent off!

1994 Aston Villa ended United's treble dream with a fine 3-1 victory in the Coca Cola Cup Final played at Wembley. Andre Kancheslskis becomes the fourth United player dismissed in five games, handling on the line in the last minute.

28

1908 Harold Halse scored after just 30 seconds on his United debut as the Reds beat The Wednesday 4-1. He joined United from Southend in the summer of 1907 where he had a reputation for being a prolific goalscorer. He played for the club for five seasons, scoring 50 goals in 124 first team games. In his first season, he won a League Championship medal and in 1908-09, an FA Cup winners' medal. Then in 1911 he won his second League Championship medal. He won one England cap, scoring twice in the 8-1 win over Austria in 1909. In the summer of 1912, he left the club to join Aston Villa, where he added a second FA Cup winners' medal to his collection and a runners-up medal in the League. The following year he moved to Chelsea where he appeared in an FA Cup Final for the third time, only to be on the losing side on this occasion. After the First World War he played for Charlton Athletic, retiring two years later.

1995 Manchester United's half-yearly accounts showed a pre-tax profit of £7.3 million, but threw up a mystery in that winger Keith Gillespie, a supposed £1 million makeweight in the Andy Cole deal with Newcastle United is valued at only £¼ million.

29

1898 A hat-trick from Boyd and two goals from Cassidy gave Newton Heath a 5-1 home win over Loughborough Town.

1906 John Peddie hit a hat-trick as the Reds beat Leicester Fosse 5-2. Glasgow-born Peddie enjoyed two spells with United. He began his career with Third Lanark but was soon signed by Newcastle United. In his first 20 games for the Magpies, the bustling centre-forward scored 17 goals and in five years at St James Park, scored 62 goals in 125 League appearances. He was going through an unusual barren spell during the 1901-02 season, prompting the Reds to sign him.

Despite scoring 15 goals in 36 games in his first season with the club, he was transferred to Plymouth Argyle. A year later, he was back with United, where he went on to enjoy three more seasons, topping the goalscoring charts in 1904-05. He had scored 58 goals in 121 games for United when he left the club to return to Scotland and join Hearts.

1919 Joe Spence scored four goals as United beat Bury 4-1 at home in the Lancashire Section (Principal Tournament) wartime match.

30

1912 Injury hit United were deprived of the services of Stacey, Bell, Roberts and Wall for the match against Aston Villa. To make matters worse, both Duckworth and Connelly were injured in the first quarter of an hour, with the latter missing the bulk of the game. Unable to produce one shot on the Villa goal, the Reds went down 6-0.

1935 United produced a decisive victory over Hull City, winning 3-0. After a goalless first-half in which many chances went begging, it wasn't until the change over that the Reds fully pressed home their advantage with Boyd hitting a hat-trick.

- March -

1972 Birth of Karel Poborsky. Signed from Slavia Prague in the summer of 1996 for a fee of £3.6 million, he had made a name for himself in Euro '96 by scoring for the Czech. national side against Portugal at Villa Park. Played on the right wing in a similar role to Andrei Kanchelskis, although taking time to settle in at Old Trafford, there was no doubt that his time would come.

31

1951 Stan Pearson scored one of his four League and Cup hat-tricks for United in a 4-1 win over Chelsea at Old Trafford.

1970 Steve James made his United debut in a 2-1 win at Nottingham Forest. A strong-tackling defender, he found himself on the side-lines following the signing of Ian Ure, but worked hard at his game and in 1971-72 made the number five shirt his own.

He made the last of his 161 first team appearances for the Reds in the final game of the 1974-75 season when United, already champions of the Second Division, beat Blackpool 4-1. Unable to force his way into the side when the club returned to the top flight, he joined York City in January 1976 and played in 105 League games for the Bootham Crescent club before returning to his native Midlands to play for Kidderminster Harriers.

1995 Eric Cantona wins his appeal against his jail sentence, receiving 120 hours' community service instead and a subsequent press conference is reduced to farce by his pseudo-philosophic utterances.

1996 Goals from Andy Cole and David Beckham give United victory by 2-1 over Chelsea at Villa Park in the FA Cup semi-final.

9 March
George Best dazzled Benfica

- March -

8 March: The last match before the War - which caused the ground damage.

(Above) 26 March - David Pegg
His penalty ensured the FA Youth Cup stayed at Old Trafford.
(Right) 31 March.
Stan Pearson hat-trick.

APRIL

1

1905 Dick Duckworth scored a hat-trick as Doncaster Rovers were beaten 6-0. The Reds' others scorers were Beddow, Peddie and Wombwell.

1954 Birth of Gordon Hill. A great favourite with the United fans he joined the club from Third Division Millwall for £70,000 and within a few months was playing for England, which cost United a further £10,000. He appeared for United in two FA Cup Finals picking up a winners' medal in 1977 after Liverpool had been beaten 2-1. Yet in both finals, he was substituted by David McCreery, the only instance of a player being substituted in two different Wembley finals. He enjoyed three seasons at Old Trafford, scoring 51 goals in 133 first team games before a dispute with the club, led to them letting him join Derby County, managed by Tommy Docherty, for £250,000. Within eighteen months he had joined Queen's Park Rangers, who by this time were also managed by Tommy Docherty, before going to the USA and playing in the NASL.

2

1898 Harry Erentz, later to find fame with Tottenham Hotspur, played at left-back in Newton Heath's 3-1 win at Grimsby Town. Six days later his brother Fred filled the position as the Heathens beat Gainsborough Trinity 1-0 before it reverted to Harry for the next match, a 3-1 win over Small Heath.

1915 Enoch West was found guilty along with other players of fixing the result of the Manchester United v Liverpool match. Because of their war records, the other players had their bans lifted after World War One, but West's remained for thirty years until 1945, when he was 62, and it was too late to resume his career!

1949 The Reds lost 1-0 in the FA Cup semi-final replay against Wolverhampton Wanderers at Goodison Park.

1955 Duncan Edwards became England's youngest international at the age of 18 years and 183 days when he played against Scotland at Wembley. Just two months earlier, he scored the first hat-trick in an Under-23 international.

1988 Brian McClair netted a hat-trick as United beat Derby County 4-1 in front of an Old Trafford crowd of 40,146. United were undefeated in their last ten games and finished the season as runners-up to Liverpool.

1989 United played five League games this month and failed to score in four of them. Their only goal was scored by Arsenal's Tony Adams in a 1-1 draw at Old Trafford.

3

1895 When Newton Heath beat Walsall Town Swifts in a Football League Division Two game, four players scored two goals each. They were Joe Cassidy, Dick Smith, Bob Donaldson and James Peters. It was also a match in which the most goals were scored in a single half, with the Heathens netting eight in the second period.

1896 Willie Kennedy netted a hat-trick as Newton Heath beat Darwen 4-0 at Clayton.

1965 Bobby Charlton fired home a splendid hat-trick as the Reds beat Blackburn Rovers 5-0 at Ewood Park. United's other scorers were John Connelly and David Herd.

1975 Two goals from Gordon Hill give United a 2-0 FA Cup semi-final win over Derby County at Hillsborough.

- April -

4

1904 Bank Street Clayton, the home of Manchester United, housed the English League v Scottish League fixture. Around 40,000 turned up, making it one of the largest attendances on record for the ground. There were no United players on show that day but Manchester City's Herbert Burgess (later to join the Reds) was in the League side that won 2-1. On the same day, United met City in the semi-final of the Manchester Senior Cup at Hyde Road, the same resulting in a 1-1 draw.

1953 Duncan Edwards at 16 years and 182 days old became Manchester United's youngest player when he made his debut in their 4-1 defeat by Cardiff City at Old Trafford.

1964 Birth of Paul Parker. He began his footballing career with Fulham where he made 15 League appearances before joining Queen's Park Rangers. At Loftus Road, Parker won 16 full caps for England and impressed with his distribution and ability to recover quickly. He had played in 125 League games for the London club when United signed him for £2 million in the summer of 1991. He won a League Cup winners' medal in 1993 and added to his collection of England caps, but injuries and the competition posed by Gary Neville limited his appearances, and at the end of the 1995-96 season he was given a free transfer.

1979 A Jimmy Greenhoff goal gave United a 1-0 FA Cup semi-final replay win over Liverpool at Goodison Park in front of a 53,069 crowd.

1988 United staged a remarkable recovery at Anfield to come away with a 3-3 draw. Although the Reds went ahead through Bryan Robson in the second minute, the Merseysiders fought back and with Beardsley, Gillespie and McMahon finding the net, United trailed 3-1. Alex Ferguson then gambled by bringing on Whiteside and Olsen, and with Colin Gibson having been sent off, were down to ten men. With 25 minutes to go, Robson scored his and United's second, and in the 77th minute Strachan levelled the scores.

5

1927 Herbert Bamlett was appointed manager of Manchester United. Before entering management, Bamlett had been one of the country's top referees and in 1914 became the youngest man to referee an FA Cup Final. It was inevitable at the end of the 1930-31 season, after United had conceded 115 goals and been relegated to the Second Division, that United would part company with him.

1930 Hugh McLenahan scored both United goals in a 2-1 win over Sunderland, the first of five consecutive League games that the Manchester-born player scored in.

1941 Following bomb damage at Old Trafford, Manchester United play their first game at their new home of Maine Road but lose 3-2 to Blackpool.

1975 Manchester United clinched the Second Division title with a 1-0 win against Southampton at the Dell and there were still three more games to play. United's goal came in the 76th minute courtesy of Lou Macari, who a minute earlier had been booked for not standing 10 yards away from a free-kick. Southampton's Mick Channon missed a penalty for Saints.

6

1930 Birth of Dave Sexton. Manager of United from 1977 to 1981, Dave Sexton had an impressive record. He had taken Chelsea to an FA Cup victory and a European Cup Winners' Cup Final and taken Queen's Park Rangers to within a whisker of a League Championship.

- April -

Appointed United's manager in July 1977, his first two seasons in charge brought very little except an FA Cup Final appearance against Arsenal. In 1979-80, United finished runners-up to Liverpool in the First Division, but at the end of the following season, Sexton was sacked, despite the club winning their last seven League games of the season. He went on to manage Coventry City and became a member of Bobby Robson's England coaching staff.

1960 Birth of Colin Gibson. He joined United from Aston Villa for £275,000 in November 1985 and made his debut in a 1-1 draw against Watford. After some impressive performances, he tore his hamstring in the second match of the 1986-87 season and though eventually he recovered to win back his place in the side, he began to face stiff competition from Irwin, Parker and Lee Martin. He played in 95 League and Cup games for the Reds before leaving to play for Leicester City in December 1990 after a short loan spell at Port Vale.

1996 United beat City 3-2, with Eric Cantona opening the scoring from a 6th minute penalty. The Frenchman had scored in all the six 'derby' matches in which he had made the starting line-up.

7 **1890** The only game in the club's history in which two brothers have scored in the same game was in Newton Heath's 9-1 beating of Small Heath in the Football Alliance when both Jack and Roger Doughty netted.

1906 George Wall made his debut for Manchester United, scoring the only goal of the game to give the Reds a 1-0 victory at Clapton Orient. Born in Boldon, County Durham, George Wall went to play for Barnsley in 1902 before Louis Rocca took him to United four years later. With United, Wall won two League Championship medals and an FA Cup winners' medal, as well as making seven appearances for England. A fast winger with a powerful shot, he scored 98 goals in 316 League and Cup appearances, including hat-tricks against Sheffield Wednesday (5-0 in 1906-07) and Leicester Fosse (4-2 in 1908-09). Had his career not been interrupted by the war, he would have played in many more games for United, but as it was, he joined Oldham, later playing for Hamilton Academicals and Rochdale.

1917 George Anderson hit three goals as United beat Manchester City 5-1 in the Lancashire Section (Subsidiary Tournament).

1928 A Bill Rawlings hat-trick helped United beat Burnley 4-3 in a seven-goal thriller at Old Trafford.

1956 United clinched their third First Division title by beating Blackpool 2-1 at Old Trafford in front of their biggest crowd of the season. United's goals were scored by Johnny Berry and Tommy Taylor.

1962 Albert Quixall, who cost the Reds a British record fee of £45,000 scored a hat-trick in a 5-0 win over Ipswich Town.

8 **1957** United's youth team lost 3-2 to Southampton at Old Trafford in the semi-final of the FA Youth Cup. It was the Reds first ever defeat in the competition, since it was formed in 1952, but they still went on to win again, as they had won the first leg at the Dell, 5-1.

1970 United beat West Bromwich Albion 7-0 at Old Trafford with Charlton, Fitzpatrick and Gowling scoring two goals apiece and George Best adding another.

1990 Manchester United drew 3-3 with Oldham Athletic in an FA Cup semi-final at Maine Road. Oldham took the lead after five minutes before United responded with two

- April -

goals from Robson and Webb. Marshall then scored for the Latics to take the tie into extra-time. Wallace put the Reds ahead before Oldham drew level when Palmer ran onto a Marshall cross.

9 **1969** Manchester United announced that the former player Wilf McGuinness will succeed Sir Matt Busby as manager, although he was not immediately given that title.

1985 Ernie Taylor died. The little man who came to the rescue of Manchester United after the Munich air crash was always admired for his magical skills. He set up the goal for Newcastle United's FA Cup win in 1951 and was the key in the 1953 Stanley Matthews final for Blackpool. But it was as Jimmy Murphy's inspired signing in 1958 that he possibly made even more impact as he steered the decimated United team to Wembley.

1991 Soccer fans arriving in Poland without tickets for United's game against Legia Warsaw in the semi-final of the European Cup Winners' Cup were to be put in prison. They were stopped at the airport at Warsaw and if they did not have a ticket were locked in cells. Polish police considered it a violation if supporters travelled without tickets because visitors to Poland must state on their Embassy Visa application their reason for their visit.

10 **1907** George Wall hit three of United's goals as Sheffield Wednesday were beaten 5-0.

1970 United beat Watford 2-0 at Highbury in the FA Cup third place play-off with two goals from Brian Kidd.

1991 The Reds beat Legia, Warsaw 3-1 in the first leg of the European Cup Winners' Cup semi-final tie in Poland with McClair, Hughes and Bruce the United scorers.

1994 Mark Hughes saved double chasing United from defeat in the FA Cup semi-final at Wembley with a brilliant and spectacular opportunist volley a minute from the end of extra-time after full-back Neil Pointon had given Oldham Athletic a deserved lead a minute into the second period.

11 **1951** Birth of Jim Holton. He was a great favourite with the Old Trafford crowd as United stormed to the Second Division championship in 1974-75. Signed from Shrewsbury Town in 1973 for £80,000, he made his United debut along with Lou Macari in a 2-2 draw with West Ham United. During that Second Division championship-winning season, he broke a leg and nine months later, broke it again in a Central League match. Sadly, it marked the end of his United days. He had played in just 69 games for the club, yet appeared in 15 full internationals for Scotland. He signed for Sunderland and later had spells with Coventry City and Sheffield Wednesday before ending his career.

1953 Les Olive made his debut in United's 2-1 home win over Newcastle United. He was at the time an amateur who worked in the club's ticket office. He later became club secretary and then a director.

1957 United lost 3-1 to Real Madrid in Spain in the European Cup semi-final first leg.

1984 A goal from substitute Alan Davies gave United a 1-1 draw against Juventus in the European Cup Winners' Cup semi-final first leg at Old Trafford in front of a 58,171 crowd.

1990 United beat Oldham Athletic 2-1 after extra-time in the FA Cup semi-final replay at Maine Road with goals from Brian McClair and Mark Robins.

45

- April -

12

1904 United lost 3-1 at Grimsby Town. It was the club's only defeat in nine April fixtures that season, seven of which were won.

1924 Joe Spence set the Old Trafford crowd alight with four spectacular goals in United's 5-1 win against Crystal Palace.

1961 United beat a Burnley side that contained six members of their Central League side 6-0, with both Dennis Viollet and Albert Quixall netting a hat-trick.

1980 Andy Ritchie stepped out of the Reserves' shadows to hit a hat-trick for Manchester United in the 4-1 win over Tottenham Hotspur at Old Trafford. It was only the second full League appearance of the season for the Manchester-born forward. Scottish international Joe Jordan had a hand in all of Ritchie's goals whilst Ray Wilkins was the scorer of United's fourth.

1992 A goal from Brian McClair gave United a 1-0 win over Nottingham Forest at Wembley in the Rumbelows Cup Final. United's Man of the Match was Mike Phelan who replaced the injured Bryan Robson. He forged a midfield partnership with Paul Ince which was the foundation of United's victory.

1995 Roy Keane was sent-off along with Crystal Palace's Darren Patterson in the FA Cup semi-final replay at Villa Park which United won 2-0 with goals from Bruce and Pallister.

13

1985 United tormented Liverpool in the FA Cup semi-final at Goodison Park, yet the Anfield side came away with a 2-2 draw. Bryan Robson opened the scoring for United but Ronnie Whealan equalised just three minutes from the end of full-time. Frank Stapleton put the Reds in front during the first-half of extra-time but with just 30 seconds to play, Paul Walsh ran Ian Rush's header into goal to set up a replay.

1994 The Reds beat Oldham Athletic 4-1 in their FA Cup semi-final replay at Maine Road. Andrei Kanchelskis gives an inspired performance, scoring one of the goals and laying the last goal on for Ryan Giggs. United's other scorers were Irwin and Robson.

1996 United crashed 3-1 at the Dell against relegation threatened Southampton. The Reds went three down before half-time whereupon they changed their kit from grey to blue! They never won in the grey kit, drawing one and losing four of the five matches. Two days later the club announce that they are to discard the grey kit and will introduce a new white kit for the 1996-97 season, with a 10% discount to fans who had bought the grey.

14

1900 United's goalkeeper Charlie Williams scored direct with a goal kick in a match against Sunderland. His opposite number managed to reach the ball on its way into the net but failed to make the save!

1941 Jack Rowley scored four of Manchester United's goals in the 7-1 win over Manchester City at Maine Road in the North Regional League.

15

1934 Birth of David Herd. The son of the former Manchester City and Stockport County inside-forward, Alex Herd, he played in the same Edgeley Park side as his father, before joining Arsenal for 8,000 in August 1954. He won five Scottish caps with the Gunners and went on to score 143 goals for them at the rate of more than one every two games.

46

- April -

In July 1961, he signed for Manchester United for £35,000, becoming a member of a great side. He brought both experience and goals to the Reds, scoring 20 goals a season on four occasions with a best of 32 in 1965-66. He scored twice in United's 3-1 FA Cup Final win over Leicester City in 1963 and was an important member of the club's championship-winning sides of 1965 and 1967. In November 1966, he hit an unusual hat-trick for the Reds against Sunderland, hitting three goals past three different goalkeepers. He missed out on United's European Cup Final and in the summer of 1968 moved to Stoke City. After a brief spell at the Victoria Ground, he left to join Waterford in the League of Ireland.

1944 Burnley are beaten 9-0 in a Football League North (Second Championship) match with Smith scoring a hat-trick and Brook, Bryant and Rowley scoring two goals apiece.

1950 United's youngest post-war League player Jeff Whitefoot, was 16 years and 105 days old when he appeared in the 2-0 home defeat by Portsmouth. He went on to spend eight seasons with United, but despite winning a League Championship medal in 1955-56, he lost his place to Eddie Colman and joined Grimsby Town. He won an England Under-23 cap whilst at Old Trafford. After just one season with the Mariners, he signed for Nottingham Forest. He played in almost 300 first team games for the City Ground club and won an FA Cup winners' medal in 1959.

1959 The highest crowd for a Youth Cup match of 35,949 saw United's home semi-final against Blackburn Rovers. United who had drawn the first leg at Ewood Park 1-1, went down 3-2 (4-3 on aggregate) in the second leg at Old Trafford.

16

1963 Despite a Denis Law hat-trick, United went down 4-3 to Leicester City in a seven-goal thriller at Filbert Street. Ken Keyworth scored a hat-trick in the space of six minutes for the home side.

1983 Facing Arsenal in the FA Cup semi-final at Villa Park, the Reds were rocked after 35 minutes when Tony Woodcock gave the Gunners the lead. Five minutes after the interval, Bryan Robson crowned his return to the game after injury with a superb equaliser, laid on by Ashley Grimes. Then in the 69th minute, Norman Whiteside raced through to smash United into the lead. Seven minutes from time, a collision in the Arsenal goalmouth left Kevin Moran clutching his forehead. The battle-scarred defender was carried off still clutching his head. United hung on to win 2-1 in front of a 46,535 crowd.

17

1926 The last England v Scotland full international to be played in England outside of Wembley Stadium took place at Old Trafford. The visitors won by the only goal of the game scored by Jackson.

1971 United struggled for the first half an hour of their League match at Selhurst Park and gifted Crystal Palace two early goals. Denis Law pulled one back just before half-time and then early in the second-half, scored United's equaliser with a spectacular scissors kick. The team then hit a brilliant spell with George Best chipping in with two goals and Law completing his hat-trick as United ran out winners 5-3.

1985 In the FA Cup semi-final replay at Maine Road, United went a goal down to Liverpool after 39 minutes when Paul McGrath put through his own goal.

- April -

Within two minutes of the start of the second-half, 'Captain Courageous' Bryan Robson equalised when his 25 yard shot whistled past Bruce Grobbelaar. Mark Hughes hit United's winner on the hour in what was a tremendous team performance.

1996 The Reds beat Leeds United 1-0 at Old Trafford to record their 100th Premier League victory. Leeds 'keeper Mark Beeney was sent off after 19 minutes for handling the ball outside the area, and with no recognised custodian on the substitute's bench, their tactics became more cautious than usual. However, Radebe who went in goal, started his career in South Africa as a goalkeeper and had played in that position for 44 minutes during another Premiership game. The stand-in 'keeper was finally beaten after 71 minutes by a shot from the edge of the area by Roy Keane.

18

1958 Matt Busby arrived home, seventy-one days after the Munich air crash. For the schoolboys of the fifties, who welcomed him home, the effect of the disaster was lasting. Though they had lost their heroes, they would find new ones under the leadership of Busby.

19

1897 Newton Heath found themselves in the end of season play-offs for the fourth time in five years. Playing away to Burnley, who had finished bottom of the First Division, the Heathens lost 2-0 but gained revenge two days later, winning by the same scoreline.

1941 Jack Rowley scored five of United's goals in a 6-4 win over Chester at Sealand Road in a North Regional League match.

1957 Billy Whealan hit a magnificent hat-trick in a 3-1 win over Burnley at Turf Moor.

1958 Billy Meredith, the Welsh bard of the right-wing, died in Withington Hospital, aged 81. Meredith's statistics are quite staggering. He played top-class football for no less than 30 years, from 1894 - when at 19 he joined Manchester City from Chirk, his home town just across the Shropshire-Wales border - to 1924 when he was accepted for every cup-tie in City's run to the semi-final. He played in 367 League games for City and another 303 for Manchester United between 1906 and 1921. He scored 181 League and 56 Cup goals. It was money that led to his move to United. Eighteen City players, Meredith among them, were suspended for receiving 'illegal payments'. Immediately after the suspension, he moved to United and within three seasons, had won League and Cup medals with his new club. Also while with the Reds, Meredith helped cause a strike as the players' union which he had helped form, went into dispute with the Football Association. He won 48 full caps for Wales, scoring 11 goals, his last coming when he was 43 years old. He returned to City as a wartime guest player and permanently in July 1921 after a row with United concerning wages.

1997 The Reds all but sealed their fourth Premier League title in five years thanks to a disappointing display by Liverpool 'keeper David James. United won 3-1 with two headers from Gary Pallister and a goal from Andy Cole. The victory put United five points clear at the top.

20

1957 A 4-0 win over Sunderland at Old Trafford clinched the League Championship for the Reds. A crowd of 58,725 watched Billy Whealan carry on where he had left off the day before, scoring after just six minutes. Whealan later grabbed his second, whilst Duncan Edwards and Tommy Taylor scored United's other goals.

- April -

1966 Despite a goal from Nobby Stiles which gave the Reds a 1-0 victory over FK Partizan Belgrade in the European Cup semi-final second leg, they went out 2-1 on aggregate. United's Pat Crerand along with Partizan's Mihaslovic was sent off in a bad tempered match.

1996 Eric Cantona is voted Footballer of the Year by the Football Writers' Association just 15 months after his kung-fu attack at Selhurst Park. The Frenchman becomes the fourth United player to win the Football Writers' vote, following in the footsteps of Johnny Carey (1949) Bobby Charlton (1966) and George Best (1968).

21
1926 Charlie Taylor scored a hat-trick as United beat Sunderland 5-1 in front of a poor Old Trafford crowd of 10,918.

1973 After seven matches without defeat, United met Manchester City at Old Trafford in a match that ironically made the Reds safe from relegation. Bobby Charlton's last derby game attracted a crowd of 61,676 and though the game ended goalless, the United fans spilled on to the pitch to celebrate survival. In fact, City officials wondered if the game might have to be replayed as it was forced to end short of the 90 minutes but thankfully for the United supporters the result stood.

1991 United lost 1-0 to a John Sheridan goal as Sheffield Wednesday won the Rumbelows Cup. United had been looking to take the Rumbelows as part of a hoped for cup double, their other objective having been the European Cup Winners' Cup.

22
1893 The Football League had decided that at the end of the season, the three bottom clubs in the new First Division (of which Newton Heath were tail-enders) would meet the first three of the Second Division for the right to play in the top flight the following year. Small Heath had finished top of the Second Division, so met Newton Heath at the Victoria Ground, Stoke, for the deciding 'Test Match'. Farman scored Newton Heath's goal in a 1-1 draw. The replay at Bramall Lane saw the Manchester side triumph 5-2 with Farman scoring a hat-trick and Cassidy and Coupar scoring one each to secure their place in the First Division for the 1893-94 season.

1904 Charlie Roberts, one of the more notable captains in United's history was signed in the mysterious dark hours from Grimsby Town. It was a typically sensational stroke by Ernest Mangnall who not only hoodwinked other interested clubs, but also the football journalists, who were usually quick to pick-up on the scent of impending transfer action.

1957 Playing at home to Burnley, United fielded eight reserve team players, along with Dennis Viollet who had not appeared in the previous first team game two days before. Matt Busby was resting his first team in preparation for the European Cup semi-final against Real Madrid in three days time. United still beat Burnley 2-0 with goals from Dawson and Webster.

1989 The Women's FA Cup Final took place at Old Trafford and was televised for the first time. Leasowe Pacific beat Fulham 3-2.

23
1904 Charlie Roberts made his debut for United in the 2-0 home win over Burton United. One of the greatest players in the club's early history, he led United to their first League Championship and their first FA Cup Final win. Signed from Grimsby Town for £400, Roberts spent ten seasons with United, making 299 appearances and scoring 23 goals. An attacking centre-half who could run the 100 yards in 11 seconds when the world record

- April -

stood at 9.6, he was one of the pioneers of the Players' Union and became its chairman. Roberts was also one of the first players to wear his shorts above his thighs, when the FA had ordered that players should cover their knees. It was perhaps his regularity of being in trouble with the games' authorities which restricted his number of England appearances to three. In August 1913 he joined Oldham Athletic and led them to runners-up in the First Division in 1914-15. He retired from playing during the war and in July 1921 became the Oldham manager.

1954 United and Wolverhampton Wanderers drew 4-4 in the first leg of the FA Youth Cup Final at Old Trafford in front of a 18,246 crowd. Duncan Edwards and David Pegg scored two goals apiece.

1966 United went down to a Colin Harvey goal in the FA Cup semi-final at Burnden Park in front of a 60,000 capacity crowd.

1977 Goals from Steve Coppell and Jimmy Greenhoff helped United beat Leeds United 2-1 at Hillsborough in the FA Cup semi-final.

1994 Eric Cantona returning from a five-match suspension scored both goals in Manchester United's 2-0 defeat of Manchester City at Old Trafford.

24

1897 Newton Heath faced Sunderland for their third play-off match The Wearsiders had been League champions in 1892, 1893 and 1895 but could only draw with the Heathens 1-1, Boyd scoring the goal. Unfortunately, two days later, Newton lost 2-0 at Roker Park in their last play-off match and had to face another season in the Second Division.

1909 Manchester United won the FA Cup for the first time in their history, beating Bristol City 1-0 in the final at the Crystal Palace. The only goal of the game came after 22 minutes when Harold Halse's shot hit the underside of the crossbar and Sandy Turnbull slammed the rebound into the empty net.

1948 United beat Blackpool 4-2 in the FA Cup Final at Wembley. Going a goal down after 12 minutes, United equalised through Jack Rowley before Blackpool took the lead just before half-time. United drew level in the 69th minute when Rowley scored his second goal. Ten minutes later, the Reds were in the lead when Pearson smashed home Anderson's through ball. Anderson himself scored United's fourth goal just minutes from time.

1968 The Reds beat Real Madrid 1-0 in the first leg of the semi-final of the European Cup with George Best scoring United's goal.

1991 A Lee Sharpe goal gave United a 1-1 draw at home to Legia Warsaw and a 4-2 win on aggregate to put them in the final of the European Cup Winners' Cup.

1994 A memorial service for Sir Matt Busby was held at Old Trafford. The hour long service was attended by 10,000 spectators along with United players past and present. The service combined singing with spoken tributes.

25

1906 United made sure of promotion to the First Division with a 3-2 win at Lincoln City with goals from Allan 2, and Wall.

1925 United beat Port Vale 4-0 with goals from Lochhead, Spence, Smith and McPherson to virtually ensure promotion from the Second Division.

- *April* -

1957 Old Trafford staged its first ever European Cup tie as Real Madrid provided the opposition. Having beaten United 3-1 in Madrid, the Spanish champions showed stiff resistance to draw 2-2. United's goals were scored by Taylor and Charlton. All United's previous home games in the European Cup had been played at Maine Road.

1984 Despite a Norman Whiteside goal, United lost 2-1 in Italy against Juventus in the European Cup Winners' Cup semi-final second leg to exit the competition 3-2 on aggregate.

1994 It is rumoured that Manchester United players will get a bonus of £30,000 each if they win the double.

26

1902 Newton Heath FC was no more, being renamed 'Manchester United' Football Club. However, the selection of the club's new title was not all that straightforward. Manchester Central was suggested, as was Manchester Celtic, but eventually Louis Rocca, who was later to play a leading role in the club's scouting staff, came forward with the name of Manchester United and it was adopted unanimously.

1952 Manchester United thrash Arsenal, the only team who could have caught them, 6-1 in the final game of the season, to capture the First Division title for the first time since 1911. Jack Rowley scored a hat-trick whilst Pearson 2 and Byrne netted the others.

1954 A David Pegg penalty in the second leg of the FA Youth Cup Final against Wolverhampton Wanderers at Molyneux gave United the trophy for the second year running.

1965 Manchester United became champions of the First Division for the sixth time after beating Arsenal 3-1 at Old Trafford, with goals from Law 2 and Best.

1996 The 11 foot high bronze statue of Sir Matt Busby was manoeuvred onto a podium below the Munich Memorial on the roof of the entrance into the executive boxes facing Sir Matt Busby Way.

27

1893 Newton Heath beat Small Heath 5-2 at Bramall Lane in the second 'Test match' with Farman scoring a hat-trick.

1908 Manchester United and Queen's Park Rangers contested the first FA Charity Shield match and drew 1-1 in front of a meagre 6,000 fans at Stamford Bridge, with Billy Meredith scoring United's goal. When they replayed at the same ground on 29 August, a crowd of 60,000 saw United win 4-0 with Jimmy Turnbull grabbing a hat-trick.

1955 United beat West Bromwich Albion 4-1 in the first leg of the FA Youth Cup Final at Old Trafford with Colman 2, Charlton and Beckett the goalscorers.

1963 A Denis Law goal gave the Reds a 1-0 FA Cup semi-final win over Southampton at Villa Park.

1974 Denis Law scored his last goal in first-class football at Old Trafford, when he was playing for Manchester City. Scoring in the 85th minute of the match, he sent his old club, Manchester United, into the Second Division.

1996 United's tribute to Sir Matt Busby is unveiled in the shape of a statue that will stand forever outside Old Trafford's East Stand. The hollow statue was filled with souvenirs and memorabilia left outside the ground following Sir Matt's death in 1994.

28

1894 After finishing bottom of the First Division again, this time with fewer points than the last season, the club were once again

- April -

involved in a 'Test Match', this time against Liverpool at Blackburn. In their first season in the Football League, Liverpool had topped the Second Division without losing a match. The odds were stacked against the Heathens, who lost 2-0 and were duly relegated.

1906 Promotion to the First Division as runners-up to Bristol City was clinched with a 6-0 win over Burton United, with goals from Sagar 2, Picken 2, Peddie and Wall. A snowstorm added to the occasion as for the first time in history, both the Manchester clubs found themselves side by side in the First Division.

1973 Bobby Charlton made the last of his 754 first team appearances for Manchester United in the Reds 1-0 defeat at Chelsea.

1996 A record Premier League attendance of 53,926 see United beat Nottingham Forest 5-0 at Old Trafford.

29

1911 United beat Sunderland 5-1 on the final day of the season at Old Trafford to take the First Division title by one point from Aston Villa. United's scorers that day were Halse 2, Turnbull and West and an own goal from Sunderland's Mitten.

1936 After leading 3-0 at Gigg Lane, United hold on to win 3-2 against Bury and so clinch promotion to the First Division. The following Saturday, the Reds draw 1-1 at Hull City and are crowned champions of the Second Division.

1950 United beat Fulham 3-0 at Old Trafford in the last game of the season in front of 11,968, the club's worst post-war home League gate.

1956 Birth of Kevin Moran. He was the first man to be sent off in an FA Cup Final, when he upended Everton's Peter Reid with a rather clumsy challenge. The referee's action seemed to spur United on and they beat Everton 1-0. Moran was not officially eligible for a medal but after the club lodged an appeal, the FA relented. It was his second FA Cup winners' medal, having won one two years earlier when United beat Brighton. A tough-tackling centre-half, Moran missed a number of games through injury. He won his first cap for the Republic of Ireland against Switzerland in 1980 and went on to appear in 71 full internationals. After playing in 288 games for the Reds, he joined Sporting Gijon in the Spanish League before returning to England to play for Blackburn Rovers.

1968 Old Trafford staged the FA Cup semi-final between Everton and Leeds United, the first to be held at the ground in the post-war years.

1986 United lost 2-0 at Maine Road in the second leg of the FA Youth Cup Final and so went down 3-1 on aggregate after only being able to draw the first leg at home to Manchester City 1-1.

30

1910 John Picken scored all four United goals as the Reds beat Middlesbrough 4-1 on the last day of the season.

1954 Birth of Gerry Daly. He joined the club from Bohemians in April 1973 for a fee of £20,000. Though he had just turned 19 years of age, he soon became part of an exciting United midfield that took the Second Division by storm in 1974-75. He also played in the FA Cup Final of 1976 when United lost to Southampton 1-0. In March 1977 his career at Old Trafford came to a rather abrupt end following a row with manager Tommy Docherty and he was transferred to Derby County for £175,000. He had appeared in 142 games for United, scoring 32 goals.

- April -

Within six months of his move to the Baseball Ground, Docherty was appointed the Derby manager and Daly was soon on his way to Coventry City for £310,000. Capped 47 times by the Republic of Ireland, he later had spells with Birmingham City, Shrewsbury, Stoke City and Doncaster Rovers.

1955 United won the FA Youth Cup for the third consecutive year with a 3-0 win at the Hawthorns. This gave them a 7-1 aggregate victory over West Bromwich Albion.

1956 The programme for the first leg of the FA Youth Cup Final at Old Trafford against Chesterfield contained a glowing pen picture of a Chesterfield youngster by the name of Gordon Banks. The future England goalkeeper played well but couldn't prevent United winning 3-2 with goals from Carolan, Pearson and Charlton. United took the trophy 4-3 on aggregate after a 1-1 draw in the second leg at Saltergate.

1960 An Alex Dawson hat-trick helped United beat Everton 5-0 in front of an Old Trafford crowd of 43,823.

1964 David Sadler scored a hat-trick as United beat Swindon Town 4-1 at Old Trafford to win the FA Youth Cup for a sixth time.

1981 Despite winning seven games in a row to end the season in eighth place in the First Division, 12 points adrift of champions Aston Villa, manager Dave Sexton and his assistant Tommy Cavanagh are sacked.

1996 The Reds' announce that 2,300 seats in the lower tier of the new stand are to cost £1,169 per season. The same places in the old cantilever stand had cost £340 per season. When the old stand was demolished, fans who were relocated were told that they would be able to claim their old seats back but then learned that it was going to cost them three times as much to do so!

9 April: Wilf McGuiness (with Nobby Styles, left) is to become the new United Manager.

- April -

(Left) 24 April United win the FA Cup for the first time

(Right) 25 April Tommy Taylor scores in the first European Cup game held at Old Trafford.

(Left) 26 April - Newton Heath become Manchester United... Louis Rocca, the man who thought of the new name.
(Above) 4 April - Colin Gibson....... gets sent off.

MAY

1

1926 The Reds end the 1925-26 season with a 3-2 win over West Bromwich Albion with Charlie Taylor scoring a hat-trick.

1948 On the final day of the season, Jack Rowley hits a hat-trick as United beat Blackburn Rovers 4-1 to finish as runners-up to Arsenal in the First Division.

1976 United lost 1-0 to Second Division Southampton in the FA Cup Final at Wembley. The Saints' winner was scored by Bobby Stokes just eight minutes from time.

2

1931 The Reds drew their last match of the season at home to Middlesbrough 4-4 in front of a crowd of just 3,969 and are relegated to the Second Division.

1975 Birth of David Beckham. A member of the 'Class of 92' that won the FA Youth Cup, he broke into the United first team at the end of the 1994-95 season. It was his first goal in the FA Cup in the semi-final win over Chelsea at Villa Park that took United to Wembley in 1996. His first full season at Old Trafford brought him both League Championship and FA Cup winners' medals. The scorer of some spectacular goals and deadly from free-kicks, Beckham is now a regular in the full England side.

1988 United won 2-0 at Oxford United's Manor Ground in front of just 8,966, the club's worst post-war away League crowd.

1992 The Stretford End was used for the last time in a League match as United played Tottenham Hotspur and after the FA Youth Cup Final three days later, the bulldozers moved in.

1994 Coventry City beat Blackburn Rovers 2-0, handing Manchester United the title trophy for the second year in succession.

3

1917 Alex 'Sandy' Turnbull who played 245 games for the Reds, scoring 100 goals was killed in action at Arras. The former Manchester City forward had made his debut against Aston Villa on New Year's Day 1907 and remained with the club until 1915 when he was banned from football for taking part in a notorious bribery scandal. He won two League Championship medals and scored the winning goal in the 1909 FA Cup Final.

1958 After the most harrowing but remarkable season in any club's history, Manchester United lose 2-0 to Bolton Wanderers in the FA Cup Final at Wembley. Bolton's second goal was one of the most controversial goals in the ground's history as Nat Lofthouse charged into United's Harry Gregg and bustled both the goalkeeper and the ball over the line. The United defenders looked on in disbelief as the referee pointed to the centre-circle.

4

1953 Manchester United's youth team beat Wolverhampton Wanderers 7-1 in the first leg of the FA Youth Cup Final. They drew the return leg at Molineux 2-2 to become the first winners of the trophy with an aggregate win of 9-3.

1957 United lost goalkeeper Ray Wood after just six minutes of the FA Cup Final against Aston Villa with a shattered cheekbone. Jackie Blanchflower went in goal but the Reds with only 10 men - for substitutes weren't allowed then - lost 2-1.

55

- May -

United had already won the League Championship and were hoping to become the first club this century to complete the double. After a goalless first-half, Peter McParland scored two goals for Villa in the space of five minutes and though Tommy Taylor pulled a goal back, it was too late and Villa with seven victories became the most prolific winners of the FA Cup of all-time.

1994 United beat Southampton 2-0 with goals from Kanchelskis and Hughes, bringing their total number of points to 91 - a new club record.

1996 Angela McDonough and Gerry McKenna become the first couple to tie the knot at Old Trafford since the ground was granted a licence to perform wedding ceremonies.

5

1928 The season ended on a spectacular note as United thrashed Liverpool 6-1 with Joe Spence hitting a hat-trick and Rawlings 2 and Hanson scoring the others. It was an important victory for the Reds, as any of six teams at the foot of the First Division could have been relegated.

1934 United were in danger towards the end of the 1933-34 season of being relegated to the Third Division (Northern Section). In an attempt to change their fortunes, they changed their colours to a design of cherry hoops on white. Their last match was at Millwall who were second from bottom with one point more than United. United won 2-0 with goals from Manley and Cape and Millwall went down. The old colours re-appeared at the beginning of the following season.

1971 United beat neighbours and rivals Manchester City 4-3 at Maine Road on the final day of the season with Best 2, Law and Charlton the scorers.

1996 David May scored his first Premiership goal for United in the title clincher at the Riverside Stadium, Middlesbrough on the last day of the season, and Alex Ferguson became the first ever manager to win three titles in Scotland and three in England.

6

1937 Birth of Shay Brennan. A member of United's FA Youth Cup winning side of 1955, he was thrown into the first team for the FA Cup game against Sheffield Wednesday immediately after the Munich air disaster. His display at outside-left was quite remarkable in that he scored two goals in United's 3-0 win. However, it was 1959-60 before he made the break into the first team on a permanent basis, going on to play in 356 games for the club. He collected two League Championship medals and was a member of the 1968 European Cup-winning team. Born in Manchester of Irish parents, he appeared in 19 full internationals for the Republic of Ireland. In fact, after playing his last game for United in January 1970, he went to join Waterford in the League of Ireland.

1967 United clinched the First Division title in style, beating West Ham United 6-1 at Upton Park. The Reds scored three goals in the first ten minutes and completely demolished the Hammers. United's scorers were Law 2, Best, Charlton, Crerand and Foulkes.

1982 United drew 4-4 at Watford after extra-time in the FA Youth Cup Final, but go down 7-6 on aggregate after losing the home leg 3-2.

7

1921 Welsh international Billy Meredith became the oldest player to appear for Manchester United when at the age of 46 years and 285 days, he played in the club's 3-0 win against Derby County at Old Trafford. Also this day, a record attendance was set, when a crowd of just 13 **paid** to watch Stockport County play Leicester City in a Second Division match.

- May -

Edgeley Park had been closed by the FA and so the game was played at Old Trafford. The attendance is somewhat misleading in that the game was watched by a lot more who had stayed on after the United v Derby County game. Over 10,000 remained inside the ground to watch the game for free.

1938 United played their last Second Division game for thirty-six years when after beating Bury 2-0, they won promotion to the First Division.

1956 United drew 1-1 at Chesterfield to win the FA Youth Cup 3-2 on aggregate for the fourth consecutive year.

1957 Mark Pearson scored a hat-trick as United beat West Ham United 5-0 in the second leg of the FA Youth Cup Final, to win 8-2 on aggregate. It was the fifth consecutive year that the Reds had lifted the trophy.

1965 Birth of Norman Whiteside. It was the Boys Brigade that gave the young Whiteside his first real taste of football. He scored a century of goals in one season before he was discovered by United's Belfast scout, Bob Bishop. After being signed by United at the age of 15, he made his League debut as a substitute a year later in a 1-0 win over Brighton. On his full debut, he grabbed the fans' attention by scoring in a 2-0 win over Stoke City - he was 17 years and 8 days old. Whiteside stepped out to make his World Cup debut in 1982 with all the confidence of a player who has done it all, yet he was just 17 years and 41 days old when he pulled on the emerald green shirt of Northern Ireland against Yugoslavia in Zaragosa. He was the youngest player ever to appear in a World Cup finals match and the youngest to be booked, being shown the yellow card in his first match! In 1983, United considered a £1.5 million offer from AC Milan, but Whiteside stayed in Manchester and scored a goal in the League Cup Final against Liverpool and in the 4-0 FA Cup Final replay win.

Against Everton in the FA Cup Final of 1985, he scored a majestic winner. A serious tendon injury threatened his career but after a clash of personalities with Alex Ferguson, he joined Everton for £650,000 in the summer of 1989. However, his appearances were limited by injury and in 1992, he retired.

8 **1956** Best remembered as a centre-half, Jackie Blanchflower, younger brother of the more famous Danny Blanchflower played in goal for the entire ninety minutes of the friendly match against Helsingborg.

1958 The Reds beat AC Milan 2-1 at Old Trafford in the European Cup semi-final first-leg with Tommy Taylor converting a penalty and Dennis Viollet scoring United's other goal.

1994 Manchester United paraded the Premiership trophy around Old Trafford after their goalless draw with Coventry City, which was also Bryan Robson's last game for the club.

9 **1953** United win the FA Youth Cup in its inaugural season by drawing 2-2 against Wolverhampton Wanderers at Molineux to win the trophy 9-3 on aggregate.

1966 The Reds produced their biggest win of the season to beat Aston Villa 6-1. Jimmy Ryan made his home debut after two away appearances and revelled in the splendid service he was given. He scored one of United's goals and made three of the others. David Sadler and David Herd scored two goals apiece and Bobby Charlton the other as United's football flowed.

10 **1995** In the very last of his seventeen home League matches, Peter Schmeichel lets in his only goal as United beat Southampton 2-1.

- May -

The Saints arrived at Old Trafford with only one defeat in their previous nine games and took the lead after just five minutes when Simon Charlton headed into an empty net. Andy Cole equalised midway through the first half before the Reds went on all-out attack during the second forty-five minutes. They were rewarded ten minutes from time when Ken Monkou pulled at Cole's shirt to give away a penalty. Denis Irwin hammered the spot-kick just wide of Dave Beasant who was only a finger-tip away from saving it.

11

1991 The shortest United career belongs to Paul Wratten who in two substitute appearances for the club, played for just 23 minutes. He came on for six minutes against Wimbledon (Home 2-1) on 2 April and then for another 17 minutes against Crystal Palace (Away 0-3) on this date.

1996 Manchester United beat Liverpool 1-0 in the FA Cup Final with an Eric Cantona special to put themselves into the record books as the first club ever to do the 'double' twice. David James who had a superb match for Liverpool was partially blocked by one of his own players as he came for a curling Giggs corner. His punch was poor and the ball fell to an off balance Cantona, who struck a superb volley through a crowded goalmouth and into the net.

12

1951 The first visit of a foreign club side to Old Trafford. Red Star Belgrade from Yugoslavia played United in a friendly as part of the Festival of Britain. Despite the visitors being the better team, United drew level with just eight minutes left when Aston was brought down inside the area and Rowley converted the spot-kick.

1965 The Reds won their Inter Cities Fairs Cup quarter-final tie first leg at RC Strasbourg 5-0 with two goals from Denis Law and one apiece from John Connelly, Bobby Charlton and David Herd.

1979 United lost 3-2 to Arsenal in one of the most exciting FA Cup Finals for years. With just four minutes left, United were trailing 2-0. Then Gordon McQueen, United's Scottish centre-half thrust out his long left leg to force the ball past Pat Jennings. Two minutes later, Sammy McIlroy weaved his way into the penalty area before stroking the ball into the Arsenal net. The Reds were back on terms with less than 90 seconds remaining, but it wasn't to be for almost on the stroke of full-time, Alan Sunderland converted Graham Rix's cross to take the Cup to Highbury.

1990 United drew 3-3 with Crystal Palace in a nerve-jangling FA Cup Final. For United it was a typical twist to their crazy season, which saw them flirt with relegation and dice with football death in the semi-final games with Oldham Athletic. Palace took the lead but United went 2-1 in front following goals from Robson and Hughes. Ian Wright, the Palace striker returning from a broken leg, scored four minutes after coming on to take the tie into extra-time. The England forward put Palace 3-2 ahead before Mark Hughes equalised following a fine run by Danny Wallace. United almost snatched a winner when Robson hit the post.

13

1994 Alex Ferguson won the Manager of the Year award on the eve of the club's appearance in the FA Cup Final.

- May -

14

1958 Manchester United suffered their heaviest defeat in the European Cup when they went down 4-0 against AC Milan in the second leg of their post-Munich semi-final. The German referee was whistle-mad and blew up for fouls that were nothing more than hard tackles.

1993 A crowd of 31,037 watched the second leg of the FA Youth Cup Final between Leeds United and Manchester United at Elland Road. 30,562 had attended the first leg at Old Trafford three days earlier to give an aggregate attendance of 61,599 spectators - a record for the competition.

1994 United beat Chelsea 4-0 in the FA Cup Final with two goals from Eric Cantona and one apiece from Mark Hughes and Brian McClair to win the elusive League and Cup double for the first time. They joined Tottenham, Arsenal and Liverpool, the only clubs to achieve that feat this century. With his goal, Mark Hughes became the only player to score at Wembley in four different club matches in one season. Hughes had already scored in the Charity Shield, League Cup Final and FA Cup semi-final.

15

1968 After beating Real Madrid 1-0 at Old Trafford in the first leg of the European Cup semi-final, United travelled to the Bernabeu Stadium for the return leg. In the first half, Real went into a 3-1 lead with goals from Pirri, Gento and Amancio. United's goal came from Tony Dunne, a 40-yard lob which trickled over the line as Kidd challenged the 'keeper. The Reds came back into the match with just a quarter of an hour to go when Sadler slipped in to convert Foulkes' header from Crerand's free-kick. Then with twelve minutes left, Best beat Sanchis and Zoco to cross for Foulkes the veteran centre-half to win the battle for United, 4-3 on aggregate.

1969 A Bobby Charlton goal helped United beat AC Milan 1-0 in the European Cup semi-final second leg in front of an Old Trafford crowd of 63,103 but it wasn't enough to take them into the final.

1982 When Norman Whiteside scored United's second goal in their 2-0 home win over Stoke City, he became the club's youngest post-war goalscorer.

1991 United met Barcelona in the European Cup Winners' Cup Final at Rotterdam, despite efforts to have it moved to a larger stadium. For Mark Hughes, the final meant so much as United's opponents were his former club. A crowd of 45,000 roared United on as they completely outplayed the Spanish giants. Two goals from Hughes, the second the team's 100th of the season, tied up victory and though Barcelona punished Les Sealey, who was suffering with a badly gashed knee sustained in the League Cup Final, United hung on for a 2-1 win.

1995 Manchester United won the FA Youth Cup Final on penalties from Spurs after Terry Cooke had put them level on aggregate in the last seconds of normal time.

16

1906 Manchester United signed Billy Meredith from neighbours Manchester City for £500 in spite of the fact that his suspension, for having offered a sum of money to an Aston Villa player, still had nearly two years to run.

1956 When England fielded its youngest post-war attack against Sweden at the Ramunda Stadium in Stockholm, United provided four of its players in Byrne, Edwards, Berry and Taylor but they disappointed in a goalless draw.

- May -

1962 United wing-half Maurice Setters was sent-off in the Reds' friendly match at Mallorca during the club's tour of Spain.

17

1990 Manchester United won the FA Cup with a player who was within an ace of being left out of the team. Lee Martin's spectacular goal gave the Reds a 1-0 win over Crystal Palace in the Final replay. Yet Alex Ferguson was concerned about the players' ability to get through extra-time without getting cramp, the youngster having been substituted in the previous three Cup games due to this problem. Also Les Sealey made his FA Cup debut for the club and became the only player to appear in the final while on loan from another club.

1994 Bryan Robson left Old Trafford after 13 years to take the position of manager at Middlesbrough.

18

1940 United lost 6-0 to New Brighton just twelve days after beating them by the same score in a West Regional League (Western Division) match.

1942 Birth of Nobby Stiles. Hailing from Collyhurst, he won five England schoolboy caps before signing for the Reds as an apprentice in 1957. He shared in United's successful FA Cup run of 1963, though he didn't win a place in the final, but in 1966-67 he hardly missed a match when the Reds won the League Championship. He wore the Number 4 shirt throughout England's triumphant World Cup in 1966. He made his mark as a world-class player with his brilliant covering, especially against Portugal's Eusebio in the semi-final. No one will forget Nobby's antics after England had won the World Cup. He put the trophy on his head and danced with delight. After United won the European Cup in 1968, his standing was at a peak, but his earlier bad boy image was reflected by his pen picture in the match programme when the Reds played Estudiantes in the World Club Championship where he was described as *'brutal, badly intentioned and a bad sportsman.'* At the age of 27 he suffered two cartilage operations and in May 1971, United accepted a £20,000 offer from Middlesbrough. He had played first team football at Old Trafford for eleven seasons, making 393 appearances. After two seasons at Ayresome Park, he moved to Preston North End for the same fee to play for Bobby Charlton. He only spent one more season playing but then spent a further seven years at Deepdale, three as coach and four as manager. He later coached Vancouver Whitecaps and West Bromwich Albion before returning to Old Trafford to work on the junior coaching staff. He won most of the honours available to a footballer - two League Championship medals, a European Cup winners' medal, England caps at Youth, Under-23 and full levels and a World Cup winners' medal.

1972 United's Republic of Ireland international full-back Tony Dunne was dismissed during the club's friendly match at Mallorca, almost ten years to the day when Maurice Setters received his marching orders.

1985 Kevin Moran was sent-off in the FA Cup Final as United beat Everton 1-0 through a Norman Whiteside goal. He is the only player ever to be dismissed in an FA Cup Final.

1997 Eric Cantona quit football for a new career in films. Though this was the third time the Frenchman has announced his retirement, United believed that on this occasion, the decision was final. Cantona spent the summer considering offers not only to develop his acting career in France but a move into the field of directing plays and films in his homeland.

19

1965 United played out a goalless draw at home to RC Strasbourg in the Inter Cities Fairs Cup quarter-final second leg just a

- May -

week after winning 5-0 in France. It was an anti-climax for the 34,188 fans who were hoping to see the Reds score plenty of goals.

1985 *'We All Follow Man Utd'* was number 10 in the British Hit Singles charts and was in the ratings for five weeks after first entering on this date. Another record which was given considerable air time but failed to make an impact on the charts was the *'Manchester United Calypso'* an upmarket tribute in some ways to the Busby Babes. It was revised in the wave of sympathy which swept over the country following the 1958 Munich air disaster.

20

1948 Sir Matt Busby managed the Great Britain team in the Olympic Games as they played their first match.

1963 Though Manchester United have had a number of black first team players, the first was Dennis Walker, who played in just one game. He appeared at outside-left in United's 3-2 defeat at Nottingham Forest, which coincidentally is the latest date the club have played a Football League game except for the first season after the Second World War.

1970 Bobby Charlton scored his last and 49th England goal against Colombia in Bogota as England won 4-0.

1995 United set a new record of 13 FA Cup Final appearances, one more than Arsenal and Everton when they played the Goodison Park side at Wembley, only to lose 1-0 to a Paul Rideout goal.

21

1977 Manchester United beat Liverpool 2-1 to win the FA Cup Final at Wembley. Liverpool, who were League Champions were the better team, but it was Stuart Pearson who gave United the lead after 50 minutes when he took a pass from Jimmy Greenhoff and shot under Ray Clemence's body. Two minutes later, Liverpool were level when Jimmy Case, turning on the edge of the penalty area, hit a cross from Joey Jones into the left-hand corner of Stepney's net. Three minutes later, United were back in front when Jimmy Greenhoff seized upon an error by Tommy Smith and his shot rebounded to Lou Macari. The little Scot's snap shot hit Greenhoff and flew past Clemence. Minutes from time, Ray Kennedy who had headed against the post in the first-half, hit the stanchion as Liverpool pressed for an equaliser. Making his debut in the final was Arthur Albiston who went on to play in 436 games for United.

1983 The Reds drew 2-2 after extra-time in the FA Cup Final. They came back from a goal down to lead Brighton 2-1 but then allowed the Seagulls to draw level. A relatively easy chance was missed by Brighton's Gordon Smith in extra-time.

22

1946 Birth of George Best. An unknown from Belfast who became a soccer superstar. He made his League debut for United on 14 September 1963, standing in for Ian Moir against West Bromwich Albion. After only 15 League games, Northern Ireland gave him his first cap against Wales at Swansea. Best initially played wide on the left, but soon began to play in a free attacking role, scoring some of the most stunning goals ever seen at Old Trafford. He won a League Championship medal in 1965 and again in 1967 but as things began to go wrong, his frustration began to show as he retaliated against harsh treatment to earn himself a reputation for indiscipline, while his taste for wine and women began to undermine his consistency on the field. However, the peak of Best's career came in 1968 when his team won the European Cup at Wembley, beating Benfica 4-1 after extra-time. It was a euphoric night for Manchester United and for Best, the pinnacle of achievement in a season that saw him gain the titles of English

- *May* -

and European Footballer of the Year. One of the most gifted players you could wish to see, he had great speed and awareness, coupled with fantastic dribbling ability. Strong and brave, he was the complete all-round forward. He was however, becoming increasingly difficult to manage - missing training and failing to turn up for a match. After sacking manager Frank O'Farrell, the club issued a statement that George Best would remain on the transfer list and would not be selected for United again. A letter from Best announcing his retirement crossed with this. He walked out on United several times and played his last game for them on New Years Day 1974. He had played in 466 games for United, scoring 178 goals. But it wasn't to be the end of his career for he played for Hibernian, Fulham, Stockport County, Bournemouth and in the United States. A footballing genius, George Best has gone down in history as one of the world's all-time greats.

23 **1996** Gary and Phil Neville played in the same England team against China to equal an 120 year old record. Not since 1876 have a pair of brothers played in a Cup Final winning side and then appeared together for their country. The last pair to do so were Frank and Hubert Heron of The Wanderers. The Nevilles were also the youngest brothers ever to win England caps together and the first pair from the same club since Frank and Fred Forman of Nottingham Forest in 1899.

24 **1908** Following their League triumph, United embarked on their first international tour, to the Austro-Hungarian Empire. After beating a Vienna XI 4-0 and Ferencvaros 6-2, the Reds faced the same Hungarian team for a return clash in Budapest. It was probably the club's first match on a Sunday but with United leading by 6-0, the referee - who could not speak English and was not acquainted with the rules - dismissed three of United's players. The players refused to leave the field and after a quarter-of-an-hours argument, United continued at full strength and won 7-0. However, as the final whistle blew, stones were thrown, players were spat at and the Hungarian police had to draw swords to disperse the crowd.

1966 Birth of Eric Cantona. The French international forward joined Leeds United in February 1992, adding some flair to the Elland Road club's League Championship win, but in November of that year, he signed for Manchester United for £1.2 million. He excelled throughout the remaining games, scoring some vital goals to help the Reds win the First Division title, thus becoming the first man ever to win a Championship medal two seasons running with two different clubs. In fact, in Cantona's first 60 appearances in the colours of Manchester United, they only lost twice - a remarkable achievement. He seemed to have found stability in a club for the first time in his career but then came a number of sendings off and his moment of infamy at Crystal Palace, from which he was suspended for nine months. He returned from this a reformed character and helped United to perform the 'double' again in 1995-96, two years after they had achieved the feat a first time. In May 1996, he was honoured by the Football Writers' Association when he was named 'Footballer of the Year'. Capped at full international level by France on 45 occasions, this most naturally gifted of strikers quit the club in the summer of 1997.

25 **1963** United won the FA Cup for the third time in their history when they beat Leicester City 3-1. Yet the Reds found themselves as underdogs as the Filbert Street side finished fourth in the First Division, 18 points ahead of United. Inspired by Denis Law who opened the scoring after half an hour, United dominated proceedings and two further goals by David Herd brought the Cup back to Old Trafford after an absence of 15 years.

- May -

26

1909 Birth of Sir Matt Busby. The greatest name in the history of Manchester United. The son of a Scottish miner, Busby was a stylish half-back with Manchester City and Liverpool before the Second World War. With City he won an FA Cup winners' medal in 1934 and although he only won one full cap for Scotland, he captained his country in several wartime matches. Appointed United manager in 1945, he moulded his first great side under the captaincy of Johnny Carey. The Reds went on to win the FA Cup in 1948 and the League Championship in 1952, the club's first League title for 41 years. In fact, in Busby's first six seasons in charge, United never finished lower than fourth. Then came his second outstanding side, the Busby Babes, who won the League Championship in 1955-56 and 1956-57 before being cruelly destroyed at Munich. With Jimmy Murphy he began to assemble a new United and won the FA Cup in 1963 and the First Division title in 1965. With Best, Law and Charlton in the side, his dream was realised when the Reds beat Benfica 4-1 in 1968 to lift the European Cup. A year later, he retired but when Wilf McGuinness was relieved of the job in December 1970, he assumed charge again, steering the club away from trouble. He was knighted after United's European triumph and was made a Freeman of Manchester before being appointed President of the club.

1947 The latest finish to a United season saw the Reds beat Sheffield United 6-2 with Jack Rowley scoring a hat-trick.

1983 When Norman Whiteside scored for Manchester United in the FA Cup Final against Brighton and Hove Albion, he was just 18 years and 19 days old, the youngest player to score during an FA Cup Final.

1995 Roy Keane was fined a further £5,000 for his red card offence in the FA Cup semi-final replay against Crystal Palace, the FA deciding to make a special case of the incident.

27

1971 Birth of Lee Sharpe. After starting his League career with Torquay United, he joined the Reds in June 1988, making his debut in a 2-0 win over West Ham United in September of that year. He was then hampered by injuries before two hernia operations and viral meningitis interrupted his career. In 1990-91 he played a significant part in United reaching the League Cup Final, scoring against Liverpool, netting a hat-trick against Arsenal at Highbury, and scoring two of the three goals by which the Reds beat Leeds United in the semi-final. At the end of the season, he was named Young Player of the Year after becoming the youngest player to represent England since Duncan Edwards, when he played against the Republic of Ireland, just two months short of his 20th birthday. In the summer of 1996, after appearing in 265 first team games and collecting both the championship and FA Cup winners' medal double for the second time in his career, he left to join Leeds United.

28

1956 Manchester United were invited by the FA to represent England in the European Cup the following season. The invitation was accepted and meant that the Reds would play home and away games with the crack Continental sides during the 1956-57 season on a knock-out basis.

29

1949 Birth of Brian Kidd. He made his senior debut for United in the Charity Shield against Tottenham Hotspur in 1967 and from that moment on, was a regular choice even though he was only 18 years old. On his 19th birthday, he scored United's third goal in the European Cup Final against Benfica to seal the Reds' victory. Capable of scoring with either foot or head, he hit 70 goals in 264 appearances for United over seven seasons before moving to Arsenal for £110,000 in 1974.

After two years at Highbury, he returned north to join Manchester City in another £100,000 move. After a successful spell at Maine Road he was on the move again, this time to Everton for £150,000. With the Goodison Park club, he had the unenviable record of becoming only the second player since World War Two to be dismissed in an FA Cup semi-final. Shortly after he joined Bolton Wanderers before going to play in US soccer. He was appointed assistant-manager at Manchester United in 1991 after Archie Knox had moved to Glasgow Rangers.

1968 Manchester United become the first English club to win the European Cup when they beat Benfica at Wembley 4-1 after extra-time. After an uninspiring first half, United took the lead when Bobby Charlton headed home David Sadler's cross. John Aston was an unlikely star and if Sadler had converted a chance created for him by the left-winger, United would have been two goals up and home and dry. However, ten minutes from the end, Graca equalised and then with under five minutes to play, Eusebio broke free and sent in a powerful shot which Stepney blocked. Two minutes into extra-time, George Best scored a goal of sheer brilliance, leaving the Benfica defence trailing before rounding goalkeeper Henrique. A minute later, birthday boy Brian Kidd headed home United's third and then Charlton rounded things off with a fourth goal, the third in the space of eight minutes.

1982 United's proposed rock concert featuring Queen, was squashed by Trafford Borough Council who refused to grant the club an entertainment licence due to the noise and nuisance the concert would cause local residents.

Despite United's protests, the decision was upheld and the concert switched to Leeds United's Elland Road.

30 **1975** United striker Stuart Pearson took a step nearer his first cap when he was named in Don Revie's squad of 35 for a June 'get together'. Pearson, top League scorer for the Reds the previous season with 17 goals, had not figured in Revie's plans, since he was invited to the 'talk-in' along with 80 other players soon after Revie became the England boss.

31 **1965** Despite Pat Crerand being sent-off, the Reds beat Ferencvaros 3-2 at Old Trafford in the Inter Cities Fairs Cup semi-final first leg. Novak put the Hungarians ahead before a subdued-looking Denis Law equalised from a penalty after his header was handled on the line. In a scintillating second half display, two goals from David Herd put United in the driving seat before goalkeeper Pat Dunne failed to hold Rakosi's half-hit shot 14 minutes from the end.

1967 United's trip from America to New Zealand before their tour of Australia was quite tiring, though in fact, the United players had three breakfasts in one day! After beating Dundee, there was the usual banquet and it was 2.00.am before the players got to bed. They had to be up again sharp at six o'clock to catch a plane for Honolulu some 2,400 miles away. They had an early breakfast at the hotel, another on the plane and then with the clock going back three hours, the club arrived at Honolulu at 11.00.am in time for another breakfast!

- May -

*(Left) 4 May
Mark Hughes.
His goal
helped secure
the record
number of
points.*

*(Right) 16 May
Billy Meredith
Signs for
United.*

*(Below left)
18 May
Kevin Moran
Unenviable
record - the
first player to
be sent off at
Wembley in an
FA Cup Final.*

*(Below right)
29 May
Brian Kidd
Birthday to
celebrate.*

JUNE

1

1909 Harold Halse made his England debut, scoring two goals in an 8-1 win over Austria in Vienna.

1926 Birth of Johnny Berry. He was signed from Birmingham City after he had scored one of the finest goals ever seen at Old Trafford when playing for the St Andrews' club against Manchester United. A tricky right-winger, he won a League Championship medal at the end of his first season with the club. The winner of three League Championship medals, he appeared in the 1957 FA Cup Final and represented England on four occasions. Though he did not play against Red Star, he made the fateful trip to Belgrade and was so seriously injured in the Munich disaster, that he never played football again. In his seven seasons at Old Trafford, the 5ft 5ins winger scored 43 goals in 273 League and Cup appearances.

1940 United fielded nine 'guest' players in the 3-0 defeat at home to Everton. The Reds' forward line included Stanley Matthews and Manchester City's Irish international Peter Doherty.

2

1950 Manchester United paid £11,000 for Reg Allen when they bought him from Queen's Park Rangers, making him the first goal-keeper to be transferred for over £10,000.

1951 Birth of Arnold Muhren. A Dutch international, he came to United from Ipswich Town in the summer of 1982 after earlier playing in Holland with Ajax and Twente Enschende. With Ipswich, he collected a UEFA Cup winners' medal but after his contract at Portman Road expired, he joined United. At the end of his first season at Old Trafford, he helped the Reds to victory in the FA Cup Final replay against Brighton, scoring a second-half penalty.

Towards the end of the 1983-84 season he seemed to lose form and thereafter struggled to retain his first team place. In June 1985 he jumped at the chance of returning to Ajax and appeared in the 1987 European Cup Winners' Cup Final. He was also in the Dutch side that won the 1988 European Championships and though he was capped before and after his United days, he never won international honours while at Old Trafford.

1962 Bobby Charlton scored one of England's goals in a 3-1 win over Argentina in a World Cup match in Rancagua, Chile.

3

1995 United's Gary Neville was a surprise choice to win his first full international cap after just 19 appearances in the Premier League.
He was on the winning side as England beat Japan 2-1 in the Umbro Cup thanks to a penalty two minutes from time.

4

1949 Birth of Lou Macari. Born in Edinburgh of Italian parents, he started his career with Celtic, where he won two League Championships and two Scottish Cups, before joining United for £200,000 in January 1973. He scored on his debut in a 2-2 draw against West Ham United, though the following season saw United relegated for the first time since 1937. In 1974-75, he scored the only goal in the win over Southampton which secured United's promotion at the first attempt. Although he never won a League Championship medal at Old Trafford, he did win an FA Cup winners' medal and a losers' medal. A hard-working inside-forward, he won 18 Scottish caps with United to add to the six he won with Celtic. He had scored 97 goals in 400 appearances before he joined Swindon Town as player-manager in the summer of 1984. He survived the 'sack' at the County Ground following a row with Harry Gregg to steer the

- *June* -

Wiltshire club to promotion from the Fourth Division. Replacing John Lyall at West Ham, he was plagued by allegations about a betting scandal and irregularities while at Swindon and in 1990 he left. He later managed Birmingham City and Celtic before taking over the reins at Stoke City.

5 **1963** Bobby Charlton scored a hat-trick for England as they beat Switzerland 8-1 in Zurich.

1965 Pat Crerand was sent off during United's 1-0 defeat at Ferencvaros to become the club's tenth sending-off in the space of twenty months.

6 **1947** United were still playing their first team home matches at Maine Road and though the reserves were playing at Old Trafford, crowds were not large. However, on this date, the gates at Old Trafford were firmly locked as a 36,000 all-ticket crowd watched the English Schools FA Final replay between Salford Schools and Leicester Schools. The first match had ended goalless and after ninety minutes of the second, the game still hadn't produced a goal. Then in extra-time, Salford scored twice to lift the trophy for the first time. There was a very strong police presence at the match to prevent spectators creeping on to the bomb damaged areas.

7 **1990** A crowd of almost 40,000 attended a rock concert at Old Trafford, starring Rod Stewart, Status Quo and Joe Cocker. The stage was built in front of the Stretford End and most of those that attended, sat on the haloed turf.

8 **1949** The transfer of Ronnie Burke to Huddersfield Town for a fee of £16,000. A powerful-built centre-forward, United signed him as a professional in August 1946 after he had been released by Liverpool.

He scored 16 goals in 28 First Division matches for the Reds before his transfer. He later played for Rotherham United and Exeter City.

9 **1971** Frank O'Farrell, the shrewd and genial Irishman was appointed as Sir Matt Busby's successor as manager of Manchester United. As a player, he made his League debut for West Ham United, soon becoming part of the 'Upton Park Academy'. He played in 210 League and Cup games for the Hammers before moving to Preston North End in a straight exchange for Eddie Lewis in November 1956. He made a further 129 first team appearances for the Deepdale club before moving into non-League football with Weymouth as their player-manager. He steered the south coast club to the Southern League championship before taking over at Torquay United, where he gained the club promotion at the end of his first season. Later at Leicester City, he led the club to the FA Cup Final and promotion to the First Division before taking over at Manchester United. He found it difficult to follow in the footsteps of Matt Busby and in December 1972 with United struggling in the First Division, he and his assistant Malcolm Musgrove were sacked. He left Old Trafford a bitter man but following a short stay at Cardiff City, accepted a lucrative offer to coach in Iran.

1996 The European Championships got underway at Old Trafford with the opening Group C match between Germany and the Czech Republic. A crowd of 37,300 saw the eventual winners, who later met their opponents in the final, win 2-0.

10 **1969** Birth of Ronnie Johnsen. Formerly Norway's most expensive player, he made his United debut at Wimbledon in the opening game of the 1996-97 season, when coming on as a substitute for Nicky Butt. He soon commanded a regular place in the United line-up being able to play at

- June -

the back or in midfield. The winner of 28 Norwegian caps, he made his debut for his country against Sweden in August 1991. Though mainly a defensive player he came close to scoring for United on a couple of occasions, especially in the match against Leeds United when his close range shot from a corner was credited as an own-goal to Leeds' 'keeper Nigel Martyn.

1994 Bobby Charlton was knighted in the Birthday Honours list, the fourth footballer to be so honoured after Sir Stanley Matthews, Sir Alf Ramsey and of course Sir Matt Busby.

11 **1931** Birth of Ray Wood. An accomplished and courageous goalkeeper he had been a professional with Darlington when United signed him in December 1949. Twelve hours later, he went straight into the League team to face Newcastle United and gave a good account of himself in a 1-1 draw. However, he was basically signed as a cover for Jack Crompton and following the signing of Reg Allen, had to wait until the 1953-54 season before gaining a regular spot. He was a member of the 1955-56 and 1956-57 Championship winning sides and was in goal in the FA Cup Final of 1957 when he fractured his cheekbone in an early collision with Aston Villa winger Peter McParland. He returned for a short spell on the wing and then went off again before returning in goal for the final few minutes. He survived the Munich air crash but by the time he was fully fit, he had lost his place to Harry Gregg. An England international, he moved to Huddersfield Town, appearing in 207 League games for the Terriers before playing for Bradford City and Barnsley.

12 **1962** Manchester United's youth team arrived home after losing in extra-time in the final of a tournament organised by Bayern Munich FC. The young Reds played four games in the three-day tournament, scoring 13 goals. A goal by Barry Fry, currently the Peterborough United manager, took the team to extra-time in the final against Bayern, but with almost the last kick of the match, United lost 2-1. The German side awarded United a special consolation cup after their fine performance.

13 **1997** Manchester United chairman Martin Edwards vowed that the club would not consider paying imports vastly more than current players such as Roy Keane and Peter Schmeichel. The club's offers of £10 million for Juninho and Marcel Desailly were both rejected and though their £5 million offer for Bayern Munich defender Markus Babbel was accepted, the club would have to smash their pay structure if they were to add him to their galaxy of stars, as he demanded £1.4 million per year!

14 **1950** James Duffy, landlord of the Church Inn in Ford Street, Salford and former landlord of the United Hotel in Mill Street off Ashton New Road in the days of the 'Loco's' - the original United team when it was composed of railway workers - died at the age of 78. For his enthusiasm in organising the first excursions to the club's away games, he was given the privilege of holding the Cup United won in 1909 all the way home.

1970 Bobby Charlton appeared in the last of his 106 games for England in the World Cup quarter-final match against West Germany in Leon. Charlton was substituted by Manchester City's Colin Bell, the consequence being that it released Beckenbauer more into open play. England lost 3-2 after extra-time.

15 **1933** Birth of Mark Jones. A fierce-tackling centre-half, he was the only ever-present in United's championship-winning team of 1955-56 and was a member of the team which retained the title one year later.

- *June* -

However, he lost his place to Jackie Blanchflower, and missed out on appearing in the 1957 FA Cup Final against Aston Villa. He had regained his place by the end of the year and played in four of United's European Cup games in 1957-58, including the game against Red Star. Only 25 years of age, he seemed to have been around Old Trafford for years, before he was killed in the Munich disaster.

16 **1965** After drawing 3-3 on aggregate against Ferencvaros, United lost 2-1 in the third match play-off in Hungary. The Hungarians had built up a two goal lead within ten minutes after the interval and though John Connelly pulled a goal back, United's long and successful season was over.

1982 Bryan Robson scored the earliest goal in any World Cup match, 27 seconds after the start of England's match against France in Bilbao. England with United's Coppell and Wilkins in the side, went on to win 3-1.

1996 Germany beat Russia 3-0 in the second Group C European Championship match at Old Trafford. The game at one stage looked like being postponed due to a bomb explosion in the centre of Manchester the previous day.

17 **1964** Birth of Graeme Hogg. Born in Aberdeen, the young centre-half made his United debut against Bournemouth in the third round of the FA Cup in January 1984. United lost 2-0 in one of the biggest cup upsets for years. But despite this disastrous start to his career, he went on to appear in 111 first team games for the club before Alex Ferguson sold him to Portsmouth for £150,000 in August 1988. Strong in the tackle and a good header of the ball, he played in 110 games for the Fratton Park club before moving to Hearts in the summer of 1991. He later moved on to Notts County, where he showed he was still a good player and a difficult man to pass.

18 **1968** Manchester United made a bid of £200,000 for West Ham United striker and England World Cup hero Geoff Hurst, but the Hammers' manager Ron Greenwood turned down the bid.

19 **1946** Birth of Jimmy Greenhoff. The elder brother of Brian Greenhoff, he started his career with Leeds United before joining Birmingham City and then Stoke City. He became a great favourite at the Victoria Ground, making 338 League and Cup appearances and scoring 97 goals. He formed an almost telepathic understanding with Alan Hudson in midfield and helped the club to their first major honour in 1972, when they beat Chelsea 2-1 to win the League Cup. In November 1976 he joined Manchester United for £100,000 to lend some experience to Tommy Docherty's young side. He appeared in two FA Cup Finals for the Reds, scoring the winner against Liverpool in 1977. He had scored 36 goals in 122 games for United when he moved to Crewe in December 1980. He later played for Toronto Blizzards and Port Vale before managing Rochdale. Though he won England honours at Under-23 level, he was surprisingly never capped at full international level.

20 **1933** Birth of Warren Bradley. When he came to Old Trafford in 1958 just after the Munich disaster, he was an amateur and had already won two FA Amateur Cup winners' medals with Bishop Auckland and 11 England Amateur international caps. Signing professional forms for United in November 1958, he won three full caps for England, the first against Italy in 1959. Though his time at Old Trafford was brief, he had a good strike rate for a winger, with 21 goals in 66 first team appearances. In March 1962, he joined Bury for £40,000 before later playing non-League football for Macclesfield Town, Northwich Victoria and Bangor City.

- June -

21 **1949** Birth of Stuart Pearson. Signed from Hull City for £200,000 at the end of United's relegation season of 1973-74, manager Tommy Docherty saw the Hull-born striker as the player to get the club back in the top flight. Pearson responded with 17 goals as United won the Second Division championship and created many more for his team-mates, especially Lou Macari. During five years at Old Trafford, he won 15 England caps, the first against Wales in 1976. He played in both the 1976 and 1977 FA Cup Finals, scoring in the latter to help United beat Liverpool 2-1. In September 1979, he left the Reds to join West Ham United in a £220,000 deal and a year later was back at Wembley as the Hammers beat Fulham. At the end of the 1981-82 season, he was released by the London club and went on Jimmy Hill's 'rebel' soccer tour to South Africa. He later played in the (USA) NASL before a knee injury forced his retirement from the professional game.

22 **1950** When Roy Paul, Swansea's international half-back came back disappointed from Bogota, his name was promptly linked with Manchester United and a £25,000 deal. The fact that Swansea Town's directors later agreed to place Paul on the transfer list added weight to United rumours. However, the rumours were completely out of step with the true position at Old Trafford. United had not made an offer and were not likely to do so. The following month, he signed for Manchester City!

23 **1995** Paul Ince at last signed for Inter Milan for £7 million but an even bigger shock was the departure of Welsh international Mark Hughes to Chelsea. Glen Hoddle let it slip that he went after the popular striker because he was out of contract.

United had paraded Hughes on the pitch at Old Trafford in February, saying that the player had agreed to sign a new contract. Though United never claimed that Hughes had signed the contract, many supporters felt they had been misled.

24 **1950** United's Charlie Mitten signed a two-year contract with the Sante Fe club in Bogota, Colombia for a promised £2,500 signing-on fee plus a salary of £2,500 a season and a win bonus of £35 a game. Leaving after a run of 113 consecutive League and Cup games for United, his Colombian adventure failed and a year later he was back in England.

1970 Birth of David May. A quick, strong central defender, he began his career with Blackburn Rovers and made 146 League and Cup appearances for the Ewood Park club before his £1.4 million transfer to Manchester United in July 1994. Good in the air and with sound positional sense, he spent the first part of the 1994-95 season in the shadows of Steve Bruce. In 1995-96 when Pallister was injured, he played alongside the United captain and then in the latter stages of the season replaced Bruce and starred in United's 1-0 FA Cup Final win over Liverpool. Though he only appeared in 18 first team games, he gained a League Championship medal as well. With Bruce departing to Birmingham City, May came into his own in 1996-97 and was capped by England.

1988 Mark Hughes completed his £1.8 million move from Barcelona back to Manchester United. Signed by the Barcelona manager Terry Venables for £2 million, he partnered Gary Lineker but the partnership never really flourished. When Venables was sacked, new manager Johan Cruyff loaned him to West German champions Bayern Munich.

- *June* -

25 **1996** Manchester United, Liverpool and Sky TV combined to allow the Reds to bring forward their 12 October Old Trafford League fixture against their Merseyside rivals by almost four hours. It meant that the glamorous clash with the Anfielders would become the first televised live match on Sky to be screened on a Saturday morning with the game having been switched to an 11.15 am kick-off.

26 **1952** Birth of Gordon McQueen. The Scottish international centre-half began his career at St Mirren before joining Leeds United in 1972, where he was seen as a replacement for Jack Charlton. At Elland Road, he played in over 150 games and won a League Championship medal before joining United for £495,000 in February 1978. After making his debut at Anfield, where United went down 3-1, McQueen went on to appear in 228 League and Cup games for the Reds, scoring 26 goals. He appeared in three Wembley finals for the club, picking up an FA Cup winners' medal in 1983 when the Reds beat Brighton over two matches. It was at Anfield in January 1984 that the popular Scot received an injury that was to keep him out of the United side for the rest of the season and though he made a few appearances in 1984-85, he was never the same. He left Old Trafford to play for Seiko of Hong Kong before later managing Airdrie.

27 **1967** Denis Law was sent off in Manchester United's 7-0 win over Western Australia at Perth in the Reds' 'Down Under' tour.

28 **1933** Birth of Fred Goodwin. He made his League debut for United as a replacement for Duncan Edwards in a 2-1 win over Arsenal in November 1954. It was only after the Munich air crash that Goodwin became a first team regular, appearing in the FA Cup Final against Bolton Wanderers and being an ever-present in 1958-59. After 106 League and Cup appearances for the Reds, he joined Leeds United in March 1960 for a fee of £10,000 but after playing in 107 League games for the Elland Road club, he moved to Scunthorpe United. He became manager of the Old Show Ground club in 1965-66 and then had a spell in charge of the New York Generals before returning to these shores as manager of Brighton and Hove Albion. He later managed Birmingham City before returning to the States as coach to Minnesota Kicks.

1947 Birth of John Aston junior. Unlike his father, he was a fast raiding winger who appeared in 185 first team games for United. He was a member of the club's FA Youth Cup winning side of 1964 and made his League debut in the 1-0 home win over Leicester City in April 1965. In 1967, he won a League Championship medal and the following year was a star of United's European Cup winning success. In the semi-final of that 1967-68 European Cup competition, he made the goal for George Best that separated United and Real Madrid at the end of the home leg. He won an Under-23 cap for England against Wales but a broken leg virtually ended his career at Old Trafford and in July 1972, he moved to Luton Town for £30,000. He enjoyed five good seasons at Kenilworth Road, playing in 174 League games before transferring to Mansfield Town. He later joined Blackburn Rovers, where he wound down his playing days.

1967 Denis Law was fined 50 dollars (£20) by the Australian Football Association after swearing at the referee in United's last game of their pre-season tour in Perth. The tour was a great success in terms of record attendances, which resulted in a record £50,000 plus profit for the Aussies.

- June -

29

1950 John Aston senior was the only United player in the England side that surprisingly lost 1-0 to the United States of America in a World Cup game at Belo Horizonte.

1996 A special concert entitled 'The Crowd are on the Pitch - Euro 96 Extravaganza' was held at Old Trafford on the eve of the Wembley Euro '96 final. The concert featured top Manchester band Simply Red, along with Madness, M People and Dodgy. There were also clowns, a troupe of acrobats and stiltwalkers. A crowd of over 60,000 attended the concert which was opened by United manager Alex Ferguson with the words *'Welcome to the Theatre of Dreams"*.

30

1965 Birth of Gary Pallister. Signed from Middlesbrough in August 1989 for a British record fee of £2.3 million, his early games in a United shirt seemed to indicate that he was a little out of his depth. However, once he settled in, the central defender, who is a tower of strength in the air and has good pace, gave a number of impressive performances and ended his first season at Old Trafford as the club's 'Player of the Year'. In that 1989-90 season, he won an FA Cup winners' medal as the Reds beat Crystal Palace after a replay. The following season he won a League Cup runners-up medal and a European Cup Winners' Cup medal after United had beaten Barcelona in the final. In 1991-92, he won a League Cup winners' medal and was voted PFA 'Player of the Year'. From 1993, he became a regular member of the England squad and despite missing a number of matches with a series of niggling back injuries, he formed an excellent partnership with David May. In 1995-96 he won League Championship and FA Cup medals as United performed the 'double' for the second time during Pallister's Old Trafford career.

29 June
Jeff Aston

In the team embarrassed by the U.S.A.!

- *June* -

Three Birth Dates:

(Top left) 4 June
Lou Macari

(Top right) 26 June
Gordon McQueen

(Left) 15 June
Mark Jones

JULY

1 **1995** Manchester United chairman Martin Edwards warned the Old Trafford faithful that they would not be allowed to influence the club's transfer activities. He said *"We have some 2.3 million supporters around the country and we cannot listen to all those voices. One man has to make the decisions and that man is the manager."* He reaffirmed manager Alex Ferguson's sell-to-buy transfer policy, arguing that the board's priority is the redevelopment work at Old Trafford.

2 **1973** Manchester City manager Johnny Hart watched Denis Law sign the contract that took him back to Maine Road after 12 years and said, *"Denis will have to fight for a place in our team. He doesn't go in automatically. We finished well last season and a team doesn't go bad overnight."* Law, who left Maine Road for Turin in 1961 after a brief stay, called in to sign for City before leaving for Scotland for a golfing and fishing holiday. Denis said, *"I'm a very lucky player to be able to come here. I have left one great club for another and they're both in Manchester, which I love. If City hadn't come along, I would have packed in the game."*

3 **1986** Manchester United and Spurs, two of the biggest spenders in English soccer were locked in a battle for Terry Butcher. Missing out on Butcher, who eventually joined Glasgow Rangers, was a major blow for United team boss Ron Atkinson who had planned to team the England star up with Paul McGrath the following season.

4 **1977** Tommy Docherty was dismissed as Manchester United manager. Directors' wives at the club, which is proud of its family image, helped to force him out. The wives acted from shock and embarrassment over his affair with the wife of the club's physiotherapist.

1988 Paul Gascoigne's business adviser warned Manchester United that they would have to make their move for the Newcastle United midfield star within 48 hours - or lose him to Spurs. He said that Gascoigne knows he cannot keep Spurs dangling for much longer, but he wants to speak to United. Newcastle insist that all the Reds need to do to be given permission to talk to the player is to match Tottenham's record-breaking £2 million offer.

5 **1971** Frank O'Farrell moved in as Manchester United's manager, knowing that his biggest problem was that the Red's fans brought up on success, are impatient for a return of the glory days. Sir Matt Busby, who introduced O'Farrell to the press, was to become a director at the next board meeting two or three weeks later.

6 **1962** Manchester United reaffirmed their offer of £115,000 for Torino's Denis Law. Yet the Italian club had failed to elect a new finance council, whose signing authority was needed, due to the late arrival of the president and three directors and are planning another election for the end of the month. But that would be after the deadline signing date of 15 July after which no players can be transferred until the season opens. United however, are hopeful that the rule can be got round.

7 **1954** Birth of Mickey Thomas. Signed from Wrexham for £300,000 in November 1978, the Welsh international forward made his debut in a 1-0 win at Chelsea.

74

- July -

He went on to appear in 110 League and Cup games for the Reds, including the FA Cup Final defeat by Arsenal in 1979. In the summer of 1981, he moved to Everton in the deal that brought John Gidman to Old Trafford. Unable to settle at Goodison Park, he joined Brighton and Hove Albion for £400,000. His wife couldn't settle on the south coast so he moved to Stoke City for £200,000. The Potteries side were forced to sell this clever footballer to Chelsea for just £75,000. Thomas later played for West Bromwich Albion, Derby County, Shrewsbury and Leeds United before returning to Stoke City for a second spell.

8

1991 Manchester United along with Arsenal and Tottenham Hotspur sign a lucrative deal with ITV for exclusive coverage of their home ties in Europe in the 1991-92 season.

9

1951 Birth of Mick Martin. When he joined United from Bohemians for £30,000 in January 1973, it was a record fee for a Republic of Ireland club. Though he was a versatile performer, he couldn't command a regular place in the United side and in December 1975, after a spell on loan with West Bromwich Albion, he joined them officially. He helped the Baggies gain promotion from the Second Division before moving to Newcastle United. The winner of 52 full caps for the Republic of Ireland, he later played League football for Cardiff City, Rotherham United, Peterborough United and Preston North End.

1955 Birth of Steve Coppell. Signed from Tranmere Rovers for £60,000, his attacking wing-play helped United reach the FA Cup Final in 1976, which they lost to Southampton, and in 1977 when they beat Liverpool. He also picked up losers' medals in the FA Cup Final of 1979 and the League Cup Final of 1983. Injury prevented him from playing in the FA Cup Final against Brighton in 1983, although he was an ever-present for four successive seasons with United, appearing in 200 consecutive League matches. An England international, winning 42 full caps, his two-year fight against a serious knee injury forced him to retire in October 1983 when he was aged just 28. A former PFA Chairman, he was appointed manger of Crystal Palace in June 1984 and was at the time, the League's youngest boss. He led the Eagles to promotion in 1988-89 and a year later took them to the FA Cup Final where they lost to United after a replay! After a short spell in charge at Manchester City, he moved back to Selhurst Park in charge of Crystal Palace.

1969 Manchester United went on trial before a four-nation jury in Geneva. They were in the dock to answer charges of hooliganism by sections of the Stretford End crowd during the European Cup semi-final second leg against AC Milan at Old Trafford, when the Italian goalkeeper was knocked out by a missile thrown from the terraces. The club were ordered to erect fences behind both goals.

10

1956 Birth of Frank Stapleton. Born in Dublin, he was on United's books as a schoolboy, but they allowed him to leave and he joined Arsenal. He played in 225 League games for the Gunners and scored in their 1979 FA Cup Final win over United. In August 1981 he signed for United for a fee of £1 million and was the top scorer in each of his first three seasons with the club. When he scored the Reds' first goal in the 1983 FA Cup Final against Brighton and Hove Albion, he became the first player to score goals for different clubs in two Wembley Cup Finals. A Republic of Ireland international, winning 70 caps for his country, he left Old Trafford in 1987-88 to join Ajax, but after only four appearances he joined Derby County. He later played for French club Le Havre and Blackburn Rovers before joining Huddersfield Town. He took over as Bradford City's manager in December 1991 and set about restoring the club

July

to its former glories, but despite two seasons challenging for promotion he parted company with the club in May 1994.

11 **1951** Mr William Mauchan, a Scot in business in Manchester, was behind a plan for Manchester United to play Barcelona at Old Trafford in the early weeks of the new season and to return the compliment in May of the following year. The businessman had a long experience of soccer tours and a close knowledge of Spanish sport.

1966 Manchester United provided three players, Nobby Stiles, Bobby Charlton and John Connelly for England's first match in the World Cup, a goalless draw against Uruguay.

12 **1962** Denis Law signed for Manchester United from Torino for a record fee of £115,000.

1967 Manchester United full-back Noel Cantwell was fined £5 at Sheffield Magistrate Court after he pleaded guilty by letter to using insulting language during United's match at Hillsborough. Inspector Peter Gratton said Cantwell was on a bench near the players entrance and that on four occasions he heard the Republic of Ireland international shout obscene expressions which must have been heard by the youngsters sitting close by. In the letter, Cantwell said he was sorry!

1991 Manchester United raked in a staggering £4.5 million in advance ticket sales. This figure was by far the biggest amount ever received by the Reds and was destined to become a record sum for English soccer. League match tickets and box seats soared to pass the 20,000 mark with over a month to go to the big kick-off.

13 **1966** The opening group match of the World Cup at Old Trafford saw Hungary and Portugal attract a crowd of 27,866. The result was a 3-1 win for the Portuguese.

1994 United's Eric Cantona, working for French TV, was arrested at the Rose Bowl and missed the Brazil v Sweden World Cup semi-final after a scuffle with a Press Box official, but was later released without being charged.

14 **1957** Birth of Arthur Albiston. A Scottish schoolboy, Under-21 and full international, Arthur Albiston appeared in 482 first team games for United. A member of their 1977, 1979, 1983 and 1985 FA Cup Final sides, he also played in the 1983 League Cup against Liverpool. He made his League debut in a goalless draw at Portsmouth in October 1974, six days after he had made his senior debut in front of 55,159 fans at Old Trafford in a 1-0 League Cup win over Manchester City. Albiston also holds the distinction of making his FA Cup debut in a Wembley Final as United beat Liverpool 2-1 in 1977. He made his international debut in the 1-1 draw with Northern Ireland in 1982, going on to win 14 caps for his country. He joined West Bromwich Albion in 1988 but after just one season at the Hawthorns, joined Dundee on a free transfer.

1971 Jack Crompton handed in his resignation after 27 years as a player and staff man at Old Trafford.

1977 Dave Sexton became Manchester United manager, claiming that he had needed less than 30 seconds to think over United's £20,000 a year offer.

- July -

15 **1989** Laurie Cunningham whose association with Manchester United came in the form of a loan spell towards the end of the 1982-83 season was killed in a car crash in Spain. He played in five League games for the Reds, scoring one of the goals when United beat Watford 2-0. Having started his career with Orient, he moved to West Bromwich Albion for £100,000. After scoring 28 goals in 110 appearances at the Hawthorns, he was transferred to Real Madrid for £1 million. In 1984 he moved to French club Marseilles and during his first season there, scored five goals in one game.

16 **1966** Bobby Charlton scored England's first goal in their 2-0 World Cup win over Mexico at Wembley.

1971 The Football League closed Old Trafford for two weeks following a knife-throwing incident during the home match against Newcastle United the previous season, which the Reds won 1-0 from a Brian Kidd goal.

17 **1932** Birth of Colin Webster. A Welsh international, he is one of the relatively few players who have served three Welsh clubs. He joined United from Cardiff City in May 1952 and had to serve his apprenticeship in the Central League, as he was to old to take part in the club's FA Youth Cup success. A utility forward, equally adept with either foot, he went on to give United good service in his six seasons at Old Trafford. He scored a hat-trick in a 4-2 win at Burnley in December 1954 and the following season he appeared in enough games to qualify for a League Championship medal. After the Munich disaster, he established himself at outside-left and played in the 1958 FA Cup Final. He played for Wales in the 1958 World Cup Finals in Sweden before later playing for Swansea Town and Newport County.

1991 Manchester United along with other leading First Division clubs sign a 'founder member document' locking them into a new Premier League.

18 **1938** Birth of John Connelly. After playing his early football with St Helens Town, he joined Burnley in November 1956. A member of the Turf Moor club's League Championship-winning side of 1959-60, when he scored 20 goals in 34 games, he also appeared in the 1962 FA Cup Final against Spurs. He scored 85 goals in 216 League games for Burnley before joining United for £56,000 in April 1964. Able to play on either wing, he made his debut for the Reds in a 2-2 home draw against West Bromwich Albion. An ever-present in his first season with the club, he won a League Championship medal, scoring 15 goals in the First Division and another five in the club's European ties. He played 20 times for England, winning his last cap against Uruguay in the opening match of the 1966 World Cup. After two years at Old Trafford he joined Blackburn Rovers before later ending his career with Bury.

19 **1993** On the same day that Manchester United sign Roy Keane from Nottingham Forest for £3.75 million, Ryan Giggs signs a 3-year sponsorship deal with boot manufacturers Reebok for an estimated £325,000.

20 **1957** Roger Byrne, Manchester United's England full-back was banned from heading a ball until he had fully recovered from a recent nose operation. The 'ban' imposed by a specialist was due to be lifted on 14 August when United were due to play in Berlin.

- July -

21 **1995** Andrei Kanchelskis left Old Trafford to sign for Everton in a £5 million deal. Alex Ferguson had wanted a meeting with the Russian winger to try and resolve the problems. Kanchelskis said he was not interested in meeting Ferguson and claimed the manager had not spoken to him for five months. He said he could not stay at Old Trafford because of the manager. Kanchelskis' agent Grigoriy Esaulenko issued the following statement: *'"If the manager goes, Kanchelskis will stay'"*. The Russian said he could not forgive Ferguson for leaving him out of United's team at Goodison Park in February. Fergsuson refused to get into what he termed a slanging match.

22 **1957** Manchester United were being called 'Busby's Greyhounds' for when the club's professionals reported to Old Trafford for pre-season training, they were told that they would be using the nearby White City Stadium!

1989 United had to pay Nottingham Forest £1.5 million for Neil Webb. This was the first time that a tribunal had decided on a fee of more than £1 million.

23 **1951** Acting on the advice of the Players Union, none of Manchester United's 31 professionals who reported for training on this day, had signed contracts with the club for the new season. The Players Union circularised all members about the dispute over contracts which they said should run from August to August. All the players stressed there was no disagreement with the club and centre-half Allenby Chilton pointed out that in witholding their signatures they were merely keeping in line with the union from whom they were awaiting instructions.

24 **1941** Birth of Tony Dunne. After beginning his career as a centre-forward with St Finbar's and Tara United in the Republic of Ireland, he joined United from Shelbourne for £3,500 in August 1960. After making his debut in a 3-2 defeat at Burnley on 15 October 1960, he went on to appear in 530 first team games for the Reds, gaining League Championship medals in 1965 and 1967, an FA Cup winners' medal in 1963 and a European Cup winners' medal in 1968. Capped 32 times by the Republic of Ireland, he was voted Ireland's Footballer of the Year in 1969, an honour the full-back thoroughly deserved. A loyal servant of the club, he gave the same loyalty to Bolton Wanderers, whom he joined in August 1973. He played in 192 League and Cup games for the Trotters, helping them win the Second Division Championship in 1977-78 before leaving to play for Detroit Express in the NASL.

1945 Birth of Martin Edwards. The multi-millionaire chairman of Manchester United took over when his father Louis suffered a fatal heart attack in 1979. He stood by Alex Ferguson when many were calling for his head in the late 1980s - a very wise decision! The United chairman also oversaw the flotation of the club on the stock exchange in 1991, making around £7 million, as the club was instantly worth £40 million.

1958 Birth of Jim Leighton. One of the best 'keepers produced by Scotland, he made his Scottish League debut for Aberdeen in 1978-79, going on to appear in over 250 games. During his time at Pitodrie, he won two League Championship medals, four Scottish Cup medals and a European Cup Winners' Cup medal. Signed by Alex Ferguson in May 1988 for £750,000, a British record for a goalkeeper, he was an ever-present in his first season at Old Trafford.

- July -

He only missed four games in 1989-90 but after being left out of United's line-up in the FA Cup Final replay against Crystal Palace, the writing was on the wall. Later playing for Hibernian, the popular Scot forced his way back into the national side at the age of 38 with hopes of playing in the World Cup Finals of 1998.

25 **1993** United's Bryan Robson was sent off in the friendly match against Arsenal.

1995 Leeds United stated that they will file an official complaint to United regarding remarks made by the club's manager Alex Ferguson in his new book 'A year in the life' in which he says, *"I almost want Leeds to be relegated because of their fans. You can feel the hatred and animosity"*. Ferguson later sent a letter of apology to the Leeds chairman saying that he does not consider there is any ill-feeling between the two clubs and that the offending paragraph was written at an emotional time!

26 **1966** Bobby Charlton scored both England's goals in their 2-1 World Cup semi-final win over Portugal.

1980 The Reds clinched the first part of a £250,000 a year sponsorship deal with Adidas in Nuremburg. The club negotiated a four-year contract which would earn them £100,000 a season. Though Adidas are a German firm, United's kit was made at Wilmslow by Umbro International!

27 **1932** Manchester United hoped to encourage the attendance of more women at their matches by the reduction of the season tickets on the ground side to 10 shillings (50 pence). Men were still to pay £1 and boys half-price!

1956 Birth of Garry Birtles. A carpet fitter by trade, he began his football career with Long Eaton before joining Nottingham Forest. Replacing Peter Withe, he ended the 1978-79 season as top scorer with 14 goals. He also scored regularly in the League and European Cups to finish the campaign with 26 goals from 53 games. In May 1980, he won the first of three England caps and played in the European Championships later that summer. At the beginning of the following season he signed for United for £1.25 million, but the move was not a success, for he failed to score for the Reds in his first 25 League outings. He had scored 12 goals in 64 first team games when he returned to the City Ground for a cut price of £250,000. Hampered by injuries, it wasn't until 1986-87 that he again emerged as a goalscorer, linking well with Nigel Clough. Surprisingly he was given a free transfer at the end of that season and joined Notts County before later ending his career with Grimsby Town.

1968 A banquet was held at the Midland Hotel, Manchester to commemorate Manchester United winning the European Cup in the 1967-68 season.

1996 Paul Scholes hit a first-half hat-trick against Portadown at Shamrock Park as United beat the League of Ireland side 5-0 in a friendly.

28 **1969** Manchester United had two players - Bobby Charlton and George Best - in the Rest of the United Kingdom side to play the Football Association of Wales team at Cardiff. The match was part of the celebrations to mark the investiture of the Prince of Wales. The United Kingdom side won 1-0 with Francis Lee of Manchester City scoring in the first-half.

29 **1957** There were rumours that Tommy Taylor had taken a day off during his holiday in the South of France resort of Juan-le-Pins to go

- July -

over the border to Milan for further talks with the officials of Inter Milan who offered him £10,000 to join them a few months earlier. Taylor said he did cross the border into Italy for a day trip, but it was to San Remo and not Milan!

30 **1963** Birth of Neil Webb. The son of the former Reading forward, Duggie Webb, he followed his father to Elm Park, signing professional forms in 1980. In July 1982, he joined Portsmouth where he began to produce some outstanding displays in midfield. After playing in 123 League games for the Fratton Park club, he signed for Nottingham Forest. An important member of the City Ground club's midfield, he was also a regular goalscorer and hit hat-tricks against Coventry City and Chelsea. An England international, he joined United in 1989, when a tribunal set a fee of £1.5 million, a figure the Old Trafford club were more than happy to meet. Hampered by injuries in his first season at the club, he came back to gain an FA Cup winners' medal in 1990 and made an appearance in that year's World Cup Finals. He later returned to the City Ground for a second spell.

1985 Manchester United played Cambridge United at the Abbey Stadium for the beneficiaries Steve Fallon and Steve Spriggs. Three match balls ended up out of the ground and one shot from Frank Stapleton soared over the terraces and landed in the brook outside the ground. The team made a quick exit after the match and drove back to Old Trafford, thus saving the expense of an overnight stay for the beneficiaries, who were both originally signed when United manager Ron Atkinson was in charge of Cambridge United.

31 **1969** Don Givens, who went on to win 56 caps for the Republic of Ireland stood in for the injured Denis Law in United's tour game against a Copenhagen Select XI in the Danish capital. The youngster had played for the Republic of Ireland in a World Cup game two months earlier, before he had even played in the Reds' first team. Though he had played in two friendlies in Ireland at the end of the previous season, this was his first real test.

1995 The FA stepped in to reprimand the club for playing Eric Cantona in the closed doors friendly at the Cliff. The FA said that the inclusion of the Frenchman in games for United against other clubs, even behind closed doors was in breach of the suspension.

5 July: Frank O'Farrell becomes the new manager

- *July* -

*(Above left) 7 July
John Gidman
Moves to United.*

*(Above right) 4 July
Tommy Docherty
Sacked!*

*(Left) 2 July
Denis Law
Signs for neighbours.*

AUGUST

1 **1932** Scott Duncan took up his duties as Manchester United's manager. The former Dumbarton, Rangers and Newcastle player had guested for the Reds during the First World War. Although he became one of the club's longest serving managers, the club experienced mixed fortunes under him. In 1933-34 United narrowly escaped relegation but two years later he led them to the Second Division championship. He resigned after 14 matches of the 1938-39 season and became manager of Ipswich Town.

1995 The club unveiled their seventh new kit in four years !

2 **1954** Birth of Sammy McIlroy. Sir Matt Busby forecast a fine future for the young Irishman when he saw him play as a 15-year-old in a schoolboy game. He joined United in September 1969 and became a professional in 1971, making his debut in November of that year with a goal at Maine Road in a 3-3 draw in front of a 63,000 crowd. He won a Second Division championship medal in 1974-75 and an FA Cup runners-up medal the following season when his glancing header hit the bar as United were beaten 1-0 by Southampton. He won an FA Cup winners' medal in 1977 as the Reds beat Liverpool 2-1. Two years later, he appeared in his third FA Cup Final in the space of four years, only for Arsenal to triumph 3-2. Capped 88 times by Northern Ireland, he left Old Trafford in February 1982 after playing in 418 first team games to join Stoke City for £350,000. Despite playing well in a struggling Potters side, he was given a free transfer at the end of the 1984-85 season and joined Manchester City. He only played 13 League games for the Maine Road club before moving to Bury.

He had a spell as player-coach at Preston North End before becoming manager of Macclesfield Town and leading them into the Football League.

1957 Birth of Ashley Grimes. He joined United from Bohemians for £20,000 in March 1977 and made his debut at the beginning of the following season in a 4-1 win at Birmingham City. A Republic of Ireland international winning 17 caps, he went on to make 103 League and Cup appearances for the Reds before being transferred to Coventry City in a £200,000 deal in the summer of 1983 after winning an FA Cup winners' medal against Brighton. He later played for Luton Town, Osasuna in Spain and Stoke City.

3 **1932** Though United returned to Old Trafford to resume training for the new season, the kicking of a football was out of the question for at least a week. A United spokesman said: *"We let the men get their wind first, commencing with simple exercises, which are increased in vigour day by day until after a week, out comes a football and we start work seriously"*.

1975 Jim Holton was sent-off in United's 3-0 win over Danish side Halskov in their opening match of their tour. Lou Macari scored two of the Reds' goals with Gerry Daly grabbing the other.

1995 Former United and England goalkeeper Alex Stepney signed up as goalkeeping coach for neighbours Manchester City. The popular 'keeper played in 535 first team games for the Reds and is still remembered for his brilliant save from Eusebio in the European Cup Final of 1968.

- August -

4

1988 Gordon Strachan turned his back on a French fortune to stay with Manchester United. The Scottish international did a smart about-turn and walked away from a lucrative move to Lens in France. Strachan wanted to finalise a new contract to give him another two years at Old Trafford, saying it would be too much hassle to move, as the French club's coach didn't really want him, he wanted a defender!

5

1970 In the Watney Cup semi-final against Hull City, a Denis Law goal 13 minutes from the end of normal time took the game to a penalty shoot-out, the first time it had been used to decide a competitive match between two senior British clubs. Best, Kidd, Charlton and Morgan were all successful, but Law failed - fortunately for United, so did Ken Wagstaffe. The last penalty was taken by Hull City 'keeper Ian McKechnie, but he blazed the ball wide of the target to put the Reds into the final.

1994 In the game against Newcastle United in the Glasgow Rangers four team competition, Peter Schmeichel kept the Reds in the game with a series of outstanding saves, only being beaten after five minutes by a Ruel Fox pile-driver. Eric Cantona equalised before half-time with a delicately judged header from a David May cross but the game went to a penalty shoot-out which Newcastle won 6-5 with Eric Cantona missing for the Reds. United therefore missed qualifying for the final against Sampdoria.

1995 United call off Andrei Kanchelskis' move to Everton saying that the Goodison club would not pay the £1.1 million sell-on clause that his former Russian club Shakhtyor Dynamo had put in the original contract with the Reds. Although terms had been agreed, no contracts had been signed. Kanchelskis still trained with Everton, refusing to report to the Cliff for training.

6

1994 United, with a somewhat weakened side, lose 1-0 to Rangers in the match for third place in the Glasgow Rangers four team competition. Frenchman Eric Cantona is introduced after half-time as a substitute, but is sent-off after receiving two bookings within the space of a couple of minutes.

7

1978 Real Madrid visited Old Trafford to play Manchester United in the club's centenary game. The game illustrated the good relationship that existed between the two clubs, built during the late fifties when the Spanish club dominated European football and which was strengthened when Real offered help after the Munich air disaster as United struggled to survive. United won the centenary game 4-0.

1993 United beat Arsenal 5-4 on penalties after a 1-1 draw to win the FA Charity Shield at Wembley. Mark Hughes scored the Reds' goal.

1995 Alex Ferguson is told that he could face a disrepute charge after criticising the FA in an article in which he was reported to have said: *"I can see no reason for them at all. It should be a professional body, not self electing. The structure is too tightly knit with too many friendships"*.

8

1959 Eighteen months after the Munich air disaster, Manchester United returned to Germany to play a friendly against Bayern Munich. Albert Quixall scored after just four seconds of the second-half but along with Joe Carolan was later sent-off. United still won 2-1.

1970 United reached the final of the Watney Cup but lost 4-1 to Derby County at the Baseball Ground.

- August -

1984 Manchester United finally win the tug-of-war with Cologne for Gordon Strachan. The German club appealed to UEFA claiming that Aberdeen had previously agreed to sell Strachan to them. Aberdeen were ordered to pay Cologne £100,000 compensation.

1985 Plans which had yet to be approved by the full football board were put forward by Manchester United to build an indoor stadium alongside their football ground at Old Trafford. The new 9,000 all-seater hall was to be the home of the club's basketball team as the club pushed ahead with their plans to become a multi-sports club.

1995 Eric Cantona rocked the club when he issued a 'let me play or I'm quitting' ultimatum regarding the club's closed door friendlies. It came just a matter of hours after the FA announced that they would not be taking any further action over the player having appeared against Rochdale but that any further appearances by Cantona would be viewed in an entirely different light.

9

1933 Birth of Albert Quixall. When he signed for United from Sheffield Wednesday in September 1958, he cost the club a British record fee of £45,000 - almost £10,000 more than the previous record. At Hillsborough, he won two Second Division championship medals and collected five full England caps to add to those won at schoolboy, Under-23 and 'B' levels. An inside-forward full of creative ideas, he scored 63 goals in 243 League games for the Owls. It appeared that his goalscoring touch had deserted him in his first season at Old Trafford, but he rediscovered it in 1959-50 and the following season scored his first hat-trick for the club in a 6-0 win over Burnley. He won an FA Cup winners' medal with United in 1963 but after scoring 56 goals in 183 first team games for the reds, he joined Oldham for £7,000. He later played for Stockport County before ending his career with non-League Altrincham.

1958 Birth of Gary Bailey. Son of former Ipswich Town goalkeeper Roy Bailey, he joined the Old Trafford staff in January 1978 from Witts University, South Africa. He made his debut in a 2-0 win over Ipswich Town and immediately established himself as the club's first-choice 'keeper. A member of United's FA Cup Final sides of 1979, 1983 and 1985, he also appeared in the club's League Cup Final team of 1983. After he had made 14 appearances for the England Under-21 side, he won his first full England cap in a 2-1 win over the Republic of Ireland at Wembley. He then began to suffer from a knee injury and at the age of only 29, after making 373 appearances for the Reds, he was forced to retire.

10

1971 Birth of Roy Keane. When he signed for United in July 1973, he set a record for a transfer deal between English clubs, joining the Old Trafford club from Nottingham Forest for £3.75 million. Forest signed the former amateur boxer from Cobh Ramblers, and after making his debut against Liverpool during the 1990-91 season, he went on to score 33 goals in 154 games for the City Ground club before his move. Hailed by many within the game as the best midfield player in the country, with plenty of stamina and coming from deep positions to score valuable goals. Always prepared to play his way out of trouble, and an excellent passer of the ball. The hard-working Republic of Ireland international wasn't really match fit when he arrived at Old Trafford, but then turned in a succession of brilliant midfield performances. He won a League Championship and an FA Cup winners' medal in 1995-96 and was voted the Littlewoods 'Man of the Match' in the final against Liverpool. The 1996-97 season was arguably his best in a red shirt as United won the League for the fourth time in five years.

1978 United beat Danish side Holstebro 1-0 to give them an undefeated four game run up to the new season.

- August -

Joe Jordan was sent-off and Martin Buchan booked in front of a partisan Danish crowd of 5,000. United's goal was scored by Lou Macari when his overhead kick went in off the underside of the bar.

1985 Everton did not just beat Manchester United 2-0 to win the FA Charity Shield, but had it handed to them on a plate! Two horrendous mistakes cost the Reds the game. The first came in the 27th minute when Paul McGrath tried to dribble out of the penalty area only to lose the ball to Kevin Sheedy who passed for Trevor Steven to score a simple goal. United's other error came courtesy of goalkeeper Gary Bailey as he dived to cut out a cross, allowing Adrian Heath to score another easy goal.

11

1991 Over 33,000 turned up at Old Trafford for a Testimonial game for Sir Matt Busby, paying £250,000 to see Manchester United draw 1-1 with a Republic of Ireland XI.

1996 United win the FA Charity Shield beating Newcastle United 4-0 at Wembley with goals from Cantona, Butt, Beckham and Keane.

12

1966 United and England World Cup star Nobby Stiles is sent-off during the club's friendly match at FK Austria.

1967 Manchester United drew 3-3 with Tottenham Hotspur in the FA Charity Shield played at Old Trafford. Bobby Charlton scored two of United's goals, whilst Denis Law hit the other. In fact, Bobby Charlton was booked for the only time in his career for time-wasting. Though the referee later decided not to report the caution as United were losing 3-2 at the time!

1994 Eric Cantona was fined two weeks wages (£20,000) by Manchester United and banned for three matches following the Broadcast Advertising Clearance Centre ban after the Frenchman had appeared in a Nike advert making a 'four- letter boast' about his 'dirty tricks' on the field.

13

1963 Republic of Ireland left-back Noel Cantwell is given his marching orders during United's friendly match in Germany against Eintracht Frankfurt.

1977 United played Liverpool in the FA Charity Shield in front of a record 82,000 crowd at Wembley. The teams were so well matched that they played each other to a standstill and the fans had to be content with a goalless draw. There was still plenty of action and United should have had a penalty when Emlyn Hughes pulled David McReery down. The linesman flagged vigorously but the referee told the United players he was too far away from the incident to be certain enough to award a penalty.

1985 Manchester United stepped up their peace plans with a big move for family support at Old Trafford. The club officially launched their new L Stand as a 1,500 seater family section.

14

1965 Manchester United and Liverpool produced an entertaining display of football in a 2-2 draw in the FA Charity Shield at Old Trafford. A crowd of 48,502 saw goals from Best and Herd for United and Yeats and Stevenson for Liverpool. For United there was the added satisfaction of seeing a reserve bolstered side perform so well.

1979 United paid a club record £825,000 for Ray Wilkins, when they signed the Chelsea and England midfielder. It was United's manager Dave Sexton who had signed the 15-year-old Wilkins for Chelsea.

1983 United lost 1-0 to Dutch champions Ajax in Holland, the goal being scored by

- August -

Danish international Jesper Olsen in the 50th minute. The winger who joined the Reds in July 1984 tormented the United defence, but despite losing, United's worst moment came when Gordon McQueen was sent-off for a violent tackle on Ajax's Jan Molby.

1994 Manchester United beat Blackburn Rovers 2-0 in the FA Charity Shield with Eric Cantona scoring his third penalty in consecutive games at Wembley. Paul Ince added United's second ten minutes from time. A Ryan Giggs corner was backheaded by Cantona to the Reds' midfielder who had his back to goal as he produced a powerful right foot overhead scissors kick from eight yards out that gave Flowers in the Blackburn goal no chance. It was United's second successive FA Charity Shield victory, a feat they had not achieved since 1957 when they beat Aston Villa 4-0 after beating neighbours Manchester City 1-0 a year earlier.

1995 The club announced that they had signed up to show twelve home games live on cinema screens at Manchester's G-Mex centre and Salford Quays. Tickets were to be priced at £8 - £10 for adults and £4 - £6 for children.

15 **1978** Sir Stanley Rous, one-time leader of world football, paid a centenary tribute to some of the men who owed their greatness to Manchester United Football Club. The former president of FIFA was guest of honour at the Old Trafford club's dinner at the Hotel Piccadilly on their 100th birthday.

16 **1991** Manchester United along with the 21 other First Division clubs, handed in their resignation to the Football League, which was preparing to start the new season virtually leaderless and without a management committee.

1994 United chairman Martin Edwards launched a scathing attack on PFA chief Gordon Taylor for his claim that English clubs are bringing foreigners in to the detriment of national interests.

17 **1963** United lost 4-0 to Everton in the FA Charity Shield on a day when they were outclassed as individuals as well as a team. United were already a well beaten side when the referee awarded the Goodison side a penalty after Maurice Setters' innocuous challenge on Roy Vernon. That they were allowed to retake the spot-kick on the intervention of a linesman after Dave Gaskell's brilliant save, was a cruel twist of the knife.

1974 United played their first game in the Second Division since they had beaten Bury 2-0 in May 1938. Playing away against Orient, the Reds won 2-0 with goals from Houston and Morgan. The Brisbane Road club only missed promotion by a point the previous season and so were a fair guide to what United fans hoped would be just one season out of the top flight. The United side rolled up their sleeves and showed they were prepared to battle as well as bask in the great name of the club.

1983 Martin Buchan's Testimonial brought United's future manager Alex Ferguson to Old Trafford as manager of the successful Scottish League side Aberdeen, Buchan's first club. Buchan was bought by Frank O'Farrell and played on for United under Docherty, Sexton and Atkinson before joining Oldham Athletic four days after his Testimonial.

1996 In the opening game of the 1996-97 season, United beat Wimbledon 3-0 with David Beckham scoring a superb goal in injury time. United's other scorers were Cantona and Irwin.

- August -

18

1946 Birth of John Fitzpatrick. The Aberdeen-born player signed professional forms in September 1963 and within twelve months, had gained an FA Youth Cup winners' medal. A tough-tackling wing-half, he was successfully converted to full-back and went on to appear in 147 League and Cup games for United. Injuries dogged his Old Trafford career and when he was finally forced to give up the game in the summer of 1973, he was still only 26 years old. He returned to Scotland on his retirement and set up his own wine business.

1951 Returning to the Old Trafford attack for the opening game of the season, after missing all the pre-season friendlies, centre-forward Jack Rowley took just eight minutes to get off the mark in the Reds' game at West Bromwich Albion. The home side then bombarded the United goal and went 3-1 ahead before Rowley scored two goals to complete his hat-trick and give United a point.

1971 United beat Chelsea 3-2 at Stamford Bridge. They finished the first-half with ten men and a goal down following George Best's dismissal but early in the second-half, Brian Kidd equalised with a header. A Willie Morgan penalty and a Bobby Charlton thunderbolt put the Reds 3-1 up before Peter Osgood pulled a goal back in the final minutes.

1989 United supremo Martin Edwards quit the club as chairman in a sensational £30 million sell-out. Millionaire property tycoon Michael Knighton became the new owner of Manchester United, promising to invest a massive amount of money into the club.

19

1950 Eddie McIlvenny, who captained the United States when they famously beat England in the 1950 World Cup made his debut for United in the opening game of the season, a 1-0 win at home to Fulham

1959 Manchester United scratched in the first round of the European Cup and the Swiss team Young Boys Berne, won on a walkover and reached the semi-finals.

1975 Alex Stepney, United's goalkeeper was taken to hospital during the away game with Birmingham City which United won 2-0 with a dislocated jaw, sustained by apparently shouting at a team-mate!

1989 Michael Knighton paraded before the Stretford End showing one or two tricks with the ball before United's opening game of the season against Arsenal. The Reds won 4-1 with goals from Bruce, Hughes, Webb and McClair.

1996 Having lost to Everton in the 1995 FA Cup Final, United's 3-1 defeat at Aston Villa was the first time in over 150 games that they had lost two consecutive competitive matches.

20

1949 Birth of Stewart Houston. Failing to make the grade at his first League club, Chelsea, Stewart Houston joined Brentford and made 77 League appearances for the Bees before signing for United in December 1973. One of a number of Scots signed by Tommy Docherty in his early days at the club, Houston went straight into the side, making his debut at Queen's Park Rangers on New Years Day 1974. In 1975 he won his one and only Scottish cap against Denmark and the following year was in United's FA Cup Final side that lost to Southampton. Unfortunately in 1977, when the Reds won the FA Cup beating Liverpool 2-1, Houston was missing, having broken his ankle at Ashton Gate two weeks before the big event. He left Old Trafford in the summer of 1980 after playing in 250 League and Cup games to join Sheffield United on a free transfer. He later played for Colchester United before becoming a member of the Arsenal coaching staff. He is now manager of Queen's Park Rangers.

- August -

1966 Two goals by Denis Law and one apiece from Best, Herd and Stiles gave United a 5-0 lead after just 22 minutes of their opening match of the season at home to West Bromwich Albion. The Reds eventually won 5-3.

1977 The Reds ran rings round Birmingham City to score a 4-1 victory at St Andrews. Lou Macari hit his first hat-trick for the club, a scoring performance that he backed up with an elusive midfield performance. Gordon Hill scored United's other goal, smashing home a volley from a ball already travelling in the direction of goal!

1982 Manchester United signed Peter Beardsley for £300,000 from Vancouver Whitecaps. Unfortunately he never made the grade at Old Trafford, appearing for just 45 minutes against Bournemouth in the League Cup.

1983 United beat Liverpool 2-0 in the FA Charity Shield at Wembley. It was United's first Charity Shield win for 25 years and Liverpool's first defeat in their last seven appearances in the competition at Wembley. There was only one team in it for the first 20 minutes and that was Liverpool, with Kenny Dalglish hitting the woodwork from a powerful drive. Bryan Robson gave United the lead after 23 minutes and added a second in the 62nd minute to give the Reds victory.

1994 Paul Parker became United's eighth player to be dismissed in the previous twelve months when he is sent-off five minutes after coming on as a substitute in the match against Queen's Park Rangers, which the Reds won 2-0.

21

1965 Manchester United's first substitute, though not used, was Noel Cantwell at home to Sheffield Wednesday on the opening day of the season. The Reds won 1-0 with David Herd grabbing the all-important goal.

1996 United's first home game of the 1996-97 season saw them fall behind to two Duncan Ferguson goals against Everton. A goal from Jordi Cruyff and an own goal by David Unsworth allowed the Reds to retain their 30 game unbeaten League run at home.

22

1936 Jack Griffiths the tall United defender who appeared in 176 first team games for the Reds was a keen sprinter and won many prizes over the sprint distances at summer meetings including the Lancashire Championships.

1951 Jack Rowley scored his second successive hat-trick in United's second game of the season as they beat Middlesbrough 4-2. He ended the season as the club's top scorer with 30 goals, including scoring other hat-tricks against West Bromwich Albion, Stoke City and Arsenal.

1953 Playing in blue jerseys which brought them luck on their last two visits to Anfield, United took the lead through Rowley after nine minutes. Liverpool were able to cash in on defensive jitters that made gifts of at least two goals, yet United challenged for every ball in a goal-shattering second-half when they had defeat staring them in the face. Crompton in goal made some brilliant saves whilst Byrne cracked in a penalty in United's 4-4 draw before accidentally turning the ball into his own net.

23

1913 Charlie Roberts signed for Oldham Athletic for a record fee of £1,500 after playing in 299 games for United and scoring 23 goals. The club's regular centre-half for nine seasons, it was his leadership and enthusiasm that had been the key to United's success as they won two League Championships and the FA Cup.

- August -

1958 Bobby Charlton gave the Reds a sixth minute lead against Chelsea at Stamford Bridge on the opening day of the season. The Ashington-born forward found the shooting form which had eluded him on the club's tour of Germany and scored a hat-trick with three unstoppable shots. ALex Dawson scored two more for United in a 5-2 win over a Chelsea side that were completely outplayed.

24

1928 Birth of Tommy Docherty. A former Scottish international, he made 324 League appearances for Preston North End before joining Arsenal in the summer of 1958. He had the misfortune of breaking his leg when playing for the Gunners against Preston and only appeared in 83 League games for the Highbury club. He packed away his boots to accept the post of senior coach to Chelsea, but during an emergency he played in four League games before becoming caretaker-manager. Four months later, his appointment was confirmed on a permanent basis and he guided the young Chelsea side to the 1967 FA Cup Final. He then managed Rotherham United, Queen's Park Rangers and Aston Villa before taking charge of Porto. He was appointed Scotland's team manager in 1971 giving them an immediate boost before replacing Frank O'Farrell at Old Trafford. In four and a half seasons with United, he assembled an exciting side. In 1977, he made his eighth appearance at Wembley, as a player and a manager, but his first as a winner. He was dismissed later that year and with his United job went his best chance of major managerial success. After coaching in Australia, he was back in Lancashire soccer as manager of Preston North End. Now a popular radio celebrity, he gets the same response from the listeners as he did from the players in his charge at Old Trafford.

1949 United returned to Old Trafford for the first time following the war and damage to the ground.

The curtain at last went up on the incomplete Old Trafford stage for the visit of Bolton Wanderers. United celebrated the occasion with a 3-0 win with Charlie Mitten hitting their first Old Trafford goal for eight years.

1952 The FA Charity Shield match between Manchester United and Newcastle United at Old Trafford was shown on live television by the BBC. However, coverage only started at 6.00pm and finished fifty minutes later. Fortunately though, five of the game's six goals were scored in this period, with United winning 4-2.

1957 A Billy Whealan hat-trick on the opening day of the season gave United a 3-0 win against Leicester City at Filbert Street.

1974 The Reds beat Millwall 4-0 at Old Trafford with Irishman Gerry Daly hitting a hat-trick.

25

1923 Frank McPherson made his United debut in the opening game of the 1923-24 season as the Reds won 2-1 at Bristol City. The former Barrow player soon established himself in the United side and was a member of the team that won promotion from the Second Division in 1924-25. In the Reds first season back in the top flight he was second top scorer with 16 goals including netting a hat-trick in a 3-1 win at Leicester City. After scoring 52 goals in 175 League and Cup games for United, he joined Manchester Central before moving to play for Watford. At Vicarage Road he scored 33 goals in 33 League games before moving to play Second Division football with Reading. When they were relegated two seasons later, he rejoined Watford before finishing his career with his home-town club, Barrow.

1989 Due to the non-arrival of membership cards for the start of the season, over 700 United fans were locked out of the club's opening fixture against Coventry City.

- August -

26 **1933** George Vose made his Manchester United debut in the opening game of the 1933-34 season at Plymouth Argyle, where the Reds went down 4-0. A natural ball-playing centre-half, he was a member of the United side which went up and down between the First and Second Divisions in the 1930s. His only honour at Old Trafford was a Second Division championship medal in 1936, the year when he played in an England trial match. He played in 211 first team games for the Reds, scoring his only goal in a 3-1 defeat by Grimsby Town at Old Trafford on Christmas Day 1933. After the war, he joined Cheshire League side, Runcorn.

1939 On what was the opening day of the 1939-40 season, United beat Grimsby Town 4-0 at Old Trafford. The Reds played a further two games, both away from home before the competition was suspended due to the outbreak of war.

1951 Birth of Jeff Wealands. A steady reliable goalkeeper, he joined the Reds as cover for Gary Bailey in February 1983, initially on loan, but later on a permanent basis after his contract with Birmingham City expired in the summer of that year. He had played his early League football with Northampton Town and Darlington but it was with Hull City that he made his name. He made 270 League and Cup appearances for the Tigers before joining Birmingham City. He only made eight appearances for the Reds and after suffering a troublesome back injury was released in 1985.

27 **1921** Arthur Lochhead, who scored 50 League and Cup goals for United in 153 appearances, made his debut for the Reds on the opening day of the 1921-22 season as they went down 5-0 at Everton. He joined United after just six games for Hearts and helped them win promotion in 1924-25, scoring 13 goals in 37 appearances.

He moved to Leicester City in October 1926 and in 303 League games for the Filberts scored 105 goals, helping them to finish as runners-up in the First Division in 1928-29. Another player to make his debut in this game was Ray Bennion. He was a right-half who joined United from Crichton Athletic in April 1920. He gained a regular first team place when Clarrie Hilditch moved to left-half and went on to appear in 301 League and Cup games for the Reds. He won ten full international caps for Wales before leaving Old Trafford in 1932 to play for Burnley.

1955 Manchester United's youngest-ever team appeared in the 3-1 win over West Bromwich Albion at Old Trafford. The average age was 22 years 106 days. The team was: Wood; Foulkes; Byrne; Whitefoot; Jones; Edwards; Webster; Blanchflower; Lewis; Viollet and Scanlon.

28 **1937** Tom Manley, scorer of two goals for United in the 3-0 home win over Newcastle United on the opening day of the season, had begun his career with his home-town club Northwich Victoria before joining United in the 1931-32 season. One of his most important goals for the Reds came on 5 May 1934 when his 80th minute strike set United on their way to a 2-0 victory against Millwall at The Den. His best season in terms of goals scored was 1935-36 when he netted 15 League and Cup goals, including four in the 7-2 win over Port Vale. After scoring 41 goals in 195 first team games, he joined Brentford, but after just three League games for the Griffin Park side, the season was abandoned because of the war. He guested for the Reds during the wartime, returning to play for the Bees after the hostilities.

29 **1908** Manchester United win the FA Charity Shield, beating Queen's Park Rangers 4-0 in a replay at Stamford Bridge.

- August -

The first match in April had ended 1-1 but there was only one team in it in the replay as Jimmy Turnbull scored a hat-trick.

1936 George Mutch had the ball in the Wolves' net within the very first few seconds of the match at Old Trafford which ended 1-1, but it was disallowed for offside.

1956 A Dennis Viollet hat-trick gave United a 3-2 win over Preston North End at Old Trafford to keep them at the top of the First Division. Also this date saw the birth of Viv Anderson. Alex Ferguson's first major signing, he was the first coloured player to gain a full England cap when he played against Czechoslovakia in November 1978. He made his League debut for Nottingham Forest in a 3-2 win at Hillsborough in September 1974, though it was 1976-77 before he established himself as the club's regular back. He remained Forest's first choice until the end of the 1983-84 season when he was transferred to Arsenal for £250,000. He had made 430 League and Cup appearances in his ten years at the City Ground, winning a League Championship medal, two League Cup winners' medals and was a member of two European Cup winning sides. After appearing in 150 League and Cup games for the Gunners, he moved to Old Trafford, again for £250,000, the fee being fixed by an independent tribunal. Plagued by injuries during his time with United, he appeared in 69 first team games before being given a free transfer and joining Sheffield Wednesday. He is now assistant-manager to Bryan Robson at Middlesbrough.

1958 As a mark of sympathy and respect following the Munich air disaster, the European Union forwarded a special invitation to United to compete in the European Cup again. It was gratefully accepted by the club with the original blessing of the FA but then they reversed their earlier decision and refused United's entry.

1985 Sir Matt Busby officially opened the new suite named after him.

30

1919 League football finally resumed after the hostilities and began exactly as it would had the 1915-16 season commenced, with the same teams in the same leagues. Manchester United travelled to Derby County who had won promotion as the war brought an end to the game. United opened the scoring after half an hour but the Rams equalised eight minutes from time. Clarrie Hilditch made his debut in this game. Born at Hartford near Northwich, he began his career with Witton Albion before playing for Altrincham, from where United signed him in 1916. During the First World War, he worked in London as a clerk in a cavalry regiment but once the game resumed in 1919 he went straight into the United side at centre-half. He played for England against Wales in a 1919 Victory International and a year later, against South Africa in the Commonwealth internationals. He was appointed United's player-manager in 1924 when John Chapman was suspended by the FA, until Herbert Bamlett took over in April 1927. During this time, he was loathe to select himself and the club slipped. Continuing to serve the club as a player, he appeared in 322 games in 16 seasons at Old Trafford, yet never won a major honour.

1941 United hammered New Brighton 13-1 in the opening game of the Football League Northern Section with Jack Rowley scoring seven of the goals.

1947 United beat Charlton Athletic 6-4 at Old Trafford with Jack Rowley scoring four of their goals.

1978 The Reds were drawn away to Stockport County in the Football League Cup but the Edgeley Park side switch the tie to Old Trafford where United win 3-2.

31

1909 For twelve months the Players Union sought affiliation to the Federation of Trade Unions.

- August -

Five days before the start of the 1909-10 season, the Football League decided that any player admitting to being a member of the union, should be suspended, have his wages stopped and be banned from playing in any game.

The Manchester United board called a players meeting and told them of the League's directive. The players told the United board that they had no grievance against them but stated that they intended to retain their membership of the Players' Union. This meant that the club's opening game of the season against Bradford City would have to be postponed, but on this date, the eve of the new season, the authorities had a change of heart and the Players' Union was recognised and suspensions removed.

1946 When football kicked off again after the Second World War, United beat Grimsby Town 2-1 with goals from Mitten and Rowley. The game was played at Maine Road because until the War Damage Commission came up with some money, and so the bomb-wrecked Old Trafford remained empty.

11 August
Matt Busby
Big crowd for
Testimonial Match

- August -

*(Right)
29 August
Jimmy Turnbull
A hat-trick in the
Charity Shield match.*

*(Below left)
Denis Viollet
28 August
Member of the youngest-ever
United team.*

*(Below right)
26 August
George Vose
Makes his debut
for United.*

93

SEPTEMBER

1

1900 Alf Schofield made his debut for Newton Heath on the opening day of the season as the Heathens went down 1-0 at Glossop. He had joined Newton Heath as a replacement for right William Bryant. A member of the team which won promotion from the Second Division in 1905-06, the Liverpool born player made 179 League and Cup appearances for the club before retiring after just ten games of the 1906-07 First Division campaign.

1959 Birth of Mike Duxbury. An adaptable well-balanced player, he made his debut against Birmingham City in 1980-81, coming on as a substitute for Kevin Moran. He went on to appear in 33 games that season, in a variety of positions as a utility player. In 1982-83 he found himself as United's right-back and was an ever-present as the Reds finished third in the First Division. It was in this position that the Blackburn-born player won his ten England caps to add to the seven won at Under-21 level. Despite losing his right-back spot to John Gidman, he continued to be an important member of the United side because of his versatility. He played in the 1983 and 1985 FA Cup winning teams and made 376 League and Cup appearances for the Reds before being given a free transfer at the end of the 1989-90 season. He joined his home-town club Blackburn Rovers before ending his League career with Bradford City.

2

1893 Alf Farman scored a hat-trick for Newton Heath on the opening day of the season as they beat Burnley 3-2.

1905 Charlie Sagar became the only United player to score a hat-trick on his debut as the Reds beat Bristol City 5-1 on the opening day of the season.

1918 The death of John James Bentley, one of Manchester United's and the Football League's greatest administrators. Possibly more than any other man, the Turton-born Bentley was responsible for the spread of football in Lancashire. In 1884 after his career was shortened by an accident, he moved into administration as secretary of Bolton Wanderers. He held the post until 1897, combining it in 1893 with the position of President of the Football League. He first became associated with Manchester United in 1902 and became the club chairman, a position he held until 1908. When Ernest Mangnall left to manage Manchester City in 1912, Bentley took over the job of secretary-manager but stepped down two years later to continue as secretary until his resignation in 1916.

1931 The lowest crowd at Old Trafford, 3,507, see United go down 3-2 to Southampton in the first game of the season.

1939 United lost 2-0 to Charlton Athletic in the third match of the season. The following morning Britain declared war on Germany and two days later the League Management Committee met to cancel the league season.

1992 Dion Dublin broke his leg on his full Old Trafford debut in United's 1-0 win over Crystal Palace.

3

1892 Having been elevated from the Football Alliance to the First Division of the Football League, Newton Heath travelled to Blackburn for their opening match. The Heathens seemed overawed by the occasion and Rovers swept into a three-goal lead. But by half-time, Newton had scored twice with Bob Donaldson privileged to score the club's first League goal and Coupar adding the second. Blackburn scored again, and though Farman hit a third for Newton Heath, the Rovers held on to win 4-3.

- September -

1921 Birth of John Aston senior. The father of John, he was originally an inside-forward, switched to wing-half but gained his reputation at left-back, from where he went on to win 17 England caps. He joined United as an amateur in 1937, turning professional in 1946. He made his League debut in the 1-1 draw with Chelsea in September of that year, going on to appear in 253 League games for the Reds. Along with Johnny Carey, he formed one of the club's most famous full-back pairings, the two internationals having a great understanding. With United he won an FA Cup winners' medal in 1948 and a League Championship prize in 1952. Occasionally, he would lend a helping hand in the forward line and in his United career, scored 30 League and Cup goals, including one in his last match against Sheffield United in April 1954. Illness forced his retirement from the playing side of the game and in 1956, he joined the backroom staff at Old Trafford. He became chief scout in 1970 following the retirement of Joe Armstrong but was sacked along with manager Frank O'Farrell two years later.

1963 United travelled to Portman Road and beat Ipswich Town 7-2 in this First Division encounter, with Denis Law hitting a hat-trick. United's other scorers were Phil Chisnall, Ian Moir, David Sadler and Maurice Setters.

4

1897 Lincoln City were beaten 5-0 on the opening day of the season with Boyd scoring a hat-trick.

1926 John Wilson made his debut for United in the 2-2 draw against Leeds United at Old Trafford. He had played his early football with Newcastle United and made 139 League appearances for the Magpies before later playing for Durham City and Stockport County. The tough-tackling wing-half spent four seasons at Edgeley Park before signing for United in the summer of 1926.

He appeared in 140 League and Cup games for the Reds before leaving Old Trafford for Bristol City in the summer of 1931 following the club's relegation.

1957 United drew 3-3 at Everton in front of a Goodison Park crowd of 72,077. This is United's best post-war away League crowd and is a League record for a midweek match.

5

1903 John Sutcliffe made his debut in goal for United in the 2-2 draw against Bristol City on the opening day of the season. After being expelled by Heckmondwike Rugby Club for alleged professionalism, he turned to soccer and signed for Bolton Wanderers. Starting out as a centre-forward, he was soon converted into a goalkeeper and won the first of five England caps in 1893. He holds the distinction of being the last Englishman to play both international soccer and rugby union. After appearing in 364 first team games for the Trotters, he left the Football League to play for Millwall, but within twelve months he had joined United. He only kept goal for the Reds in season 1903-04 when they missed promotion to the First Division by one point before joining Southern League Plymouth Argyle.

1936 United went down 5-4 at Derby County despite Bamford netting a hat-trick for the Reds.

1979 The Reds beat Tottenham Hotspur 3-1 in the Football League Cup second round second leg tie at Old Trafford to go through to the next round 4-3 on aggregate. They are indebted to Spurs' Paul Miller, whose own goal in the last few minutes gave United victory.

6

1902 Having emerged from Newton Heath to become the Manchester United of 1902 in colours of red and white, their first

- September -

match was away at Gainsborough Trinity, whom they beat 1-0 with a goal by Richards. The first United team was: Whitehouse; Stafford(capt); Read; Morgan; Griffiths; Cartwright; Schofield; Richards; Peddie; Williams; Hurst.

7 **1907** In their second game of the season, United beat Liverpool 4-0 at Clayton to go top of the First Division. Sandy Turnbull scored the first of his four hat-tricks for the club and it was only the fine form of Sam Hardy in the Liverpool goal that prevented the Anfield side from suffering a real drubbing.

1996 Eric Cantona missed a penalty in the match against his former club Leeds United at Elland Road. However, the Reds still won 4-0 with the Frenchman making up for the miss with a stunning goal in the dying minutes of the game.

8 **1917** George Anderson scored four goals for the Reds as they beat Blackburn Rovers 6-1 in a Lancashire Section (Principal Tournament) wartime game.

1934 Barnsley took a shock 6th minute lead against Manchester United at Old Trafford but the Reds inspired by George Mutch came back to win 4-1. The Scot scored a first-half hat-trick in the space of seven minutes, scoring in the 24th, 26th and 30th minutes as he adopted a shoot on sight approach. United's fourth goal came five minutes after the restart when Manley headed home from close range.

1951 United had won 15 successive matches at Old Trafford when they faced lowly Stoke City, still waiting their first win. The Reds went ahead after seven minutes when Jack Rowley shot home following Harry McShane's corner kick.

Although dictating the run of play, United didn't find their real measure until the last 20 minutes when they made full use of their shooting power and Rowley completed his hat-trick.

1973 Brian Greenhoff made his debut for United in a 2-1 defeat at Ipswich Town. The younger brother of Jimmy Greenhoff, he turned professional in 1970 two months after his 17th birthday. The Reds converted him from full-back to centre-half in the latter part of the 1974-75 season and he held that position until Christmas 1977. He appeared in the 1976, 1977 and 1979 FA Cup Finals and gained 18 full England caps and four at Under-23 level. In 1979 after appearing in 270 League and Cup games for the Reds he was transferred to Leeds United for £350,000. He went on Jimmy Hill's 'rebel' soccer tour to South Africa in the summer of 1982 before joining his brother Jimmy at Rochdale the following year.

9 **1922** Frank Barson made his debut in the 1-0 win against Wolverhampton Wanderers at Molineux. He had started his career with Barnsley before joining Aston Villa in 1919. A member of their FA Cup winning side of 1920, he also won his only England cap that year when Wales beat the home side 2-1 at Highbury for their first victory on English soil for 39 years. Despite all the rumours, which included the centre-half supposedly pulling a gun on the Villa manager, United had no qualms about paying £5,000 for the defender in the summer of 1922. He helped the Reds win promotion to the First Division in 1924-25 and played in 152 games before being given a free transfer and joining Watford.

1959 The Reds beat Leeds United 6-0 at Old Trafford in front of a 48,407 crowd. Though the Yorkshire side were unlucky to be three goals down at the interval, they folded up later in the game.

- September -

Even with Albert Quixall limping on the wing for most of the game, United tore the Leeds defence to ribbons. Warren Bradley and Dennis Viollet scored two goals apiece, whilst Bobby Charlton and Albert Quixall added the others.

10 **1892** The first ever Football League match was played in the city. Burnley were the visitors, with the result a 1-1 draw. Bob Donaldson scored Newton Heath's goal. The Heathens line-up was: Warner; Mitchell; Brown; Perrins; Stewart; Erentz; Hood; Donaldson; Coupar; Carson and Matthieson.

1924 The city of Manchester showed its appreciation of Ernest Mangnall's contribution to football with a Testimonial game at Maine Road between an Everton and Liverpool side against a City and United side. Under Mangnall's leadership, United won the First Division championship in 1908 and 1911 and the FA Cup in 1909. Not only was he influential in the construction of Old Trafford but of Maine Road too, after joining City as their secretary-manager.

1927 United have only twice conceded seven goals in the Football League at home and on both occasions to Newcastle United! The Magpies won this encounter 7-1 with Joe Spence scoring United's consolation goal.

11 **1897** United's Boyd scored his second hat-trick of the season in the club's second match as the Reds won 4-0 at Burton Swifts.

1937 United beat Barnsley 4-1 at Old Trafford in a game that is remembered for the remarkable ill-fortune that the visitors suffered. After 25 minutes, their goalkeeper Binns was taken to hospital with two broken fingers sustained in attempting to stop United's first goal scored by Manley.

Then full-back Ives had to leave the field with broken ribs. With nine men Barnsley put up a great fight, but a second-half hat-trick by Tommy Bamford put the game out of their reach although former United player Hine scored a last minute penalty.

1946 Liverpool were beaten 5-0 with Stan Pearson grabbing a hat-trick as the Reds win their fourth successive game since the start of the season.

1993 Manchester United lose their unbeaten record in the Premier League, going down 1-0 to Chelsea at Stamford Bridge, their first defeat in 17 League matches.

12 **1908** Jimmy Turnbull scored four of Manchester United's goals as they beat Middlesbrough 6-3. The Reds' other goals are scored by Halse and Wall.

1936 In what was generally a disappointing season for United, a crowd of 68,796 turned up to see them beat prospective League champions Manchester City 3-2 with goals from Bamford, Bryant and Manley.

1956 United's first competitive match on the Continent was in Brussels against Anderlecht the Belgian champions, when goals from Dennis Viollet and Tommy Taylor saw them to a 2-0 win.

13 **1902** Manchester United's first home game under their new name saw a crowd of 20,000 - 8,000 of them under cover as a result of ground improvements during the summer - gathered to see them beat Burton United 1-0 with a goal from Hurst.

- September -

1930 Despite a hat-trick from Tom Reid, United's robust centre-forward, the Reds lost 7-4 at home to Newcastle United, which made a total of thirteen goals conceded at home in a period of four days! They had also conceded six goals at Chelsea in their previous away game. Not surprisingly, the Reds were relegated at the end of the season.

1941 Jack Rowley scored four of United's goals as they beat Stockport County 5-1 in a Football League Northern Section (First Championship) wartime match.

1957 Birth of Mal Donaghy. He joined Luton Town from Irish League side Larne in the summer of 1978 and was an ever-present for the Hatters in seasons 1979-80, 1980-81, 1981-82, 1984-85, 1985-86 and 1986-87. He had made 483 first team appearances for the Kenilworth Road club before signing for United for £650,000 in October 1988. Initially, the Northern Ireland international, who won 91 caps, played alongside Steve Bruce, but on the arrival of Gary Pallister he moved to right-back. He continued to remain a valuable squad member and was unlucky not to pick up a League Cup winners' medal against Nottingham Forest after appearing in the Reds' first team in the weeks prior to the final. He appeared in 119 first team games for the Old Trafford club before joining Chelsea in August 1992.

1980 Yugoslavian international Nikola Jovanovic scored two of United's goals as they beat Leicester City 5-0.

14

1923 Birth of Henry Cockburn. He made his first team debut for United in wartime football against Tranmere Rovers in 1943 in a match that was abandoned after 85 minutes. However, the 6-3 scoreline in United's favour was allowed to stand. He won the first of his 13 full caps for England after just six League appearances for the Reds. Though he only stood 5ft 4ins, he was a great player in the United side because he worked so hard for the team and his enthusiasm rubbed off on to other people. He won an FA Cup winners' medal in 1948 and a League Championship medal in 1951-52. After playing in 275 games for United he left to join Bury but after just 35 League games for the Gigg Lane club he entered non-League football.

1929 A hat-trick by Bill Rawlings gave United a 3-2 win at Middlesbrough.

1956 Birth of Ray Wilkins. He became Chelsea's youngest-ever captain when he was 18 and led them to promotion from the Second Division in 1976-77. He played in 179 League games for the Stamford Bridge club before transferring to United for £825,000 in August 1979. He took a while to settle at Old Trafford but eventually he replaced Martin Buchan as club captain. He later captained England but lost both jobs to Bryan Robson. He scored a memorable goal in the 1983 FA Cup Final against Brighton which ended 2-2 and picked up a winners' medal after the Reds won the replay 4-0. The holder of 84 England caps, he joined Italian League side AC Milan for £1.5 million in the summer of 1984. He later played for Paris St Germain before Graeme Souness signed him for Glasgow Rangers. He won League Championship and Skol Cup winners' medals with the Ibrox club before joining Queen's Park Rangers. Awarded an OBE in the honours list, he became the Loftus Road club's manager, but parted company after they were relegated from the Premier League in 1995-96.

1960 United beat West Ham United 6-1 with two goals apiece from Bobby Charlton and Dennis Viollet and one each from Scanlon and Quixall.

1963 Matt Busby gave George Best his first game, playing him at outside-right against West Bromwich Albion at Old Trafford, David Sadler scored United's goal in a 1-0 win.

- September -

1966 United suffered their worst-ever League Cup defeat, going down 5-1 to Blackpool at Bloomfield Road, with a team that consisted of nine internationals.

15

1930 John Mellor made his debut for United in a 3-0 defeat at Huddersfield Town. Signed from Witton Albion, he played in one of United's poorest teams. In fact, the Reds lost their first twelve fixtures that season and not surprisingly were relegated to the Second Division. Mellor therefore played most of his 116 League games for the Reds in Division Two, for when United won promotion in 1935-36, he only appeared in two top flight games before leaving Old Trafford to play for Cardiff City.

1965 The club's programme for the match against Newcastle United contained a warning notice referring to the obscene chanting at the referee in the club's previous home game against Stoke City. It was during this game that eight youths between the ages of 15 and 21 were removed from the Stretford End and banned for the rest of the season.

1976 United played their first match in the UEFA Cup, losing 1-0 away to Ajax of Amsterdam. They won the second leg 2-0 at Old Trafford with goals from McIlroy and Macari to progress to the next round.

1993 Manchester United celebrated their return to the European Cup after 25 years with a 3-2 win over Honved in Hungary. Roy Keane twice and Eric Cantona found the net for United, but they came close to throwing the game away, missing a number of easy chances and conceding two soft goals late in the game.

16

1918 Birth of Allenby Chilton. He made his debut for United on 2 September 1939 against Charlton Athletic at The Valley and the very next day war was declared, so he had to wait a further seven years before he played his next League game! Despite being wounded on service in Normandy, he guested for Charlton Athletic in wartime football and won a Wartime South Cup winners' medal. There was a time in his early days with United that he gave up football to try boxing, but after six months in the ring, he returned to soccer. He represented England on two occasions and was United's only ever-present when they won the League title in 1951-52. Succeeding Johnny Carey as club captain, he eventually lost his place to Mark Jones after a run of 166 consecutive League games. It was a record until broken by Steve Coppell during the 1980-81 season. Scanlon played in 390 League and Cup games for the Reds, winning an FA Cup winners' medal in 1948 and League Championship medal in 1951-52. He left Old Trafford in 1955 to become player-manager at Grimsby Town.

1957 Birth of David McCreery. A more than able deputy for United's midfield or front-line player, nearly half of his 109 first team appearances were as a substitute. He wore the number 12 shirt in both the 1976 and 1977 FA Cup Finals and substituted Gordon Hill on both occasions. In August 1979, he went to Queen's Park Rangers for £200,000 and in the summer months played for Tulsa Roughnecks in the NASL. In October 1982 he joined Newcastle United and at the end of 1983-84 helped the Magpies win promotion to the First Division. Capped 67 times by Northern Ireland he later played for Hearts before returning to the Football League to play for Hartlepool United.

1989 United beat Millwall 5-1 in front of a 42,746 crowd with Mark Hughes grabbing a hat-trick.

- September -

17

1958 Albert Scanlon hit a fine hat-trick in United's 4-1 win over West Ham United at Old Trafford in what was probably the best performance of his career. Yet it was a great team performance with goalkeeper Harry Gregg in particularly fine form. The Hammers would have had a couple of early goals but for the Irishman's anticipation, and he was only inches away from thwarting their penalty because John Bond only scored after Gregg had punched out his spot-kick. United's win was revenge for their 3-2 defeat against the Hammers nine days earlier.

1981 Manchester United's Old Trafford housed the Lambert and Butler seven-a-side cricket tournament, with Lancashire playing Yorkshire and Derbyshire facing Nottinghamshire. The two winners then played each other for the right to play in the final at Stamford Bridge. Black sight-screens were installed and the goalposts removed. Over 3,000 spectators saw Lancashire win through to the final.

18

1942 Birth of Alex Stepney. He began his career as an amateur with Tooting and Mitcham before turning professional with Millwall in 1963. He made 137 League appearances for the Lions before joining Chelsea three years later. However, he only made one League appearance for the Stamford Bridge club before United paid £55,000 for his services in September 1966. Apart from a brief spell in 1970-71, he was United's first-choice goalkeeper for 12 seasons, appearing in 535 League and Cup games. He won a League Championship medal in 1967, a European Cup winners' medal in 1968, when he made two instinctive saves from Eusebio in the closing minutes of normal time, and an FA Cup winners' medal in 1977. Halfway through United's relegation season of 1973-74, Stepney was joint leading scorer after converting two penalties!

He made just one appearance for England in a 3-1 win over Sweden in May 1968. After leaving Old Trafford he went to play in the USA with Dallas Tornadoes and later with non-League Altrincham.

1965 A Denis Law hat-trick helped United defeat Chelsea 4-1 at Old Trafford. Bobby Charlton scored the Reds' other goal.

1968 United played Waterford in the European Cup first round first leg at Old Trafford. A Denis Law hat-trick helped the Reds to a 3-1 win.

1971 United beat West Ham United 4-2 with George Best scoring a hat-trick.

1972 Though Manchester United had yet to win in a Football League game that season, the fans put all that behind them to pay tribute to Bobby Charlton, who had graced the game for a good number of years. A crowd of 60,538 packed into Old Trafford for his Testimonial match.

19

1908 Harold Hardman who served the club for over half a century as a director made his debut in the derby match at Manchester City. The Reds won 2-1 and though Hardman played in only four games for United he had won four full England caps whilst with Everton and an Olympic Games soccer gold medal with the 1908 Great Britain team. One of only three amateurs to win FA Cup winners' medals this century, he was United's chairman from 1951 until his death in the summer of 1965. One of the game's greatest administrators, he was President of the Lancashire FA and an FA Councillor.

20

1924 William Henderson scored all United's goals in a 3-0 win over Oldham Athletic at Boundary Park.

- September -

21

1933 Birth of Dennis Viollet. An England schoolboy international, he succeeded Stan Pearson in United's League side, making his debut in a 2-1 win at Newcastle in April 1953. He had good ball control, a deceptive swerve and a powerful shot. His 32 goals in 1959-60 when he skippered the team is still a United record. Capped twice by the full England team in 1960 and 1961, he also represented the Football League in the late 1950s. After scoring 178 goals in 291 games, in which he won two League Championship medals and an FA Cup runners-up medal, he left Old Trafford to join Stoke City in January 1962 for £25,000. He helped the Potters win the Second Division championship in 1962-63 and scored 59 goals in 182 League games before signing for NASL side Baltimore Boys. After a short spell with Witton Albion, he won an Irish FA Cup winners' medal with Linfield.

1935 Birth of David Pegg. An elusive outside-left, he joined United as an amateur in 1950 and made his first team debut at Middlesbrough in December 1952, three months after turning professional. An England schoolboy, 'B' and Under-23 international, he played just once for the full England side in a World Cup qualifying match against the Republic of Ireland which ended in a 1-1 draw. He won two League Championship medals and played in the FA Cup Final defeat by Aston Villa. He had lost his place to Albert Scanlon shortly before the Red Star European Cup match but still made the trip, losing his life on the Munich runway.

1941 Jack Rowley scored four of United's goals in a 7-1 win over Stockport County in a Football League Northern Section (First Championship).

1947 A record derby crowd of 71,364 watch United and City play out a goalless draw at Maine Road.

1889 Newton Heath played their first match in the Football Alliance, a League inferior only to the Football League itself and destined to become the future Second Division. They beat Sunderland Albion 4-1 with goals from Wilson 2, J.Doughty and Stewart.

1912 Birth of George Mutch. Arriving at Old Trafford from Arbroath in May 1934, the Aberdeen-born forward soon made a name for himself and was the club's leading scorer in his first season. He headed the club's goalscoring charts again in 1935-36 when the Reds won the Second Division championship with 21 goals. He had scored 49 goals in 120 first team appearances when Preston North End secured his services for £5,000 in September 1937. In his first season at Deepdale, he helped the Lilywhites to third place in the First Division and to the FA Cup Final. At Wembley, he scored the only goal of the game from a penalty just 30 seconds from full-time to take the Cup to Preston. Capped once by Scotland, he later played for Bury before ending his career with Southport.

1935 Hubert Redwood made his debut for United in the goalless draw at home to Tottenham Hotspur. It was his only game that season but the former Sherdley Albion right-back went on to appear in 96 League and Cup games before the outbreak of war. He only scored two goals for United, both of them coming in a 3-3 draw at Southampton during the club's promotion season of 1937-38. He continued to play for the Reds in wartime football but died from tuberculosis at the age of 30 after he had been invalided out of the army.

1994 Paul Scholes scored both United goals on his debut in a 2-1 Football League Cup win at Port Vale. The last home-grown player to achieve this feat was Bobby Charlton in 1956.

- September -

22

1965 The Reds won 3-2 at HJK Helsinki in the European Cup first round first leg tie with goals from Connelly, Herd and Law.

1993 Manchester United are accused of fielding a reserve side when they are beaten 2-1 by Stoke City in a second round first leg Coca Cola Cup match.

23

1933 Neil Dewar scored four goals as Manchester United beat Burnley 5-2 at Old Trafford.

1961 Nobby Stiles scored for both sides in United's 3-2 derby win over Manchester City and had the misfortune to score another own goal for City at Maine Road in January 1967.

1964 Birth of Clayton Blackmore. A Welsh international, he made his United debut at Nottingham Forest in the final game of the 1983-84 season. He went on to appear in 251 first team games for the Reds, winning a European Cup Winners' Cup medal in the 1991 final against Barcelona. He also appeared in the League Cup Final of 1991 against Sheffield Wednesday and in the European Super Cup against Red Star Belgrade, but joined Middlesbrough on a free transfer in the summer of 1994.

1964 Manchester United played their first game in the Inter-Cities Fairs Cup and drew 1-1 against Djurgardens IF, with David Herd scoring the Reds' goal.

1987 The Reds beat Hull City 5-0 in the Football League Cup first round first leg tie at Old Trafford with goals from McGrath, Davenport, Whiteside, Strachan and McClair.

1989 Danny Wallace made his United debut in a 5-1 defeat by Manchester City at Maine Road. At 16 years 313 days, he became Southampton's youngest-ever League debutant when he played against Manchester United on 29 November 1980. He won a regular place in the Saints' line-up in 1982-83, finishing the season as the club's top scorer. The following season he missed just one game as Southampton finished second to Liverpool in the First Division championship just three points behind the Anfield club. In 1986 he made his one and only appearance for England against Egypt in Cairo, scoring once in a 4-0 win. He joined United in September 1989 for £1.2 million and though a regular in the Reds' side, he failed to lift the side. However, he had the consolation of receiving an FA Cup winners' medal when United beat Crystal Palace after a replay. Injuries then hampered his career and in October 1993 he moved to Birmingham City for £250,000.

24

1952 United beat Newcastle United 4-2 at Old Trafford in the FA Charity Shield with goals from Rowley 2, Downie and Byrne.

1962 Birth of Mike Phelan. After playing with Burnley for a number of seasons, he joined Norwich City for £45,000 and almost immediately became team captain. He had made 194 appearances for the Carrow Road club when United signed him for £750,000 in July 1989. He won his first England cap in 1990 when he came on as substitute for Bryan Robson in the match against Italy. Primarily a midfield player, he won a European Cup Winners' Cup medal, an FA Cup winners' medal, a League Cup winners' medal and a League Championship medal in his 146 games for the Reds. He joined West Bromwich Albion in the summer of 1994 but later returned to Norwich as reserve team coach before joining Gary Megson at Blackpool.

- September -

25

1911 The Reds beat Swindon Town 8-4 in the FA Charity Shield at Stamford Bridge with Harold Halse scoring six of United's goals. This is the most goals scored by a United player in one match and was equalled by George Best at Northampton Town in the FA Cup in February 1970.

1957 United produced their best away win in Europe, beating Shamrock Rovers 6-0 in the European Cup. The goalscorers were Taylor 2, Whealan 2, Pegg and Berry.

1963 Manchester United played their first game in the European Cup Winners Cup competition, drawing 1-1 against German side Willem II with David Herd netting the Reds' goal before later being sent-off!

1968 Nobby Stiles was sent off 11 minutes from the end of the World Club Championship match against Estudiantes which United lost 1-0. Though regarded as a controversial character, it was only the second time he had been sent off in his career. The dismissal came when he angrily flung his arm in the air at the decision of the linesman flagging him offside. The game netted total receipts of £87,500, a record for a soccer match in Argentina.

1994 Old Trafford was taken over by the BBC as they recorded their popular Sunday programme 'Songs of Praise'. Over 40,000 worshippers from all parts of the county flocked to the ground and made it just as colourful a scene as any United matchday.

26

1896 Joe Cassidy hit a hat-trick as Newton Heath beat Newcastle United 4-0.

1903 Eddie Pegg scored all the Reds' goals as they beat Bradford City 3-1 in a Second Division encounter.

1925 Charlie Rennox scored three of United's goals as they overpowered Burnley 6-1 at Old Trafford.

1951 The first visit of a non-European team to Old Trafford. Hapoel of Tel Aviv, Israel were beaten 6-0 in a game which kicked off at 5.25 pm and attracted only 12,000 spectators.

1956 Manchester United recorded their highest total in a single match when they beat Anderlecht 10-0 in a preliminary round of the European Cup with goals from Dennis Viollet 4, Tommy Taylor 3, Liam Whealan 2 and Johnny Berry.

1984 Burnley are beaten 4-0 in the Football League Cup second round first leg at Old Trafford with Welsh international Mark Hughes scoring a hat-trick.

1990 Manchester United played Halifax Town, then bottom of the Fourth Division in the League Cup. The Shaymen had yet to score in the League that season, yet scored in each leg against the Reds. However, they lost 5-2 on aggregate.

1995 A last minute goal by goalkeeper Peter Schmeichel saved United's unbeaten home record in European competition, but unfortunately it was not enough to put the Reds through as Volgograd won on the away goals rule. For the record, Schmeichel also scored in open play when playing in the Danish Third Division.

27

1983 When United drew 2-2 at Dukla Prague in a first round second leg European Cup Winners' Cup tie, it was the only occasion in the club's history that they have won on the away goals rule, after drawing the first leg 1-1 at Old Trafford.

- September -

1995 Peter Schmeichel won a hat-trick of Best European goalkeeper awards. Following his success in 1992 and 1993, the popular Dane missed out in 1994 but won it again this year. In the world rankings, calculated by the International Federation of Football Historians and Statisticians, he finished second to Argentina's Jose Luis Chilavert.

28

1895 Newton Heath beat Crewe Alexandra 2-0. It is the last time the two clubs have met in the League and is the longest gap since any two current League clubs last played each other.

1903 James West who had been at United since 1900 after joining the club from Lincoln, resigned his post as secretary. Though he had put the club on a firm administrative footing, promotion from the Second Division still eluded the club.

1968 Birth of Russell Beardsmore. The Wigan-born player made his debut as a substitute in the 2-0 home win over West Ham United in September 1988. Having looked as if he had secured a place in the first team squad, he lost out with the arrival of new players and the keen competition for places. He had appeared in 75 first team games when at the end of the 1992-93 season, he joined Bournemouth. An England Under-21 international, he has gone on to play in over 150 games for the Dean Court club.

29

1957 Birth of Les Sealey. After starting his League career with Coventry City, he joined Luton Town for £80,000 in the summer of 1983. He had a loan spell with United before Alex Ferguson took him on a free transfer as cover for Jim Leighton. He made his name replacing the Scottish international in United's FA Cup final victory over Crystal Palace in 1990.

He won a European Cup Winners' Cup medal in 1991, but after the arrival of Peter Schmeichel his Old Trafford days were numbered. He had played in 54 first team games in a hectic 16 months before joining Aston Villa. He returned to United in 1992 to appear in a couple of matches but then played for Blackpool and West Ham United before joining Leyton Orient.

1976 With the UEFA Cup first round tie against Ajax poised at a goal apiece on aggregate thanks to Lou Macari's 43 rd minute goal, United manager Tommy Docherty played his part in United's 2-0 victory on the hour. He substituted Gerry Daly with Arthur Albiston and moved Stewart Houston to centre-back and Brian Greenhoff into a roving role in midfield. The gamble paid off with Greenhoff providing the cross from which Sammy McIlroy scored to take United through 2-1 on aggregate.

1992 Welsh international Mark Hughes was sent off in the first round second leg UEFA Cup clash against Russian side Moscow Torpedo. Both games ended goalless before the Reds lost 4-3 on penalties.

1993 Just before United's European Cup tie against Hungarian side Honved, Frank Taylor, the only surviving journalist from the Munich air disaster unveiled a new Press Memorial Plaque in the club's press lounge.

30

1903 United secured the services of Ernest Mangnall the Burnley secretary. Along with the club's first great benefactor, J.H.Davis, he transformed Manchester United into one of the First Division's top teams, winning the Championship for the first time in 1907-08. In 1909 they beat Bristol City 1-0 to win the FA Cup. In 1912, when the United team started to wane, he moved across to join Manchester City. He built a new stadium at Maine Road to compare with the one he had just built at Old Trafford.

- September -

*(Above)
10 September
Joe Spence*

Scored the consolation goal in the embarrassing defeat!

*(Above right)
9 September
Frank Barson*

Made his debut for United

*(Right)
8 September
George Mutch*

Hat-trick in seven minutes.

- *September* -

14 September

(Above left)
Ray Wilkins
&
(Above)
Henry Cockburn

Birth dates.

(Left)
30 September
Ernest Mangnall
One of United's greatest managers,
joined as secretary.

OCTOBER

1 **1936** Birth of Duncan Edwards. Matt Busby was so convinced that he had the makings of an outstanding player that he even travelled to his home in Dudley to secure his signature. Once at Old Trafford he soon impressed, making an immediate impact in the newly launched FA Youth Cup in 1952-53. United won the competition for five successive seasons from its inception with Edwards playing in the first three. He was 16 years 185 days old when he made his first team debut against Cardiff City in April 1953, whilst on the international front, he was the youngest to play for England when given his first cap in April 1955 at the age of 18 years 183 days. He starred in a 7-2 triumph over Scotland. He won 18 full caps and in addition, received four England 'B' caps and hit six goals in one of his six matches at Under-23 level, as he played up front. Over the next few seasons, he went on to win two League Championship medals and an FA Cup losers' medal. 'Big Dunk' was the golden youth who could have well become the greatest soccer immortal of them all had his football not been denied to all supporters before he had barely started living. After 15 days of fighting valiantly for his life following the Munich air crash, this soccer prodigy died. Today, he is remembered in his home town, by a stained glass window at St Francis' Church.

1960 The great Real Madrid side, winners of the European Cup for four successive seasons since its inception in 1956, arrived at Old Trafford to unleash a devastating defeat on United by 6-1 to emphasise their position as the greatest club side in Europe. The following month, United only lost 6-5 to the Spanish giants after a dazzling exhibition of attacking play by both teams.

1980 United drew 0-0 at Widzew Lodz in the UEFA Cup first round second leg but after only drawing the first leg at Old Trafford 1-1, went out on the away goals rule.

1995 Eric Cantona made a sensational comeback for Manchester United after his eight-month suspension, taking just sixty seconds to lay on the club's opening goal for Nicky Butt in the match against Liverpool at Old Trafford. The Anfield side then take a 2-1 lead before Cantona put Giggs through to win a 71st minute penalty which the Frenchman converted for the equaliser.

2 **1944** Birth of Willie Morgan. The Scottish international winger began his League career with Burnley but after deciding he needed to leave Turf Moor to benefit his career, he asked for a transfer. The club refused his request and so his own game began to deteriorate. At one stage, Burnley refused to let him play in any of their sides and banned him from the training ground. However, in August 1968, United paid £117,000 to take him to Old Trafford. Although he scored a hat-trick in an 8-1 win over Queen's Park Rangers, he wasn't renowned for his goalscoring ability. He nevertheless created many for Best, Charlton, Law, Macari and Pearson. He left United in the summer of 1975 to rejoin Burnley but a short time later signed for Bolton Wanderers. During his time at Burnden Park, the Trotters became one of the classiest sides in the Second Division and won the title in 1977-78. In 1978, former United manager Tommy Docherty instigated court proceedings against him and Granada Television but the action collapsed when Docherty admitted lying in court. Willie later ended his League career with Blackpool before playing in the NASL with Minnesota Kicks.

October

1957 Shamrock Rovers became United's first-ever Old Trafford European victims when they are beaten 3-2 in the European Cup with goals by Viollet 2 and Pegg.

1968 Denis Law scored four of United's goals as they beat Waterford 7-1 in the European Cup first round second leg tie at Old Trafford. Stiles, Burns and Charlton were the others scorers, as the Reds won 10-2 on aggregate.

3

1942 John Smith hit a hat-trick in United's 5-2 win over Blackburn Rovers in a Football League North (First Championship) wartime game.

1981 When Bryan Robson moved from West Bromwich Albion to Manchester United, the fee of £1.5 million paid for him set a British club record. He was too late to play in United's 5-0 win over Wolves in which Sammy McIlroy scored a hat-trick but was paraded before an Old Trafford crowd of 46,837. He eventually made his League debut for United in the derby game at Maine Road seven days later. He gave a commanding performance in a goalless draw.

4

1890 Newton Heath were drawn away to Higher Walton in the First Qualifying Round of the FA Cup, but the opposition agreed to play at North Road in order to collect greater receipts. The Heathens won 2-0 with goals from Farman and Evans.

1958 United were guinea pigs in an experiment for playing League football on a Saturday night. They met Wolverhampton Wanderers at Molineux without Harry Gregg, Bobby Charlton and Wilf McGuinness, who were on international duty in the Northern Ireland v England game in Belfast. The weakened United side lost 4-0.

1993 Former Manchester United and Scotland defender Jim Holton aged just 42, died at the wheel of his car, apparently from a heart attack.

5

1934 Birth of Ron Cope. The Crewe-born centre-half made his first team debut for United in a 2-1 win at Arsenal in September 1958, five years after he had turned professional. He came into his own following the Munich air crash and appeared in United's FA Cup Final side of 1958 that lost to Bolton Wanderers. He appeared in 106 League and Cup games for the Reds before joining Luton Town.

1940 Birth of Dave Gaskell. Capped at England schoolboy and youth level, goalkeeper Dave Gaskell spent his early years at Old Trafford as understudy to Harry Gregg. Though never an automatic choice, his occasional appearances added up and by the time he left the club to join Wrexham, he had played in 118 games for United. He came in for Ray Wood in the 1956 FA Charity Shield win over Manchester City and kept goal in the 1963 FA Cup Final when United beat Leicester City 3-1.

1977 The Reds were forced to play their European Cup Winners' Cup first round second leg tie against St Etienne at Plymouth Argyle's Home Park ground, as a punishment for bad behaviour by their fans during the first leg. It was a reprieve as UEFA had initially expelled the club from the competition. United won the match 2-0 (3-1 on aggregate). Stuart Pearson scored the first goal after 33 minutes following a brilliant cross from Steve Coppell and it was the United winger who added a second for United on the hour when he turned inside two men and netted with a cross shot.

1985 United drew 1-1 at Luton Town after winning their first ten League games from 17 August to 28 September. They therefore fell one short of Tottenham Hotspur's record of 11 successive opening League wins in 1960-61.

-October-

6

1923 Sam Wynne of Oldham Athletic scored two goals for his side and two own goals for Manchester United in his side's 3-2 win at Boundary Park. This has happened only twice in Football League history.

1928 James Hanson and Joe Spence scored two goals apiece as United beat Burnley 4-3 at Turf Moor.

1948 United lost 4-3 to Arsenal at Highbury in the FA Charity Shield.

1956 Bobby Charlton made his United debut at Old Trafford against his namesake team, Charlton Athletic. He scored twice in United's 4-2 win and in the return game hit a hat-trick.

1965 The Reds beat HJK Helsinki 6-0 in the European Cup preliminary round second leg match with John Connelly scoring a hat-trick.

1973 After scoring from the penalty spot in a pre-season friendly shoot out against Uruguayan side Penarol and two in the League against Leicester City and Birmingham City, goalkeeper Alex Stepney missed one in United's 2-1 defeat at home to Wolverhampton Wanderers. However, he remained the club's joint top scorer until 29 December!

1991 Mark Hughes was sent off in the goalless draw against Liverpool at Old Trafford.

7

1920 Birth of Jack Rowley. One of the most prolific goalscorers in United's history, he joined the club from Third Division Bournemouth for £3,000 towards the end of 1937. Needing time to settle into his new surroundings he asked to play in the reserves. A few weeks later, he returned to first team action and scored four goals as United beat Swansea 5-1, During wartime, he 'guested' for Spurs, Wolves and Distillery. He played for Spurs one week and scored seven goals and then a few days later, scored all eight goals in a victory for Wolves over Derby County. The England international dominated United's scoring in the early post-war years, especially on the big occasions - he hit two in the 1948 FA Cup Final victory over Blackpool. He started the 1951-52 season in fine style, scoring a hat-trick in each of the first two games. He scored goals right to the end of his career with United - 208 in 422 League and Cup games. In that 1951-52 season he scored 30 in 40 Championship-winning fixtures - a United record until it was broken by Dennis Viollet in 1959-60. After 18 years with the club, he was given a free transfer and joined Plymouth Argyle as player-manager. He later held similar posts with Oldham Athletic, Ajax of Amsterdam, Wrexham and Bradford Park Avenue.

1926 United manager John Chapman was suspended from football for 'improper conduct' in his position as secretary-manager of Manchester United Football Club. Nothing further was added and no explanation was given.

1950 Billy Redman made his debut for United in the 3-1 win over Sheffield Wednesday, four years after being picked for the first team at the age of 18, when the game was postponed.

1967 Scottish internationals Denis Law and Ian Ure were sent off in a fiery First Division clash between United and Arsenal at Old Trafford. A John Aston goal gave United the points in front of 60,197 fans.

1986 The Reds beat Port Vale 5-2 in the Football League Cup second round second leg at Vale Park to win 7-2 on aggregate. Former West Bromwich Albion midfielder Remi Moses scored two of United's goals.

October

1995 A crowd of 21,502 watched the reserve game against Leeds United at Old Trafford because Eric Cantona was playing only his second game after his eight-month suspension from the game.

8

1927 United lost 5-2 at Goodison Park with Everton centre-forward Dixie Dean scoring all his club's five goals.

1994 Club officials decided to ban a huge 130' x 60' red, black and white flag from the ground. They said the flag, owned by United fan Mike Edroff, was a breach of safety regulations and that they were afraid of it being ignited. However, they did say that if its owner could provide a safety certificate they would allow it back in the ground!

9

1915 United lose 7-3 at home to Burnley in a Lancashire Section (Principal Tournament) wartime game.

1920 Ted Partridge made his debut for United in a 4-1 win over Oldham Athletic at Old Trafford. The talented left-winger joined United from Welsh club Ebbw Vale and over the next nine seasons created many a goal for his fellow forwards. He held down a first team place for three seasons before making way for new signing Frank McPherson. He returned to the side on a regular basis in 1927-28 but the following season, after scoring 18 goals in his 160 appearances, he joined Halifax Town.

1926 Clarrie Hilditch was appointed as temporary player-manager of Manchester United. To date, the Northwich-born half-back remains the only player-manager in the club's history. He made 322 appearances for the Reds and played for England against Wales in a 1919 Victory International match and against South Africa in the 1920 Commonwealth internationals.

1943 An Alf Bellis hat-trick gave United a 3-1 Football League North (First Championship) victory over Chester.

1954 Tommy Taylor scored four of United's goals in their 5-2 win over Cardiff City at Old Trafford. Dennis Viollet was the Reds' other scorer.

1974 A Gerry Daly goal gave United a 1-0 Football League Cup third round win over rivals Manchester City.

10

1903 Harry Moger made his debut for United, keeping a clean sheet as the Reds beat Barnsley 4-0. He came to United from Southern League Southampton and was the club's first choice goalkeeper over the next nine seasons. During that time, he won two League Championship medals and starred in the FA Cup Final victory over Bristol City. Yet despite winning these major honours with United, he was never recognised by England at international level and after appearing in 264 games he retired.

1935 Birth of Albert Scanlon. The nephew of Charlie Mitten, he starred in the 1953 and 1954 Youth Cup winning sides and in November 1954 made his League debut against Arsenal. However his appearances were limited over the next few seasons and it was only six weeks before the Munich air disaster that he established himself in the first team. He survived the Munich crash but the injuries he suffered meant that he missed the remainder of the season. He returned for the 1958-59 season and scored 16 goals, including a hat-trick in a 4-1 win over West Ham United. In 1960 he joined Newcastle United before later playing for Lincoln City and Mansfield Town.

1987 Bryan Robson scored for both United and Sheffield Wednesday in the Reds 4-2 win at Hillsborough.

- October -

11 **1919** John Greenwood made his debut for United in the derby match at Maine Road which ended all-square at 3-3. He had joined United during the First World War from South Shields and by the end of his first season at Old Trafford had become a first team regular at half-back. He gave the Reds great service over the next eight seasons, appearing in 205 League and Cup games and helping the club win promotion to the First Division in 1924-25. He later joined Aldershot, who were then a non-League club, before ending his career with Blackpool.

1937 Birth of Bobby Charlton. Nephew of the legendary centre-forward Jackie Milburn, he was a member of the sides which won the FA Youth Cup in 1954-55 and 1955-56. He made his debut for United on 6 October 1956 and though he scored twice in a 4-2 victory over Charlton Athletic, manager Matt Busby felt that the young striker needed time to mature! It wasn't too long before he won a regular place in the United line-up. He had scored two goals in United's 3-3 draw at Red Star Belgrade and when the plane carrying the Manchester United team crashed in thick snow at Munich Airport, Charlton was thrown 50 yards and escaped with just a deep cut on his head. Within two months, he made his international debut against Scotland, marking the occasion with a spectacular goal. In 1966 he helped England win the World Cup and won both the Footballer of the Year and European player awards. In 1967 he won his third League Championship medal and in 1968 scored two goals in the emotionally charged European Cup Final against Benfica. After 106 caps and 49 goals, his international career ended in the 1970 World Cup in Mexico. In 1973 he pulled on a United jersey for the last time. He had set appearance records for both club and country and had become a footballing legend. He later had spells managing Preston and Wigan and established the famous Bobby Charlton soccer schools for children. Manchester United honoured him with a place on the board. He had helped them to become one of the most famous clubs in the world and was one of the most popular and talented footballers of all time.

12 **1895** The Reds lost 7-1 at Liverpool in a Second Division game in front of just 7,000 spectators.

1907 George Stacey made his debut for Manchester United in the Reds' tremendous 6-1 win against Newcastle United at St James' Park. He had joined United from Barnsley for £400. Originally a coalminer, he soon established himself at right-back before later switching to left-back. He was in the United side that won the FA Cup in 1909 and received League Championship medals in 1907-08 and 1910-11. He played in an England trial match in 1912 but never won a full cap. One of the club's unsung heroes, he played in 267 League and Cup games for United before returning to work down the pits at the outbreak of war.

1988 A Brian McClair hat-trick helped United to beat Rotherham United 5-0 in a Football League Cup second round second leg tie to give them a 6-0 aggregate win.

1996 Injury-hit United beat Liverpool 1-0 thanks to a superb right-footed strike from David Beckham in the 22nd minute. If Liverpool had won the game, which kicked off at 11.15am, they would have been seven points clear at the top of the Premiership. Instead, the Anfield side's lead was cut to just one point.

13 **1951** Manchester United earned many high praises after their 5-2 win at Aston Villa. United's attack in the second-half transformation erased all the weak points noted in recent matches and made goalscoring a mere formality. Jack Rowley and Stan Pearson scored two goals apiece for the Reds with Bond adding the fifth.

-October-

1984 United, with Remi Moses in outstanding form, completely demolished West Ham United 5-1. The pulsating performance brought great relief for Alan Brazil as he scored his first League goal for the Reds. Gordon McQueen had opened the scoring for United to mark his return after a 10 month absence, whilst Strachan, Hughes and deservedly Moses got United's other goals.

14 **1980** Manchester United's ground hosted the 'B' international match against the United States with the home side winning 1-0.

1995 A 4th minute Paul Scholes goal gave the Reds a 1-0 win over Manchester City. With no City fans present, there was an unusual one-sided atmosphere for a derby match!

15 **1892** Newton Heath beat Wolverhampton Wanderers 10-1 for their record win in the Football League with Bob Donaldson scoring the club's first League hat-trick.

1955 United and Aston Villa drew 4-4 in an exciting match at Villa Park. David Pegg scored two of the Reds' goals with Blanchflower and Webster the other scorers.

1960 Despite a Dennis Viollet hat-trick, United lost 5-3 at Turf Moor against League Champions, Burnley.

1963 United beat Willem II Tilburg 6-1 in a first round second leg European Cup Winners' Cup tie at Old Trafford with Denis Law grabbing a hat-trick.

1971 Birth of Andy Cole. He made his League debut for Arsenal in December 1990, coming on as a substitute in the match against Sheffield United.

He made no further appearances for the Gunners but gained League experience in two extended loan spells at Fulham and Bristol City. He proved to be a sensation at Ashton Gate with eight goals in 12 games and in March 1992 they signed him on a permanent basis for £500,000. Within eight months, he had joined Newcastle United for £1.75 million, and promptly picked up a First Division championship medal. In 1993-94 he became the first player to score 40 League goals in a season for Newcastle. He ended the season as the country's leading goalscorer and was voted the PFA's Young Player of the Year. He joined United in January 1995 in exchange for Keith Gillespie and £6 million. He then became the first United player to score five goals in a League game as the Reds beat Ipswich 9-0, and in March 1995 won his first England cap against Uruguay. However, having not scored as many goals for United as expected, he had to convince many people that he was worth the money paid for him.

16 **1954** A crowd of 55,966 saw United beat Chelsea 6-5 at Stamford Bridge with Dennis Viollet scoring a hat-trick and Tommy Taylor two of their goals. United's sixth goal was scored by Jackie Blanchflower.

1965 The first Manchester United substitute to be brought on to the field of play was John Fitzpatrick who replaced Denis Law in United's 5-1 defeat against Tottenham Hotspur at White Hart Lane.

1968 United played Estudiantes of Argentina in the second leg of the World Club Championship at Old Trafford. Although the fixture between the European Champions and the South American Champions had an unhappy history of violence, United were not prepared for the general hostility that met them in Buenos Aires. United lost the first-leg 1-0 and then drew 1-1 at home with Willie Morgan scoring United's goal.

October

1991 Ryan Giggs became the youngest man ever to play for Wales when at the age of 17 years and 321 days he came on as substitute against West Germany.

17

1930 There was a meeting of 3,000 supporters at the Hulme Town Hall under the chairmanship of S.Mason. Dissatisfaction and even revolution was in the air as United suffered a run of deplorable defeats of ten games without a single point and were bottom of the division! It was decided by a large majority to boycott United's game with Arsenal at Old Trafford the following day. A crowd of around 50,000 was expected but in the event 23,406 made the effort, although that was the highest gate of the season. Heavy rain also discouraged some from making the trip and it was never known how many actually boycotted the game. United lost 2-1 and then lost 4-1 at Portsmouth the week after. They had by now lost all 12 of their opening fixtures.

1948 Birth of Francis Burns. Born in Glenboig, Lanarkshire, he joined United as a 15-year-old in 1964. Three years later, he made his debut at left-back against West Ham United. He held the position for most of that season, playing in all the club's European Cup matches until injury ruled him out of the semi-final second leg match against Real Madrid. Over the next five seasons he was hampered by injuries, otherwise he would have made many more than the 155 appearances he did make. Ironically after he left Old Trafford to join Southampton for £60,000 in the summer of 1972, his injury problems seemed to clear up. He was capped at every level by Scotland but only won one cap at full level, against Austria in 1970. After a year at The Dell, he joined former team-mate Bobby Charlton at Preston before ending his playing career with League of Ireland club, Shamrock Rovers.

1956 United's 3-2 win over Borussia Dortmund in the European Cup first round first leg tie was played in front of 75,598 at Maine Road - the club's best home European crowd.

18

1913 A George Anderson hat-trick gave United a 3-0 home win over Preston North End in a First Division game.

1941 Jack Rowley scored four of United's goals in their 8-1 win over Chester in the Football League Northern Section (First Championship).

1952 United made nine changes, five positional and four new faces, following their 2-0 defeat against Stoke. They beat Preston North End 5-0 at Deepdale with Johnny Aston and Stan Pearson scoring two goals apiece and Jack Rowley the other.

19

1907 A hat-trick from Sandy Turnbull and two goals from James Turnbull gave United a 5-1 win against Blackburn Rovers at Ewood Park.

1960 Manchester United played their first match in the newly formed Football League Cup but could only manage a 1-1 draw with Exeter City at St James' Park. Exeter, fifth from bottom of the Fourth Division played like heroes. It wasn't until 12 minutes from time that Alex Dawson snatched the equaliser. However, United could claim justifiably to have won a penalty when Dawson was pulled down by the Exeter 'keeper when he only had to tap the ball over the line!

1977 The Reds lost 4-0 at FC Porto in the European Cup Winners' Cup second round first-leg tie.

October

1994 United drew 2-2 with Barcelona in the UEFA Champions League. The match was beamed to no fewer than 107 countries, and it was estimated that around 80 million people worldwide tuned in. The game certainly lived up to its billing as Old Trafford's match of the season. Alex Ferguson dropped something of a bombshell by leaving out skipper Steve Bruce. Barcelona came to Manchester on the back of four successive Spanish Championships but Kanchelskis and Sharpe put on a magnificent display of wing football to take the Spaniards apart. Hughes opened the scoring after 18 minutes with a downward header but Barcelona's Brazilian ace Romario equalised before the break. Parker's lack of height was exposed four minutes into the second-half when Bakero took a long ball from Koeman to fire past Schmeichel. United lifted their pace and deserved their equaliser with just ten minutes to go. Lee Sharpe under a lot of pressure from goalkeeper Busquets and a defender, scored with a brilliant back heel flick to crown a magnificent night of football.

20

1956 United lost 5-2 to Everton at Old Trafford where they had been unbeaten for eighteen months; the men from Goodison Park were the last team to beat them at home in March 1955.

1973 Though not fully match fit, George Best reappeared in United's colours for the game at home to Birmingham City and displayed great skill in United's 1-0 win. The Reds' goal was scored by goalkeeper Alex Stepney from the penalty spot - his second such goal of the season!

1976 A Gordon Hill goal gave the Reds a 1-0 UEFA Cup second round first leg win over Juventus in front of a 59,000 crowd.

1990 Manchester United and Arsenal were both fined £50,000 by the FA following a brawl involving both sets of players during a League game at Old Trafford. The two teams also had points deducted for their part in the incident; Arsenal two and United one. It was the first time the Football Association had deducted points for 'on the field' activities. For the record, United lost 1-0.

1993 Manchester United were two goals up in 13 minutes against Galatasaray in the European Cup but then conceded three goals and needed a late Cantona strike to salvage a 3-3 draw against the Turkish champions. It ended a sequence of 17 successive home wins in the competition stretching back to September 1957.

21

1967 Birth of Paul Ince. The Ilford-born midfielder began his League career with West Ham United and after making 91 League and Cup appearances for the Hammers joined United for £1 million in August 1989. It appeared that his much publicised transfer to the Reds was about to fall through because he failed his medical. A fortnight later however and an independent medical panel reported that his pelvic problem was not so serious, and the fee reduced. He won his first full England cap whilst with United, maturing into a strong-running midfield player. He won a European Cup Winners' Cup medal and a League Cup winners' medal before winning a League Championship medal in 1992-93. He played in 275 first team games for the reds before leaving to join Inter Milan in the summer of 1995.

1989 Rugby League history was made at Old Trafford when Paul Newlove became the youngest Great Britain international at the age of 18 years and 72 days in the match against New Zealand which the Kiwis won 24-16.

- *October* -

22 **1927** A Joe Spence hat-trick helped the Reds beat Derby County 5-0. The Reds' other scorers were Johnston and McPherson.

1932 Tom Reid hit a hat-trick in United's 7-1 win over Millwall with Brown 2, Gallimore and Spence the Reds' other goalscorers.

1957 Manchester United beat Aston Villa 4-0 at Old Trafford in the FA Charity Shield in front of a crowd of 27,923. with a hat-trick from Tommy Taylor and a fourth goal from Johnny Berry. Peter McParland, Villa's Northern Ireland international winger thought the United fans were wonderful. He expected a 'roasting' for his part in the accident to Ray Wood in the FA Cup Final a few months earlier.

23 **1909** Jimmy Turnbull is sent-off during United's game against Sheffield United at Bramall Lane but the Reds still won 1-0 with George Wall netting the goal.

1920 Alf Steward kept a clean sheet on his United debut as the Reds beat Preston North End 1-0 at Old Trafford. Signed from Stalybridge Celtic, he had to wait three years before being handed the goalkeeper's jersey on a permanent basis. It was unfortunate for him that he was the last line of defence in such an indifferent United team. He played in 326 games for the Reds, his last being in 1932. Just before the outbreak of the Second World War he managed Torquay United.

1965 After being dropped for the previous three games, David Herd returned to the United line-up and scored a hat-trick in a 4-1 win over Fulham. Though it took the Reds some time to find the goal trail, they always looked the more creative side. Fulham had a couple of unlucky moments with the ball twice bouncing off the post and into Pat Dunne's hands in the United goal.

1982 Football triumphed in one of the most breathtaking Manchester derby matches in years. The Reds were two goals down just into the second-half and it seemed that they were destined never to score. But two goals from Frank Stapleton in the 53rd and 80th minutes gave United a share of the spoils. Both sides gave the 57,334 fans - Britain's biggest gate of the season - great entertainment.

24 **1891** Newton Heath's FA Cup opponents Heywood scratched from the competition to give the Heathens an outright win. The two teams played a friendly match which Newton Heath won 3-2.

1896 A Joe Cassidy hat-trick gave the Reds a 3-0 win over Burton Wanderers. They ended the season as runners-up to Notts County and won promotion to the First Division.

1956 United's youngest post-war player was goalkeeper Dave Gaskell when he appeared as a substitute for Ray Wood in the FA Charity Shield against Manchester City at the age of 16 years and 19 days. He kept a clean sheet in United's 1-0 win with Dennis Viollet scoring the Reds' goal.

1964 Denis Law scored four of United's goals as they beat Aston Villa 7-0 at Old Trafford.

1994 The Football League decided not to fine Manchester United for fielding weakened teams in their second round Coca Cola ties against Port Vale. They decided to recommend that clubs involved in European competition should be exempt in future until the third round.

25 **1890** Newton Heath fielded their reserve side in the FA Cup second qualifying round against Bootle, and lost 1-0.

- October -

1932 Birth of Harry Gregg. He began his footballing career with Dundalk and was a part-timer with Coleraine and Linfield, before he was snapped up by Doncaster Rovers in the summer of 1951. Matt Busby signed him for United in December 1957 for what was then a record for a goalkeeper - £23,000. The plane that was carrying home the victorious United team from their match against Red Star Belgrade crashed on the runway at Munich Airport, killing many of the players. Harry Gregg crawled virtually unscathed from the wreckage. Three weeks later, he kept goal in the 3-0 FA Cup win over Sheffield Wednesday. In the 1958 FA Cup Final, he was bundled over the line by Nat Lofthouse for Bolton's second goal in a 2-0 win over United. Also that year, Northern Ireland, for whom Gregg won 25 caps, reached the quarter- finals of the World Cup and he was acclaimed by the viewing public as the best 'keeper in those finals. He played in 247 League and Cup games for the Reds before joining Stoke City in 1966. He later managed Shrewsbury, Swansea and Crewe before becoming Lou Macari's assistant at Swindon Town. However, in April 1985, he departed after the two former United stars ended up not speaking to each other!

1937 Birth of Wilf McGuinness. United player and manager, he was one of the stars of the club's highly successful Youth team of the 1950s, appearing in three FA Youth Cup winning elevens and captaining England Youth. He had played in 83 first team games for United, when he broke his leg in a Central League fixture and was forced to retire at the age of 22. United gave him a coaching job and the FA later appointed him as trainer of England's Youth team. He was also used by Alf Ramsey as a training assistant in the 1966 World Cup. Then in April 1969 he was sensationally chosen to replace Matt Busby as United's manager. He lost the position in December 1970, reverting back to trainer-coach of the reserve team. He later had brief spells managing in Greece and with York City before becoming Bury's trainer.

1986 Old Trafford staged the Whitbread Trophy Bitter first Rugby League Test between Great Britain and Australia.

26

1901 Jimmy Coupar scored a hat-trick in the Reds' 6-0 win over Doncaster Rovers. The club's other scorers were Griffiths and Preston with a Doncaster defender putting through his own goal to complete the rout.

1952 Birth of Arthur Graham. An exciting winger, he turned professional with Aberdeen in 1970. A great favourite at Pittodrie, he won a Scottish League Cup winners' medal in 1977 and scored 40 goals in over 300 appearances for the Dons. In the summer of 1977 he moved to Leeds United for £125,000 and in six seasons at Elland Road scored 47 goals in 280 matches. He arrived at Old Trafford just prior to the start of the 1983-84 season and in that campaign made exactly 50 appearances, scoring seven goals. Capped ten times by Scotland, he made just one appearance the following season before moving to Bradford City, where he ended his League career.

1960 In the first Football League cup tie to take place at Old Trafford, Albert Quixall scored two of United's goals in a 4-1 first round replay win over Fourth Division Exeter City.

27

1928 Henry Rowley made his debut for Manchester United in the 2-1 win at Huddersfield Town. Signed from non-League Shrewsbury Town, his career was somewhat unusual in that he enjoyed two separate spells with United. He was joint top scorer in 1929-30 but the following season, the goals didn't seem to come so easily and after just one game in the Second Division he returned to the top flight with Manchester City. He found life at Maine Road difficult and two years later, after playing in 18 games, joined Oldham Athletic.

116

-October-

He rejoined United in 1935-36 and he enjoyed his best spell with the club, scoring 19 goals as the Reds clinched the Second Division championship. But the following season, as United were again relegated, saw him struggle and at the end of the campaign, he retired.

1945 Matt Busby's first match as manager saw the Reds beat Bolton Wanderers 2-1 in a Football League North match.

1964 United beat Djurgardens IF 6-1 in a first round second leg Inter Cities Fairs Cup tie at Old Trafford with Denis Law scoring a hat-trick. Bobby Charlton 2, and George Best were the other United scorers.

1976 United produced their biggest League Cup win in beating Newcastle United 7-2 at Old Trafford in front of a 52,002 crowd. Gordon Hill, who cost United £70,000 when signed from Millwall, scored a hat-trick.

1990 United and City drew 3-3 in the Manchester derby at Maine Road. Brian McClair scored two of United's goals with Mark Hughes netting the other.

28 **1978** The Greenhoff brothers both got on the scoresheet as United beat Wolverhampton Wanderers 4-2 at Molineux.

1995 Republic of Ireland international Roy Keane was sent-off in the Premier League match against Middlesbrough. It was his third dismissal in six months. United still won 2-0 with goals from Pallister and Cole.

29 **1921** Joe Spence scored a hat-trick for Manchester United as the Reds defeated Manchester City 3-1 in the derby match at Old Trafford. Joining United at the end of the First World War, he went on to create a club record of 481 League appearances which was only beaten by Bill Foulkes some 40 years later. The scorer of some memorable goals, he was the club's top or joint-top scorer for seven of his 14 seasons at Old Trafford. His best season was 1927-28 when he netted 24 goals in 43 League and Cup appearances. On 12 April 1924 he scored four in a 5-1 win over Crystal Palace. In that 1927-28 season he scored hat-tricks against Derby County and Liverpool and two seasons later again scored four goals as the Reds beat West Ham United 4-2. All told he scored 168 goals in 510 League and Cup games before signing for Bradford City in 1933. Two years later, he joined Chesterfield, continuing to work for the Saltergate club after his playing days were over.

1932 Tommy Frame, United's centre-half was sent-off in the Second Division game at Port Vale which ended all-square at 3-3. Bill Ridding who also played for Manchester City before managing Bolton Wanderers, scored two of the goals.

1986 The first match to be played under the club's new floodlighting system was a Littlewoods Cup-tie against Southampton which ended goalless.

1994 United beat Newcastle United 2-0 at Old Trafford. At one point during the game, the Reds played with full internationals from eight countries. They were Schmeichel (Denmark) Irwin (Republic of Ireland) Pallister (England) Gillespie (Northern Ireland) Cantona (France) Hughes (Wales) McClair (Scotland) and Kanchelskis (Russia).

30 **1886** Newton Heath played their first game in the FA Cup, drawing 2-2 at Fleetwood Rangers with Jim Doughty scoring both their goals. But the referee, Mr Norris awarded the tie to Fleetwood because Newton Heath refused to play extra-time.

October

1948 United won 6-1 at Deepdale against Preston North End with Charlie Mitten and Stan Pearson scoring two goals apiece. United's other scorers are Johnny Morris and Jack Rowley.

1957 Former Nottingham Forest manager Brian Clough became the second player to score five goals in a Representative game when playing for an FA XI against the Army.

31

1965 Birth of Denis Irwin. He began his footballing days with Leeds United before joining Oldham Athletic on a free transfer in the summer of 1986. It was at Boundary Park that his career began to take off, as he became a vital member of the best team the Latics ever had.

He appeared for Oldham in the League Cup Final of 1990 against Nottingham Forest and the same season impressed United in the club's two epic duels with the Boundary Park club in the semi-finals of the FA Cup. By the end of that summer, he had signed for United for £625,000 and appeared in the club's League Cup Finals of 1991 and 1992. He made his first full appearance for the Republic of Ireland against Morocco in 1990 and became first choice for his country. Able to play in both full-back positions, he is still recognised as a specialist at both free-kicks and corners and has scored a number of memorable goals during his stay at Old Trafford.

*(Left) 3 October: Sammy McIlroy scores a hat-trick.
(Right) 5 October: Ron Cope - Birthday*

-October-

(Left) 1 October - Eric Cantona, makes a sensational comeback
(Right) 14 September - Bryan Robson, big money signing from West Brom.

NOVEMBER

1

1921 John Chapman who had been manager at Aidrieonians for 15 years took up his duties as manager of Manchester United. At the end of his first season the Reds were relegated and it took the club three seasons to get back into the top flight. One of his best signings was Frank Barson, but in 1926, Chapman was suspended from all involvement with football because of alleged improper conduct whilst acting as United's secretary-manager. Though details of the charges were never made public, the club had no option but to dispense with his services.

1959 United's Johnny Giles became the Republic of Ireland's youngest player when he played against Sweden at the age of 18 years and 360 days.

1963 Birth of Mark Hughes. One of the club's all-time favourites, his first major contribution for United was in the FA Youth Cup of 1981-82, when he teamed up with Norman Whiteside to give the Reds a powerful strike force at junior level. He scored in his first match against Leicester City and made an encouraging start, scoring four goals in his seven full appearances in that 1983-84 season. He made his Welsh international debut against England in May 1984, scoring the only goal of the game. He has scored some very spectacular goals but the one he netted for Wales against Spain in 1985 in a World Cup qualifying game will linger long in the memory. In 1984-85 he scored 25 goals in all competitions, the best individual performance at Old Trafford for 13 years. He hit hat-tricks against Aston Villa in the League and Burnley in the League Cup. He collected an FA Cup winners' medal and was voted the PFA Young Player of the Year. In the summer of 1986 he was sold to Barcelona for £2.5 million but he couldn't settle and in his second season, he was sent out on loan to Bayern Munich, where he was much happier. In July 1988, he returned to Old Trafford for £1.5 million and soon began to repay some of the fee. Voted PFA Player of the Year in 1989 and 1991, 'Sparky' went on to appear in 472 first team games for the Reds in his two spells, scoring 162 goals, before surprisingly being allowed to join Chelsea for £1.5 million in the summer of 1995.

1993 Manchester United got a hostile greeting from Galatasaray fans when they arrived in Turkey. 'Welcome to Hell' was the message on banners at Istanbul Airport. Two days later a lack-lustre performance allowed Galatasaray to draw 0-0 and so go through to the lucrative League stage of the European Cup. To compound the Reds' misery, Eric Cantona was sent-off after the final whistle and he and Bryan Robson were struck by police in the players' tunnel.

2

1895 James Peters hit a hat-trick as the Reds beat Liverpool 5-2 in a Division Two game.

1960 Dennis Viollet scored United's goal in a 2-1 defeat at Bradford City in the second round of the Football League Cup. The crowd of just 4,670 is the lowest post-war attendance to watch United in a competitive game.

1974 Stuart Pearson scored a hat-trick and Lou Macari another as United went 4-0 up by half-time against Oxford United at Old Trafford. They relaxed in the second-half after a 45 minute display that produced bold attacking football. They tightened their grip on the Second Division and increased their lead at the top to five points.

- *November* -

1977 Murca of the Portuguese side Porto scored two own goals for Manchester United in the European Cup Winners' Cup second leg at Old Trafford. They helped the Reds win 5-2 but as they had lost the first leg 4-0 in Portugal, they went out 6-5 on aggregate.

1983 Frank Stapleton hit both United goals as the Reds beat Spartak Varna 2-0 in the European Cup Winners' Cup second round second leg tie at Old Trafford to give the club a 4-1 aggregate win.

3

1894 Manchester's first Football League derby was played at Ardwick, the home of Manchester City. Though the two clubs had met in the Manchester Cup, Football Alliance and FA Cup, this first League meeting was a memorable one for the Heathens as they ran out winners 5-2 with Dick Smith scoring four of the goals. Newton Heath also won the return fixture 4-1.

1934 William Bryant made his debut for United in the 2-1 win at Blackpool, scoring the Reds opening goal. Given his first taste of League football with Wolves, he later joined Wrexham before signing for United in October 1934. A goalscoring outside-right, he scored 44 goals in 160 League and Cup appearances, remaining with United throughout the war years. When the hostilities ceased, he joined Bradford City for a brief spell before leaving the game.

1945 United beat Preston North End 6-1 in the Football League North competition with Rowley and Smith both scoring two goals and Warner and Worrall one apiece.

1962 Denis Law scored four times for Manchester United in their 5-3 win over Ipswich Town at Old Trafford and four times for Scotland against Norway four days later.

1973 Chelsea were winning 2-0 at Old Trafford with just five minutes remaining but goals by Brian Grenhoff and Tony Young made the final score 2-2.

1976 Veteran goalkeeper Alex Stepney salvaged the pride of Manchester United in their UEFA Cup defeat against Juventus in Turin. The Reds' 'keeper kept the score respectable with a series of fine saves in a 3-0 defeat. United's only chance in a one-sided game came after 11 minutes when Gordon Hill headed wide from Steve Coppell's cross.

4

1981 A Manchester United XI beat Sydney Olympic 2-1 in a friendly match. The club officials decided that there should be free admission and a crowd of just over 3,000 turned up for the 2.00 pm kick-off much to the disgust of schoolteachers and employers!

1986 Manchester United played their last game under Ron Atkinson in an FA Cup replay against Southampton at the Dell. An injury hit United went down 4-1 with Peter Davenport netting the Reds' consolation goal.

5

1892 Newton Heath and Blackburn Rovers shared eight goals in an exciting match at the North Road ground, Monsall, with Alf Farman netting two of the Heathen's goals.

1938 John Warner made his debut for Manchester United in the Reds 2-0 win at Aston Villa. Signed from Swansea Town, his career spanned the immediate periods before and after the Second World War. He appeared in 118 games for the club, but like a number of other players if the war hadn't brought an end to League football, he may well have become one of United's greatest players.

- November -

Though he was 35 when football resumed after the hostilities he was still able to hold down a first team place. In the summer of 1951, he moved to Oldham Athletic before later joining Rochdale, playing his last game for the Spotland club at the age of 42.

1949 'Sonny' Feehan made his debut in goal for United for the injured Jack Crompton whilst in complete contrast, Huddersfield Town recalled their long-service 'keeper Bob Hesford. Torrential rain early in the day made the ground very heavy, a factor suited to United's style. Jack Rowley opened the scoring after seven minutes and added another in the second-half in United's 6-0 win. The Reds' other scorers were Pearson 2, Delaney and Mitten.

1958 Local Rugby League club, Salford hired the Old Trafford ground to try playing a match under floodlights. A crowd of over 8,000 turned up to see their opponents Leeds win 22-17.

6

1965 Harry Gregg became the first United goalkeeper to be sent-off in a first team match, when he was dismissed during the Reds 2-2 draw at home to Blackburn Rovers.

1971 Outplayed for three-quarters of the derby game with Manchester City, United emerged from the Maine Road encounter with a point in a 3-3 draw. Sammy McIlroy scored for the Reds on his debut and Brian Kidd and John Aston were the other scorers. Colin Bell and Francis Lee, with a penalty, scored for City before Mike Summerbee equalised in the last minute.

1986 The contracts of manager Ron Atkinson and his coach Mick Brown were terminated by United chairman Martin Edwards. Atkinson had brought some success to the club and had sold two players, Hughes and Wilkins for record amounts, yet there were those who questioned his judgement on the buying side.

Though he signed Robson, Moses, Strachan, Olsen, Gidman, Muhren and Gibson, he allowed Peter Beardsley to slip through the club and missed the opportunity of signing Gary Lineker before the England striker moved from Leicester City to Everton.

7

1981 United went top of the First Division with a superb 5-1 win against Sunderland at Roker Park. Kevin Moran headed the Reds into the lead only for the home side to equalise just before half-time. In the second-half, Bryan Robson scored his first goal since his transfer from West Bromwich Albion and Frank Stapleton headed a couple of goals, before Gary Birtles got on the scoresheet with just two minutes to play.

1984 A Gordon Strachan goal in the UEFA Cup second round second leg tie at Old Trafford gave United a 1-0 aggregate win over Dutch side PSV Eindhoven.

1993 In the first derby game played on a Sunday, Manchester United restored their 11 point lead at the top of the Premier League with a stirring 3-2 win at Maine Road after Manchester City had taken a 2-0 half-time lead through Niall Quinn. Eric Cantona, atoning for his lapse in Turkey, scored two goals with Roy Keane hitting an 87th minute winner.

8

1924 Tom Jones made his United debut in a 1-1 draw at Portsmouth. Joining United from Oswestry Town, he played at either right or left full-back depending on the availability of Charlie Moore or John Silcock. In 1926, he won the first of his four Welsh caps but it wasn't until 1933-34 that he became the club's first choice left-back. He appeared in 200 League and Cup games for the club in 11 seasons before moving into non-League football with Scunthorpe and Lindsay United.

- November -

1930 Jimmy Bullock scored a hat-trick for United but the Reds still went down 5-4 to Leicester City at Filbert Street.

1941 Jack Rowley scored five of United's goals as they beat Tranmere Rovers 6-1 in a Football League Northern Section (First Championship) match.

1993 UEFA contact Manchester United regarding Eric Cantona's reported bribery allegations against the referee of their European tie in Istanbul.

9

1963 Denis Law's third hat-trick of the season helped Manchester United beat Tottenham Hotspur 4-1 in front of an Old Trafford crowd of 57,413. He was the outstanding performer in a United side in which Moore, Herd and Quixall also shone. It was the former Sheffield Wednesday player who scored United's other goal.

1985 United began the 1985-86 season with an undefeated League run of 15 matches (13 won and two drawn), until they travelled to Hillsborough and lost 1-0 to Sheffield Wednesday.

10

1976 Jonathan Clark had the shortest single showing, being one of three players to have made just one substitute appearance. Coming on for Colin Waldron, he played for just 30 minutes in the 3-3 draw with Sunderland at Old Trafford.

1994 Andrei Kanchelskis became the first Manchester United player to score a hat-trick in the Premier League when he hit three goals in the Reds 5-0 win over neighbours Manchester City. The match at Old Trafford was played 100 years to the week after the first ever derby clash. United's other scorers in their biggest ever win over City were Cantona and Hughes. The win also equalled United's biggest ever Premier League win to date. Kanchelskis went on to end the season as United's top scorer with 14 League goals.

11

1964 United travelled to Borussia Dortmund for their second round first leg tie in the Inter-Cities Fairs Cup. The German side made shock changes to their line-up, bringing in tearaway centre-forward Harold Beyer. The Germans however, had no answer to the individual brilliance of Charlton, Best and Law. In one of United's best performances on the continent, the Reds won 6-1 with Bobby Charlton grabbing a hat-trick.

1993 UEFA clear Eric Cantona of making bribery allegations against the referee in Istanbul.

12

1955 Eddie Colman made his United debut in a 3-1 defeat at Bolton Wanderers. A product of United's youth teams, he appeared in three FA Youth Cup winning sides before making his debut. He played in 25 League games that season and picked up a League Championship medal. He won a second Championship medal the following season, scoring his first goal for the club in a 2-2 draw at Tottenham Hotspur. The natural successor to Henry Cockburn, he had played in 107 games for the club, and was just 21 years old, when he was killed in the Munich air disaster.

1975 Manchester United were hung, drawn and quartered in one of the great derby drubbings of all time, as the Reds crashed out of the Football League Cup fourth round at Maine Road. Dennis Tueart shot Manchester City ahead as early as 35 seconds and then Asa Hartford added a second after 14 minutes. A mistake by Martin Buchan in the 29th minute let in Tueart for his second and City's third.

- November -

Joe Royle headed the fourth for City in the 79th minute and though it would be easy to make Paddy Roche the scapegoat after he had replaced Alex Stepney, the whole United side were below par.

1993 UEFA slapped a four-match suspension on Eric Cantona in European club competition and fined Manchester United £2,500 for 'incorrect conduct' (three bookings and Cantona's dismissal) and Galatasaray £7,000 for use of fireworks in the stadium plus £2,500 for inadequate security.

13

1937 United won 7-1 at Chesterfield in a Football League Division Two game with Tommy Bamford scoring four of the Reds' goals. For this game, Stan Pearson made his debut for United but failed to get on the scoresheet.

1965 The Reds produced a stunning display to beat Leicester City 5-0 at Filbert Street, usually a bogey ground for United. It was undoubtedly the club's best display in the League home or away that season. United's goals were scored by Herd 2, Best, Charlton and Connelly with Denis Law being the only forward not to score.

1968 European champions Manchester United beat Belgian champions Anderlecht 3-0 at Old Trafford in the European Cup quarter-final first leg tie with goals from Denis Law 2, and Brian Kidd. Promoted wingers Carlo Sartori and Jimmy Ryan were the players who helped turn the game so dramatically in the second-half as the Reds began to capture the adventurous spirit of the football that has marked many of their European ties.

14

1931 United won 5-1 at Oldham Athletic with Johnston and Spence grabbing two goals apiece and Frank Mann hitting a spectacular fifth.

1942 The Reds beat Manchester City 5-0 at Maine Road with John Smith netting a hat-trick and William Bryant scoring the other two goals.

1960 Birth of Remi Moses. Born in Manchester and a lifelong United supporter, he jumped at the chance to return to Old Trafford in the dual transaction that took Bryan Robson to United in October 1981. Moses was rated at around £650,000, having signed before the Robson part of the deal was finalised. An aggressive England Under-21 international, his appearances were limited due to injury, and in 1988, after playing in 198 League and Cup games for the Reds, he announced his retirement.

15

1895 Birth of Neil McBain. The oldest player ever to appear in a League match when he kept goal for New Brighton against Hartlepool United at the age of 51 years fourth months, he had joined United as a wing-half from Ayr United. The Reds paid £4,600 for him in 1921, and a year later he won the first of his three Scottish caps. His stay at Old Trafford was a short one, in that he only played in 43 games before signing for Everton in January 1923. He later played for St Johnstone, Liverpool and Watford, where he eventually became manager. He later managed Ayr United, Luton and Leyton Orient before ending his days as coach of the great Argentinian side Estudiantes.

1924 James Hanson made his debut for United in the 2-0 win over Hull City at Old Trafford and celebrated by scoring the opening goal. He also scored in his next two outings, but then had to step down for Bill Henderson who was United's regular choice in attack, and who had been injured. Midway through the 1925-26 season Hanson made the breakthrough and though the goals were slow to arrive, they eventually did. In 1928-29, he was an ever-present and the club's leading scorer with 19 goals.

- November -

In the Christmas Day match of 1929 against Birmingham City, he suffered an injury and never played again.

1958 Despite two goals from the 'Black Prince', Alex Dawson, the Reds lost 6-3 to Bolton Wanderers at a fog-shrouded Burnden Park.

1967 United travelled to Yugoslavia to play FK Sarajevo in the European Cup second round first leg. A tremendous rearguard action allowed the Reds to play out a goalless draw.

1986 United drew 1-1 with Liverpool, whose goalkeeper Bruce Grobbelaar claimed that he was subjected to the constant throwing of missiles from the Stretford End; coins, eggs and bananas littered the goalmouth.

16

1895 The Reds drew 5-5 at home to Lincoln City in a Second Division match with goals from Clarkin 2, Cassidy, Collinson and Peters.

1929 United suffered one of their heaviest defeats, losing 7-2 to Sheffield Wednesday at Hillsborough.

1938 Old Trafford witnessed the fastest ever hat-trick in International football as Willie Hall of Tottenham Hotspur netted a treble inside three and a half minutes of the match against Ireland. Hall went on to score five times in succession, thus equalling the England record, as the home side won 7-0.

1974 Birth of Paul Scholes. Equally at home playing in midfield or up front, he made a sensational debut for United, scoring both goals in a 2-1 Coca Cola Cup victory over Port Vale in September 1994. His first Premier League appearance saw him score within 11 minutes of him coming on as a substitute in a 3-2 defeat against Ipswich Town at Portman Road.

In 1995-96 he scored 11 goals in his first 23 games, a remarkable achievement considering he only completed five of those games. He came on for Andy Cole in the FA Cup Final victory over Liverpool to collect a winners' medal, having already won one for the League Championship. During the 1996/97 season he won his second Championship medal and forced his way into the England squad.

1990 The European Super Cup was contested between Manchester United and Red Star Belgrade. Because of the Civil War in Yugoslavia, the tie was just played at Old Trafford instead of over two legs. A Brian McClair goal after Steve Bruce had missed a penalty gave United a 1-0 win.

1996 United beat Arsenal 1-0 in a game tarnished by accusations of racist remarks from United's Danish international 'keeper Peter Schmeichel, after a clash with Ian Wright. The Reds stumbled to the three points when left-back Nigel Winterburn chested the ball over his own line after a poor clearance from England 'keeper David Seaman.

17

1944 The War Commission wrote to the Manchester United directors to say that the Old Trafford ground was 'not considered a total loss' but it was still quite a time before any repair work could be proposed.

1965 After building their own Berlin Wall in East Germany for their first round European Cup match against AEK Vorwaerts, United broke away in the last ten minutes and scored two goals through Law and Connelly. The 2-0 win flattered United who gave a disappointing display.

- November -

18 **1968** Birth of Peter Schmeichel. After his impressive performances for Denmark when they won the European Championships in the summer of 1992, Schmeichel was rated the best goalkeeper in the world. When United signed him from Brondby for £850,000 in August 1991, he was already an established Danish international. In his first season, he helped the Reds to win the League Cup against Nottingham Forest and kept clean sheets in his first four games. All told, he kept 17 clean sheets that season, but bettered it by one in 1993-94 as United won the Premier League. In 1995-96 he became the first United goalkeeper since Alex Stepney to get his name on the scoresheet when heading home a last minute equaliser against Rotor Volgograd in the UEFA Cup. He kept 22 clean sheets that season and was instrumental in the club's double success.

1995 United beat Southampton 4-1 in what was the first time that visiting supporters had been allowed in at Old Trafford for a Premier League game that season. Southampton kicked-off, but just 15 seconds had passed, when Ryan Giggs slotted home United's first goal. Four minutes later, the Welshman added a second after a misunderstanding in the Saints defence. Only eight minutes had gone when United scored their third through Paul Scholes. With the game wrapped up, United used all their three substitutes before Cole added a fourth goal. The visitors pulled one back in the closing minutes but couldn't prevent United from recording their 50th home win in the Premier League.

19 **1983** Republic of Ireland international Frank Stapleton demolished Watford with a first-half hat-trick for Manchester United in a 4-1 win over the visitors. He scored twice in the first-half and then completed his hat-trick in the 83rd minute to win a standing ovation from the fans.

1991 The Reds won the Super Cup beating Red Star Belgrade 1-0 with a goal by Brian McClair after 67 minutes but the plaudits went to the visitors who emphasized what English supporters had been missing during the five-year ban on English clubs playing in the European competitions. The Reds fielded eight non-English players in their squad but this did not have a significant effect. Steve Bruce missed a 2nd minute penalty but it was the performance of Dejan Savicevic which caught the eye.

20 **1911** Manchester United had begun the 1907-08 season being floated as a limited public company. The Football Association supervised the club's affairs until at last a note in the minute book said: *'The Commission has gone exhaustively into the position of the club and satisfactory arrangements have now been made which will put the club in proper working condition.'* At that point, shares were issued to the general public with a capital of £15,000 in £1 shares. Arrangements with the firm of Walker and Pomfray Brewers - the owners of the Old Trafford land - resulted in 24 acres and 12 poles being leased to the club for an annual rent of £1,492 with the directors holding the option to purchase within seven years.

1943 Charlie Mitten scored four of United's goals as they beat Tranmere Rovers 6-3 in the Football League North (First Championship). In fact, the match was abandoned after 85 minutes but the score stood.

1957 After a goalless first-half against Dukla Prague in the first round first leg European Cup tie, United scored three goals in the space of 12 minutes through Webster, Taylor and Pegg. At the banquet attended by both teams after the match, one of the Czech club's officials publicly wished Manchester United the best of luck in the next round of the competition, even though the second leg in Prague was two weeks away!

- *November* -

21

1891 United achieved their biggest win in the Football Alliance when they beat Lincoln City 10-1 with Bob Donaldson scoring a hat-trick.

1953 Although the absence of Stanley Matthews was a big disappointment, there was the best gate of the season at Old Trafford for the visit of Blackpool. In a close fought first-half, Tommy Taylor scored for United, equalising Bill Perry's goal for the Seasiders. Despite the visitors having seven internationals in their side, it was the young and eager soccer students of Manchester United that won the day 4-1, with Taylor finally grabbing a hat-trick in front of the 49,853 crowd.

22

1890 Newton Heath lost 8-2 when they visited Nottingham Forest to record one of their heaviest defeats in the Football Alliance.

1902 Alex Downie made a goalscoring debut for Manchester United in a 1-1 draw at Leicester Fosse. Having played his early football with Third Lanark and Bristol City, he joined United from Swindon Town. He played regularly in the side that won promotion from the Second Division in 1905-06 but two seasons later when the Reds won the League Championship he only appeared in ten games. He was left out of the side to face one of his former clubs, Bristol City in the FA Cup final, and in 1910 after scoring 14 goals in 191 games, he joined Oldham Athletic before later ending his career with Crewe Alexandra.

23

1907 Sandy Turnbull scored all four of United's goals as they defeated Woolwich Arsenal 4-2.

1935 United beat Norwich City 5-3 at a rain soaked Carrow Road with Jack Rowley grabbing a hat-trick and Tom Manley two goals. As well as scoring his two goals, the tall Welsh international created all of Rowley's goals as the United forwards gave the Norwich defence little rest.

1988 At the Manchester United v Sheffield Wednesday game at Old Trafford, which the Reds drew 1-1, the Football Supporters Association had a banner at the Scoreboard End declaring 'Fans say no to ID'.

1994 Paul Ince was sent-off in the European Champions League match in Gothenburg which United lost 3-1. United's longest run in European competition without a win now stretched to four games.

24

1945 The Reds beat Leeds United 6-1 with Wrigglesworth and Buckle grabbing two goals apiece and Hanlon and Rowley scoring one each.

1979 Joe Jordan hit two of United's goals as they beat Norwich City 5-0 at Old Trafford. The Reds' other scorers were Coppell, Macari and Moran.

1984 United's Mark Hughes and Sunderland's David Hodgson were sent-off in a stormy clash at Roker Park. The Welsh international had scored the Reds' first goal but it wasn't enough as the home side held out for a 3-2 win.

1988 Manchester United director Bobby Charlton was embarrassed at his name being linked with the job of England's manager. The former United and England star who won 106 caps between 1958 and 1970 made it quite clear that he had no ambitions to crown his distinguished international career by becoming the boss.

25

1939 William Wrigglesworth, United's left-winger played an important part in the Reds' 8-1 runaway success over Port Vale in the Western Division of the War League. Much of the credit for his five goals went to the fine prompting of United's young inside-forward Stan Pearson. The pair formed a good understanding which always troubled an overworked Port Vale defence.

26

1966 David Herd scored a goal against three different goalkeepers at Old Trafford when Manchester United beat Sunderland 5-0. Herd scored four times, the first against three against Jim Montgomery, Charlie Hurley and John Parks in that order. The other United goal was scored by Denis Law.

1994 Mark Hughes was sent-off for the fifth time in his United career as the Reds drew 0-0 at Arsenal. It was the second season in succession that the Old Trafford side had a player dismissed at Highbury following Eric Cantona's dispatch in 1993-94.

27

1948 Travelling from their overnight quarters at Saltburn-on-Sea along frost-bound roads, United were pleasantly surprised to find Ayresome Park in good condition for their match against Middlesbrough. The home side wore black arm bands in memory of their old centre-forward George Elliott who had died earlier in the day, aged 59. The Reds were the first to get to grips with the conditions and Rowley gave them to lead after 12 minutes. United went on to win 4-1 with Jack Rowley netting a hat-trick in an exhibition of flowing football.

1968 United went down in the European Cup second round second leg against RSC Anderlecht in Belgium, but Carlo Sartori's goal was enough to take the Reds into the next round, 4-3 on aggregate.

1971 United crushed Southampton 5-2 with George Best scoring his second hat-trick of the season, before limping off with a leg injury 20 minutes from the end. A young Sammy McIlroy scored again to maintain his goal-a-game average in his three full League appearances. United's other scorer was Brian Kidd who shot on sight at every opportunity.

28

1891 A Bob Donaldson hat-trick helped the Heathens beat Walsall Town Swifts 4-1.

1936 Walter Winterbottom, later to become manager of England, made his debut for United in a 2-1 defeat at Leeds United. He was working as a schoolteacher when Louis Rocca spotted him playing for Cheshire League side Mossley. He went on to make 23 appearances that season at wing-half, and had played in just four games in 1937-38 when a spinal injury ended his career. After the war, he was offered the FA's top coaching job, as well as being appointed team manager of England. He guided England to four successive World Cup finals before being replaced by Alf Ramsey in 1963.

1936 Manchester goalkeeper Tommy Breen conceded a goal after just 60 seconds of his League debut at Leeds United before he had even touched the ball! The following season, the Irish international was the club's first choice 'keeper as they won promotion to the First Division. The former Belfast Celtic custodian appeared in 71 League and Cup games for the Reds before losing his place to John Breedon.

1990 United inflicted Arsenal's biggest Highbury defeat since the war, beating the Gunners 6-2 in a fourth round Rumbelows Cup tie. Arsenal who had gone the previous 17 games without defeat were completely outplayed. The Reds made a dream start with Clayton Blackmore firing home after just two minutes.

November

Goals from Hughes and Sharpe just before the interval were decisive, but Alan Smith pulled two back for Arsenal. The Reds wobbled for a while but 19-year-old Lee Sharpe completed his hat-trick and Danny Wallace hit United's sixth.

29 **1902** A hat-trick by Edward Pegg helped the Reds beat Stockport Central 4-1 in an FA Cup fifth qualifying round.

1947 Chelsea were destroyed 4-0 by United at Stamford Bridge with Johnny Morris scoring a hat-trick.

1967 Goals from Best and Aston gave the Reds a 2-1 European Cup second round second leg win against FK Sarajevo in front of 62,801 fans at Old Trafford.

1973 Birth of Ryan Giggs. Although he was born in Cardiff, he was brought up in the Manchester area where his father played Rugby League after a successful career in Rugby Union. Then known as Ryan Wilson, he was actually at Manchester City's School of Excellence and captained England Schoolboys against Scotland at Old Trafford before United snapped him up in the summer of 1990. It was around this time that his mother changed her name to Giggs and though young Ryan's talent was obvious for all to see, United were careful to develop him slowly. He made his first team debut against Everton on 2 March 1991, and on 16 October 1991 became the youngest ever Welsh full international when he played against Germany at the age of 17 years 321 days. He set another record when he became the first player to win the PFA's Young Player of the Year Award in successive seasons, a feat he achieved in 1991/92 and 1992-93. One of the game's leading players, he has won four League Championship medals, two FA Cup winners' medals and a League Cup winners' medal in his Old Trafford career.

1988 Manchester United turned out for nothing at St Andrews to support a testimonial for Birmingham City's Ian Handysides. The Birmingham midfielder had to quit the game at the age of 27 after undergoing major brain surgery.

30 **1935** Bert Whalley made his debut for United in the goalless draw at home to Doncaster Rovers. Though he only appeared in 33 League games for the reds, he played for the club before, during, and after the Second World War. Signed from Stalybridge Celtic, he was a virtual ever-present during the war years, turning out in 188 games. After playing in just three games after the hostilities had ended, he took up a coaching position. Partly responsible for the development of so many of the club's youngsters, he should not even have been on the fateful European Cup trip to Belgrade but with Jimmy Murphy on international duty as manager of Wales, he volunteered to take his place, and lost his life.

1957 Not having been beaten by a London club at Old Trafford since October 1938, when Charlton Athletic won 2-0, United finally lost 4-3 to Tottenham Hotspur in front of a 43,077 crowd. The Reds then proceeded to lose their very next home game, 1-0 to another London outfit, Chelsea!

1974 United beat Sunderland 3-2 at Old Trafford in front of 60,585 - the club's best ever Second Division crowd - home or away.

- November -

(Left)
6 November
Gordon Strachan.
Signed for United.

(Below left)
5 November - Jimmy Delaney
Scores in United's 6-0 win.

(Below centre)
14 November - Frank Mann
Scores the spectacular fifth goal.

(Right)
28 November
Walter
Winterbottom
Makes his debut
for United.

130

DECEMBER

1 1951 United beat Blackpool 4-1 with John Downie grabbing a hat-trick.

1961 A letter to the Manchester Evening News from a Mr. L. R. Cunningham of Whitefield complained bitterly about the United forward-line! He wrote: *'United have players who are not pulling their weight and the strain is being shouldered by those who are playing flat out. The failure of Herd, Quixall and Charlton this year must be a terrific blow to the defence. When the forwards learn to play together and not as individuals then we may see a Red revival.'*

1965 A David Herd hat-trick gave United a 3-1 second leg victory in the European Cup first round match against ASK Vorwarts to take them through to the second round with a 5-1 aggregate win.

1994 France rocked Manchester United with an international call up for Eric Cantona, which left the Reds without either of their top strikers for the clash at Queen's Park Rangers. Mark Hughes was already out of the match with a one match ban following his dismissal against Arsenal, but the French decision to pull their captain out in readiness for the European Championship qualifier shocked Alex Ferguson. The United boss offered to fly Eric out on the Sunday, but the French FA wouldn't wear it.

2 1964 Manchester United completed the eclipse of Borussia Dortmund to win through to the last 12 of the Inter Cities Fairs Cup with a crushing 10-1 aggregate win over the Germans. Winning the second leg 4-0, United showed that they had the ability to pierce a continental-style packed defence. Two early goals from Bobby Charlton and one apiece from Denis Law and John Connelly saw United home.

3 1969 United lost 2-1 to Manchester City in the first leg of the Football League Cup at Maine Road. Colin Bell gave City the lead but Bobby Charlton equalised in the 66th minute. The game looked to be heading for a draw when with just two minutes left, Ian Ure brought down Francis Lee for the England forward to score from the spot and give the Blues their first leg lead.

1994 Alex Ferguson opened the new Mega Store situated behind the Stretford End of the ground. Kicking a ball through a paper net, the United manager declared the store open. Remarkably the day's takings were reported as being £250,000!

4 1937 Jack Rowley became United's, and it is thought the Football League's, youngest hat-trick scorer when he hit four goals in the Reds 5-1 win over Swansea Town at Old Trafford. Rowley who was 17 years and 58 days old was playing in only his second game for the club. Pearson and Rowley, probably the youngest left-wing pairing ever to play for United, showed a real understanding in a forward line that was on top throughout. United's other scorer was William Bryant.

1959 Birth of Paul McGrath. Born of Irish parents in Ealing, London, he was discovered by United playing for St Patrick's Athletic in the League of Ireland. He made his debut for the Reds against Tottenham Hotspur in November 1982 and eventually won a regular place. He won an FA Cup winners' medal in 1985 as United beat Everton at Wembley and earlier that season won the first of his many full caps for the Republic of Ireland when he came on as substitute against Italy. Despite being injured for much of the 1987-88 season he recovered in time to star in the Irish midfield during the 1988 European Championships.

- December -

Injuries again took their toll the following season and in August 1989, he joined Aston Villa for £400,000. He proved to be an inspirational signing for the Villa Park side, helping them to runners-up in the First Division in 1989-90. He represented the Football League XI and was the mainstay of Jack Charlton's Republic of Ireland side that qualified for the 1990 World Cup Finals. He was voted PFA Player of the Year in 1991-92, and though he continued to play on 'borrowed' time for Villa he amassed 322 first team appearances before signing for Derby County.

5 **1942** A John Smith hat-trick helped United to a 6-1 win over Wrexham in a Football League North (First Championship) wartime match.

1995 Manchester United lost 2-1 to an International Select XI in Belfast. The Reds sent a team for the game, staged by Co-operation North, a non-political organisation for the promotion of understanding between the two communities of Northern Ireland. Paul Scholes scored United's goal in a match which raised £160,000 for the charity.

6 **1941** United beat Wrexham 10-3 in the Northern Section First Championship with Johnny Carey scoring four of the goals and Jack Rowley a hat-trick. The other scorers were Smith 2, and Bryant.

1992 In the first-ever Premier League meeting between United and Manchester City, Paul Ince got his first goal of the season in the Reds' 2-1 win. In a red-blooded and at times over physical contest, Ince's shot from well outside the box after 20 minutes gave United a 1-0 half-time lead. Mark Hughes too produced one of his specials, also scoring from outside the penalty area with a dipping, swerving left-foot volley that gave Tony Coton no chance.

Niall Quinn pulled a goal back for City a minute later and United had to hang on for the last 15 minutes as City staged a barnstorming finish.

7 **1940** In an exciting North Regional League wartime match, Manchester United drew 5-5 with Blackburn Rovers at Ewood Park.

1946 Jack Rowley scored United's first goal in their 4-1 win over Brentford, inside the opening minute, after Gorman had almost put through his own goal. It was the only gaol of the first-half, but in the second period, a poor Brentford side conceded three further goals, two scored by Jack Rowley to complete his hat-trick, and one by Charlie Mitten. United finished the first season of League football after the Second World War as runners-up in the First Division.

1963 Denis Law gave a virtuoso performance in a 5-2 win over Stoke City with four fabulous goals. Dave Gaskell in the United goal produced three excellent saves and Peter Dobing hit the post after Law and Herd had given the Reds a 2-0 lead. Law's efforts put a different complexion on the game in a second-half completely dominated by the home side.

1991 For the first time ever, the League Cup and FA Cup draws were made on the same day. At lunchtime, United were drawn away to Leeds United who were currently top of the First Division in the quarter final of the League Cup. That evening, the Reds were again drawn away to Leeds in the FA Cup third round. United won 3-1 in the League Cup and 1-0 in the FA Cup.

1993 After Manchester United's 3-0 win at Sheffield United, the bookies stopped taking bets on the Reds winning the title, although you could still bet on how many points they would win it with!

132

- December -

8   **1963** The birth of Brian McClair. He joined Celtic from Motherwell for £100,000 and in 145 appearances for the Parkhead club, scored 99 goals before Alex Ferguson brought him to Old Trafford in June 1987 for £850,000. In his first season with the Reds, he became the first United player since George Best to score 20 League goals in a campaign. However, following Mark Hughes' return to Old Trafford, McClair found goalscoring more difficult and was moved into a midfield role. First capped by Scotland when he played for Celtic, he went on to win 30 caps for his country and in 1987 was voted Scottish Player of the Year. Though now mainly used as a substitute, he has won just about every medal the English game can offer.

9   **1939** Manchester United beat Stockport County 7-4 at Edgeley Park in a War Regional League (Western Division) match with goals from Pearson 2, Smith 2, Hanlon, McKay and an own goal.

10   **1904** United beat Gainsborough Trinity 3-1. It was the first goal that the club had conceded in eight League games, the other seven matches all also being won. During this spell, they scored 14 goals with Harry Moger being United's 'keeper keeping the clean sheets.

1963 United reached the quarter-final of the European Cup Winners' Cup by beating Tottenham Hotspur 4-1 at Old Trafford. Spurs' Dave Mackay broke his leg in the eighth minute, but by then the Reds had taken the lead through Bobby Charlton. Maurice Setters kept Jimmy Greaves in check despite having to leave the field to have six stitches inserted in a head wound. Charlton scored a second goal and David Herd two to give United a 4-3 aggregate win over their North London opponents.

1977 An inexperienced United side went down 2-1 to West Ham United at Upton Park as their defence went walkabouts towards the end of the game. Also conspicuous by their absence were the Manchester United fans who were banned from the ground as a security precaution.

11   **1943** Stan Pearson netted a hat-trick as United beat Wrexham 5-0 in the Football League North (First Championship) wartime match.

1954 Without a point from their last three away matches, United travelled to Turf Moor for a fixture in which Geoff Bent made his debut for the injured Roger Byrne. There was a blow for the Reds after 14 minutes when Don Gibson put through his own goal. But 21-year-old Welshman Colin Webster, deputising for Tommy Taylor scored a hat-trick, a just reward for his courage and tenacity.

1974 After United had drawn 0-0 at Ayresome Park in a fifth round League Cup tie against Middlesbrough, both managers - Jack Charlton and Tommy Docherty - wanted referee Peter Reeves changed for the replay because he was 'whistle happy'. Docherty went so far as to say that his present Manchester United team were 'fairies' compared with the players of his day. He also added that, *'the game is changing and I don't like it. I was brought up differently, when tackling was an art. Now all the bodily contact is going out of the game.'* For the record, United won the replay 3-0 two weeks later with goals from McIlroy, Pearson and Macari.

12   **1896** Newton Heath beat West Manchester 7-0 in the FA Cup third qualifying round with Cassidy, Gillespie and Rothwell scoring two goals each and Bryant, a spectacular strike from distance.

133

- December -

1908 A George Wall hat-trick helped United to a 4-3 home win over Leicester Fosse with John Picken grabbing the Reds' winner.

1959 Wilf McGuinness broke a leg playing for United's reserves against Stoke City at Old Trafford. It was a bad break and though it virtually ended his playing career, it opened the way to a rise on the managerial side. A Manchester and England schoolboy international, he first played in the United League team in 1955 and continued his international career with the England Youth and Under-23 side before gaining two full caps. At his original appointment, after retiring from the playing side, he was assistant-trainer to Jack Crompton. He was in charge of the reserve side with a special interest in the United Youth side. When he took up his duties as Chief Coach in June 1969, he became one of the youngest coaches in charge of a First Division side.

1984 Celtic were ordered to replay their European Cup tie with Rapid Vienna at Old Trafford after crowd trouble at Parkhead and were well beaten by the Austrians.

13
1980 United drew 2-2 at home to Stoke City. The Reds' goalscorers were Joe Jordan and Lou Macari, both of whom went on to manage the Potters.

14
1912 United beat Newcastle United 3-1 at St James' Park with Enoch West scoring all the Reds' goals.

1963 With Denis Law out of the United side, David Herd thrived on the support he received from his colleagues to score a well-taken hat-trick against Sheffield Wednesday in a 3-1 win for the home side.

1985 Chris Turner made his United debut in a 3-1 win at Aston Villa. Signed from Sunderland for what was then a club record fee for a goalkeeper of £250,000, he had to wait until Gary Bailey was injured before gaining a regular place. Turner then kept his spot until a young Gary Walsh was given his chance. Turner played in 79 League and Cup games for the Reds before leaving Old Trafford in 1988 to play for Sheffield Wednesday for a second time.

15
1951 Birth of Joe Jordan. He began his footballing days with Morton before Leeds United paid £15,000 to bring him to Elland Road in October 1970. He played an important role in the Yorkshire club's League Championship winning team of 1974 and in two losing European Cup Final teams of 1973 and 1975. In January 1978, United paid £350,000 for his services. An old-fashioned type of centre-forward, he was one of the most feared strikers in the top flight. He played in 126 games for the Reds, scoring 41 goals, with his best season being 1980-81 when he netted 15 goals in 33 League games. In the summer of 1981 he signed for AC Milan before later playing for Verona. Capped 52 times by Scotland, he returned to England in 1984 to play for Southampton, before joining Bristol City, where he eventually took over as manager. He later managed Hearts and Stoke City, before returning to Ashton Gate for a second spell as manager.

16
1936 Birth of Maurice Setters. He began his days with Exeter City, but after just ten League appearances, was snapped up by West Bromwich Albion. He spent five seasons at the Hawthorns before joining United in January 1960. Though he was never honoured at full level, he won another five England Under-23 caps whilst at Old Trafford to go with the 11 he gained whilst at West Brom.

- *December* -

His only honour at United came in 1963 when the Reds beat Leicester City 3-1 to win the FA Cup. His final game for United was in October 1964 as Aston Villa were thrashed 7-0. A few weeks later he joined Stoke City for £30,000. He later had spells at Coventry City and Charlton Athletic, before entering management with Doncaster Rovers. He then worked with Jack Charlton at Sheffield Wednesday and Newcastle United, before teaming up with him again in charge of the Republic of Ireland international side.

1970 United struggled against Third Division Aston Villa in the League Cup semi-final first leg at Old Trafford. Andy Lochhead gave the visitors the lead in the 41st minute and it was just seconds before the interval when Brian Kidd converted Carlo Sartori's cross to save United's blushes!

1982 The first live television showing of a Football League match came from Old Trafford when Manchester United played Tottenham Hotspur. The match shown on BBC 1 between 7.05 and 9.00 pm saw the Reds win 4-2 with Arthur Graham and Kevin Moran scoring two goals apiece. The game however, only attracted a crowd of 33,616, forcing the Football League to pay United compensation of £50,000, as normally this fixture would have attracted a crowd in the region of 50,000.

17 **1904** A John Peddie hat-trick helped United pick up valuable points in the Second Division away match at Burton United which the Reds won 3-2.

1932 United beat Lincoln City 4-1 with former Liverpool forward Tom Reid netting a hat-trick. John Silcock at full-back gave a wonderful display and the experiment of playing Chalmers and Stewart on the left-wing was a great success.

1966 The Reds visited the Hawthorns and beat West Bromwich Albion 4-3 in a most exciting match. David Herd scored a hat-trick and Denis Law the winner as United maintained their position at the top of the First Division.

1969 In the Football League Cup semi-final second leg tie against Manchester City at Old Trafford, the Reds could only draw 2-2 and so went out of the competition 4-3 on aggregate. It was a classic encounter with Ian Bowyer giving City the lead after 17 minutes. Six minutes later, Paul Edwards drew United level and on the hour, Denis Law put United 2-1 in front on the night, 3-3 on aggregate. With just eight minutes remaining, Alex Stepney failed to read the indirect free-kick award and parried Lee's shot when he could safely have let it in. Mike Summerbee gratefully smashed home the rebound for the goal that took City to Wembley.

1994 Manchester United conceded their first goal in League matches at Old Trafford that season after 1,135 minutes when losing 2-1 to Nottingham Forest.

1995 The clash with Liverpool at Anfield, which United lost 2-0, was interrupted by two male streakers, who with anti-Cantona graffiti painted on their bodies, ran onto the pitch.

18 **1921** Birth of Jack Crompton. Known as 'Mr Dependable' at Old Trafford, he was United's goalkeeper in the 1948 FA Cup Final against Blackpool, bringing off a spectacular save in the dying minutes that kept the Seasiders at bay. Yet only 48 hours earlier, he had been on the operating table for the removal of an abscess on his spine. After playing in 211 League and Cup games and losing his place to Ray Wood, he left Old Trafford to work as Luton Town's coach. He returned to Old Trafford following the Munich disaster to help Jimmy Murphy rebuild the side.

Later he managed Barrow and became Preston North End coach under Bobby Charlton, before returning to Old Trafford for a third time in 1974 as United's reserve team trainer.

1978 Manchester United's plans to raise a million pounds sailed through the club's extraordinary general meeting of shareholders at Old Trafford. The controversial scheme was pushed through on an overwhelming vote of 37 for and only three against on a show of hands. The meeting lasted 22 minutes with only six shareholders questioning the new rights issue of shares to raise £1,015,000 new capital.

19

1903 Dick Duckworth made his debut for United in the 4-2 home win over Gainsborough Trinity, scoring the Reds' second goal. One of the greatest players ever to wear a United shirt, it was another couple of seasons before he established himself fully. A member of the club's outstanding half-back line of Duckworth, Roberts and Bell, he was the only one who did not win full international honours. The nearest he came to it was when he played in a Commonwealth international during the 1901 tour of South Africa. He also made five appearances for the Football League XI and won two League Championship medals and an FA Cup winners' medal with United.

1972 Manchester United sacked manager Frank O'Farrell and his two assistants and said that their truant Irish international, George Best, would never play for the club again. But when the United directors drew up that part of the statement dealing with Best, they did not know he had already sent them a letter announcing that he would never play football again!

20

1950 Manchester United are to install floodlighting at their practice ground, The Cliff, at Broughton to enable junior players and part-time professionals to train at night. Matt Busby said *'floodlighting will be used only during off-peak electricity periods. It will be a boon to young players who are at work during the day'*. To cover the lighting installation, United have obtained licences which will also allow them to repair parts of The Cliff, the former home of Broughton Rangers Rugby League Club.

21

1907 Sandy Turnbull became the first United player to be sent-off in a League match against Manchester City. He had scored two goals in the Reds' 3-1 win before he got his marching orders.

1918 William Woodcock scored four of United's goals in a 5-1 home win over Port Vale in the Lancashire Section (Principal Tournament) wartime game.

1929 George McLachlan made his debut for United in the 3-1 win over Leeds United at Old Trafford. Having started his career with Clyde, he joined Cardiff City and played in the Welsh club's 1927 FA Cup winning team, the first and only time that the trophy has been won by a non-English club. A ball-playing winger, United had hoped that his goals would help their flagging fortunes but in 116 appearances for the Reds, he only scored four goals. He later joined Third Division (North) club, Chester.

22

1917 United beat Burnley 5-0 at Turf Moor in a Lancashire Section (Principal Tournament) wartime match with George Anderson scoring a hat-trick.

1923 A hat-trick from Bain and goals from Lochhead and Spence gave United a 5-0 win over bottom club Port Vale in a Division Two encounter.

1956 United were due to face West Bromwich Albion in a First Division game at 2.15.pm. The reds were lined up ready to go out

- December -

as were the referee and linesmen, but there was no sign of West Brom or United manager Matt Busby for that matter. The kick-off was delayed until 2.30.pm, but it was 4.00.pm before the Midlands side arrived due to their train being held up in the dense fog. By then of course, the game had been postponed and the crowd had made their way home.

1969 Birth of Mark Robins. Having joined the club as an apprentice, he was the first graduate of the FA National School to make an impact in League football. In reserve football he had been scoring at the rate of over 50 goals a season for a couple of years, and though he only scored 16 goals in 63 games for the first team, he did net the winner in the FA Cup semi-final of 1990 to take the Reds through to Wembley. In the summer of 1992, he joined Norwich City for £800,000, and in his first season scored 15 goals as the Canaries finished third in Division One. In January 1995, he signed for Leicester City for £1 million helping the Foxes into the Premiership the following season.

23 **1962** Birth of Terry Gibson. After winning England Youth honours, little Terry Gibson signed professional forms for Spurs and played in two epic FA Cup ties against Manchester United. Later allowed to move to Coventry City, he scored 43 goals in 97 League games before being transferred to United in the deal that took Alan Brazil in the opposite direction. He never really had an opportunity to prove himself at Old Trafford and after a miserable 18 months, he joined Wimbledon, helping the Dons to their shock FA Cup Final victory over Liverpool in 1988.

1970 Manchester United were knocked out of the Football League Cup at the semi-final stage by Third Division Aston Villa after going down 2-1 at Villa Park.

Brian Kidd scored a brilliant solo goal, but if it had not been for some outstanding saves by Jimmy Rimmer, who later played for Villa, United's defeat would have been much heavier.

1972 United's first League game under Tommy Docherty's leadership saw 46,382 turn up to see the Reds play Leeds United. At a time of the year when attendances at football matches usually drop to their lowest, it was an increase of over 13,000 from the 'same' Saturday of the previous two seasons. Ted MacDougall scored United's goal in a 1-1 draw.

24 **1898** Newton Heath beat Darwen 9-0 in a Football League Division Two fixture with William Bryant and Joe Cassidy both scoring hat-tricks.

1904 One of United's most memorable tussles with their great rivals Liverpool came when goals from Williams, Roberts and Arkesden gave them a 3-1 win. Though it was only a Second Division game, the 'Athletic News' described it as the game of the day. The clubs had only met twice in the League, Liverpool winning the first meeting 7-1 and United the return, 5-2. The two had met in a Test Match in 1894 when Liverpool won 2-0 thus consigning the Reds to the Second Division.

1955 United beat West Bromwich Albion 4-1 at the Hawthorns with Dennis Viollet grabbing a hat-trick.

25 **1931** United beat Wolverhampton Wanderers 3-2 at Old Trafford, only to lose 7-0 at Molineux on Boxing Day, one of the club's three all-time worst defeats.

- December -

1941 Goals from Rowley and Smith enabled United to draw 2-2 with neighbours Manchester City in front of the season's largest crowd of 20,000 in a Football League Northern Section (First Championship) wartime match.

1953 A hat-trick from Tommy Taylor and goals from Jackie Blanchflower and Dennis Viollet gave United a 5-2 win over Sheffield Wednesday.

1957 United's last Christmas Day fixture saw them beat Luton Town 3-0 with goals from Charlton, Edwards and Taylor.

26

1899 Newton Heath won away at Grimsby Town 7-0, the club's best away win in a Football League fixture.

1931 The Reds lost 7-0 at Wolverhampton Wanderers to equal their biggest away defeat in the Football League. It was also United's second consecutive Christmas 7-0 defeat!

1933 United lost 7-3 at Grimsby Town, who were lying top of the Second Division. The Mariners were three up by half-time and at one stage, led 6-1. United's scorers were Byrne 2, and Frame, but it was a miserable season for the Reds who used 38 players in the 42-match programme.

1960 Alex Dawson hit a hat-trick as United beat Chelsea 6-0 at Old Trafford.

1961 United beat Nottingham Forest 6-3 at Old Trafford with Nobby Lawton netting a hat-trick.

1991 United won 6-3 against Oldham Athletic at Boundary Park with former Latics full-back Denis Irwin scoring two of the goals. United's other scorers were McClair 2, Kanchelskis and Giggs.

27

1909 Arthur Whalley made his debut for United at Hillsborough, but the Reds went down to Sheffield Wednesday 4-1. Signed from Blackpool, he won a League Championship medal in 1910-11, and when Charlie Roberts joined Oldham Athletic, he became United's regular centre-half. He played for the Football League against the Irish League in 1913 and in an England trial match the following year. He returned to Old Trafford after the First World War, but in the summer of 1920 he left to join Southend United before later playing for Charlton, Millwall and Barrow.

1913 Though James Hodge played in 86 games for Manchester United between 1910 and 1919 and his brother John made 30 appearances for the club between 1913 and 1915, the only time they played together was in the 2-1 win over Sheffield Wednesday at Old Trafford when Meredith and Wall were the United scorers.

1920 The record attendance for a Football League game at Old Trafford was set at 70,504 for the visit of Aston Villa, who ran out winners 3-1.

1930 United lost 7-0 at Aston Villa to equal their worst defeat in the Football League.

1943 A Stan Pearson hat-trick helped United beat Halifax Town 6-2 in the Football League North(First Championship) wartime match.

1965 Originally an evening kick-off, the game against West Bromwich Albion had to be changed to 2.00.pm, as Norweb wouldn't give permission for the club's floodlights to be used during a 'peak demand' period.

1983 When United drew 3-3 with Notts County, nine of the visiting team were booked - seven of them for refusing to move back ten yards at a United free-kick.

- December -

28

1914 John Robson was appointed United manager. Prior to coming to Old Trafford, he had been in charge at Brighton, and before that been involved with Middlesbrough and Crystal Palace. Although his stay at United lasted seven years, much of his time was spent supervising the club's wartime games rather than Football League games. Throughout his stay, United remained a First Division club, but once their fortunes began to decline when League soccer resumed after the war, he stepped aside, though for a little while he worked as assistant to his successor, John Chapman.

1925 Frank McPherson scored all United's goals as the Reds beat Leicester City at Filbert Street 3-1.

1940 United beat Blackburn Rovers 9-0 in the North Regional League with John Smith, who was later to join the Ewood Park club, scoring five of the goals.

29

1970 Wilf McGuinness was reduced to the ranks of trainer of United's Central League side and Sir Matt Busby recalled from his position as general manager to take charge of the team again.

30

1972 Tommy Docherty replaced Frank O'Farrell as Manchester United manager. At the time, Docherty was managing the Scottish national team, a team of outstanding talents that included United's Denis Law and Willie Morgan.

31

1892 Newton Heath beat Derby County 7-1 with both Alf Farman and Bob Donaldson hitting hat-tricks.

1904 A hat-trick by Allan helped the Reds beat Burslem Port Vale 6-1.

1941 Birth of Alex Ferguson. Replacing Ron Atkinson in November 1986, he has served the longest spell as United manager since Sir Matt Busby. A former player with St Mirren and Glasgow Rangers, he first entered management with East Stirling before taking St Mirren to the First Division championship. In 1978 he took charge at Aberdeen, and during his stay at Pittodrie, led the Dons to three Scottish League championships, the Scottish Cup four times, and the League Cup on one occasion. On top of all those domestic honours, his greatest success came in the winning of the European Cup Winners' Cup. He had declined offers to manage a number of top English clubs but he could not resist the temptation to join Manchester United. Initially he found life more difficult, and in 1989-90 there was a real threat of relegation and inevitably there was a great deal of speculation surrounding Ferguson's future. However, he encouraged the development of a youth policy and spent wisely in order to realise his ambitions, and in the end it all began to pay dividends. United won the FA Cup in 1990. The following year they lifted the European Cup Winners' Cup, and then went on to win the European Super Cup and League. Then in May 1993, he helped bring the League Championship home to Old Trafford for the first time in 26 years, making him the first manager to win the title in both England and Scotland. In 1993-94 he led the club to their first 'double' and repeated the feat in 1995-96, after finishing runners-up to Blackburn Rovers in 1994-95. In 1996-97, United won the Premier League title for the fourth time in five seasons under the managership of Alex Ferguson.

1955 A post-war record crowd of 60,956 witnessed the Manchester derby at Old Trafford. The turnstiles closed ten minutes before kick-off with thousands of fans still outside the stadium. Goals from Tommy Taylor and Dennis Viollet gave United a 2-1 victory.

- December -

1960 Birth of Steve Bruce. A former England Youth and 'B' international, he started his career at Gillingham before Norwich City paid £135,000 for his services in July 1984. He helped the Canaries win promotion in 1985-86 and to their highest (at that time) League position of fifth in the First Division in 1986-87. He joined United for £825,000 in December 1987 and went straight into their side for the match against Portsmouth. He made a disastrous debut as he conceded a penalty and then broke his nose!

He soon became an automatic choice, and over the years had the knack of scoring important goals for a central defender; 52 total in 425 first team games for the Reds. An inspiring captain, he won three League Championship medals, two FA Cup winners' medals and a League Cup winners' medal before in the summer of 1996, he rejected the prospect of a lucrative testimonial at Old Trafford to join Birmingham City.

*(Left) 10 December - Maurice Setters. Six stiches in a head wound.
(Right) 9 December - John Hanlon. Scores in an 11 goal War-time thriller.*

- December -

*(Above) 31 December
Alex Ferguson - Birthday.*

*(Right) 24 December
Charlie Roberts - Scores a
goal in the 'Game of the Day'.*

- YEAR INDEX -

Year	Pages
1884	36, 94
1886	117
1889	101
1890	19, 44, 108, 115, 127
1891	115, 127, 128
1892	14, 50, 94, 97, 112, 121
1893	6, 49-51, 94, 95
1894	33, 48, 51, 121, 137
1895	32, 42, 50, 104, 111, 120, 124, 125
1896	4, 22, 42, 103, 115, 133
1897	15, 48, 50, 94, 95, 97
1898	26, 39, 42, 137
1899	17, 32, 35, 62, 138
1900	5, 11, 23, 46, 94, 104
1901	21, 26, 39, 116, 136
1902	6, 10, 44, 51, 94, 95, 97, 127, 129
1903	12, 95, 103, 104, 110, 136
1904	7, 39, 43, 46, 49, 133, 135, 137, 139
1905	4, 5, 12, 23, 34, 42, 94, 127
1906	4, 8, 20, 25, 34, 39, 44, 48, 50, 52, 59, 94
1907	4, 22, 39, 45, 55, 96, 104, 111, 113, 126, 127, 136
1908	12, 37, 39, 44, 51, 62, 90, 94, 97, 100, 134
1909	12, 24, 31, 33, 38, 39, 50, 55, 62, 66, 68, 91, 92, 97, 104, 111, 115, 138
1910	11, 23, 26, 52, 111, 127, 138
1911	35, 39, 51, 52, 97, 103, 126
1912	18, 27, 39, 134
1913	30, 50, 88, 113, 138
1913	30
1914	43, 50, 139
1915	4, 42, 55, 91, 110, 138
1916	6, 91, 94
1917	37, 44, 55, 96, 136
1918	94, 99, 136
1919	7, 24, 39, 91, 96, 110, 111, 138
1920	30, 34, 90, 96, 109, 110, 115, 138
1921	9, 21, 48, 50, 56, 90, 95, 117, 120, 124, 135
1922	96
1923	20, 89, 98, 109, 124, 136
1924	30, 46, 48, 89-91, 96, 97, 100, 111, 117, 122, 124
1925	17, 19, 50, 55, 103, 124, 139
1926	12, 30, 47, 49, 55, 66, 90, 95, 109, 110, 120, 122
1927	4, 10, 18, 30, 31, 43, 91, 97, 110, 115, 117, 136
1928	8, 18, 44, 56, 89, 90, 109, 116, 124
1929	17-19, 98, 116, 125, 136
1930	17, 43, 98, 99, 113, 123, 138
1931	7, 55, 68, 90, 94, 95, 124, 137, 138
1932	5, 14, 15, 23, 27, 38, 77, 79, 82, 90, 115-117, 135
1933	4, 17, 31, 56, 68, 69, 71, 82, 84, 90, 101, 102, 117, 122, 138
1934	46, 56, 63, 90, 96, 101, 108, 121
1935	17, 39, 90, 99, 101, 110, 117, 127, 129
1936	18, 20, 24, 52, 88, 90, 91, 95, 97, 107, 128, 134
1937	7, 24, 56, 66, 90, 95, 97, 101, 109, 111, 116, 124, 128, 131
1938	11, 57, 77, 82, 86, 121, 125, 129
1939	6, 23, 35, 38, 90, 94, 99, 128, 133
1940	5, 24, 25, 38, 60, 66, 108, 132, 139
1941	32, 33, 43, 46, 48, 78, 91, 98, 101, 113, 123, 132, 139
1942	35, 60, 100, 108, 124, 132
1943	9, 98, 110, 126, 133, 138
1944	47, 107, 125
1945	10, 24, 42, 63, 78, 117, 121, 127
1946	8, 9, 13, 18, 22, 25, 32, 34-36, 61, 67, 69, 87, 92, 95, 97, 132
1947	34, 63, 67, 71, 91, 101, 129
1948	4, 7, 9, 10, 12, 19, 21, 25, 33, 50, 55, 61, 63, 95, 98, 99, 109, 113, 118, 128, 135
1949	5, 6, 14, 21, 25, 31, 33, 34, 36, 38, 42, 49, 63, 66-68, 70, 87, 89, 122
1950	4, 10, 32, 47, 52, 66, 68, 70, 72, 87, 101, 109, 136
1951	5, 7, 13, 19, 21, 22, 25, 31, 32, 40, 45, 58, 66, 75, 76, 78, 87, 88, 90, 96, 98-100, 103, 109, 111, 116, 122, 131, 134
1952	5, 18, 27, 44, 51, 63, 71, 77, 89, 95, 101, 102, 107, 113, 116
1953	14, 15, 23, 30, 31, 43, 45, 55, 57, 68, 88, 101, 107, 110, 127, 138
1954	4, 5, 7-9, 14, 42, 46, 50-52, 71, 74, 77, 82, 95, 110-112, 133
1955	8, 12, 14, 32, 38, 42, 47, 51, 53, 56, 63, 68, 75, 90, 99, 107, 111, 112, 114, 123, 134, 137, 139
1956	5, 25, 27, 38, 44, 52, 53, 57, 59, 63, 67, 68, 75, 77, 79, 91, 95, 97, 98, 101, 103, 107-109, 111, 113-115, 136
1957	5, 8-10, 14, 17, 19, 20, 22, 23, 30, 32, 38, 44, 45, 48, 49, 51, 55, 57, 60, 66, 68, 69, 76-79, 82, 86, 89, 95, 98, 99, 103, 104, 108, 114-116, 118, 126, 129, 138
1958	9, 10, 17-20, 24, 33, 34, 36-38, 45, 48, 55, 57, 58, 61, 69, 71, 77, 78, 84, 89, 91,100, 108, 110, 116, 122, 125, 127
1959	6, 15, 22, 24, 35, 36, 47, 56, 69, 77, 83, 84, 87, 94, 96, 101, 109, 120, 131, 134
1960	4, 18, 21, 25-27, 44, 53, 71, 78, 98, 101, 107, 108, 110, 112, 113, 116, 120, 124, 134, 138
1961	6, 9, 17, 24, 25, 36, 37, 46, 47, 74, 101, 102, 131, 138
1962	15, 25, 35, 37, 44, 59, 66, 68, 69, 74, 76, 77, 101, 102, 121, 137
1963	5, 6, 18, 23, 27, 30, 38, 47, 51, 60-63, 67, 78, 80, 84-87, 95, 98, 100, 103, 108, 112, 120, 123, 128, 132-135
1964	6, 12, 18, 21, 24-27, 32, 35, 38, 43, 53, 69, 71, 77, 102, 113, 115, 117, 123, 131, 135
1965	5, 11, 20, 22, 35, 39, 42, 47, 51, 57, 58, 60, 61, 63, 64, 67, 69, 71, 72, 78, 85, 88, 99, 100, 102, 109, 112,115, 118, 122, 124, 125, 131, 138
1966	17, 26, 32, 35, 47, 49, 50, 57, 60, 62, 76, 77, 79, 85, 88, 99, 100, 111, 116, 128, 135
1967	5, 18, 21, 30, 47, 56, 61, 63, 64, 71, 76, 78, 79, 85, 89, 100, 102, 109, 111, 114, 125, 129

(Year Index continued)

1968 .. 4-6, 13, 18, 21, 22, 27, 36, 47, 49, 50, 52, 56, 59-61, 63, 64, 69, 78, 79, 82, 100, 103, 104, 107, 108, 111, 112, 124, 126, 128

1969 .. 6, 9, 10, 12, 26, 35, 45, 59, 67, 75, 78-80, 82, 116, 131, 134, 135, 137

1970 .. 18, 19, 23, 31, 40, 44, 45, 56, 61, 63, 68, 70, 83, 95, 96, 100, 103, 111, 113, 116, 127, 134, 135, 137, 139

1971 . 5, 6, 24, 26, 33-35, 40, 47, 56, 60, 63, 67, 74, 76, 77, 82, 84, 87, 89, 100, 112, 122, 128

1972 .... 6, 9, 10, 18, 27, 34, 40, 60, 67, 69, 71, 100, 113, 136, 137, 139

1973 .. 5, 6, 8, 11, 18, 24-26, 45, 49, 52, 66, 70, 74, 75, 78, 84, 87, 96, 100, 109, 111, 114, 121, 129, 134

1974 . 5-7, 10, 21, 22, 25, 31, 34, 40, 45, 51, 52, 62, 63, 66, 76, 82, 86, 87, 89, 91, 96, 110, 120, 125, 129, 133, 134, 136

1975 .... 5, 6, 9, 11, 21, 23, 27, 42, 43, 55, 64, 75, 82, 87, 107, 123, 134

1976 ...... 8, 18, 24, 31, 40, 52, 55, 69, 70, 75, 91, 96, 98, 99, 104, 114, 117, 121, 123

1977 . 7, 11, 18, 20, 24, 27, 31, 42-44, 50, 52, 61, 69, 70, 74-76, 78, 82, 85, 87-89, 96, 99, 100, 107, 108, 113, 116, 121, 133

1978 .... 6, 18, 34, 71, 74, 78, 79, 83, 84, 86, 91, 98, 107, 117, 134, 136, 139

1979 ... 7, 13, 27, 31, 37, 43, 44, 58, 70, 75, 76, 78, 84, 85, 95, 96, 98, 99, 127

1980 .... 6, 8, 14, 20, 21, 26, 30, 37, 46, 52, 69, 79, 80, 87, 94, 98, 99, 102, 107, 112, 134

1981 .. 7, 8, 18, 43, 53, 70, 75, 98, 100, 108, 120-122, 124, 134

1982 . 5, 8, 18, 27, 34, 56, 57, 59, 64, 66, 69, 76, 77, 80, 82, 88, 94, 96, 99, 102, 115, 131,135

1983 ... 8, 21, 22, 25, 27, 31, 35, 38, 47, 57, 61, 63, 66, 71, 75, 76, 82, 84-86, 88, 90, 91, 94, 98, 99, 102-104, 116,

1983 (contd.) 120, 121, 126, 138

1984 ... 7, 13, 15, 19, 27, 36, 45, 51, 66, 69, 71, 75, 77, 82, 84, ... 86, 98, 103, 112, 120, 122, 127, 134, 140

1985 ... 35-37, 44-47, 57, 60, 61, 66, 76, 80, 84, 85, 90, 91, 94, 98, 108, 116, 120, 123, 131, 134, 140

1986 ... 8, 13, 24, 35-37, 44, 52, 74, 79, 98, 102, 109, 116-118, 120-122, 125, 139, 140

1987 .... 5, 7, 36, 66, 75, 102, 110, 131, 133, 140

1988 .... 18, 42, 43, 55, 63, 66, 69, 70, 74-76, 78, 83, 98, 104, 111, 120, 124, 127, 129, 131, 134, 137

1989 .... 19, 20, 27, 42, 49, 57, 72, 77-80, 87, 89, 94, 99, 102, 114, 120, 132, 139

1990 ..... 19, 37, 44, 45, 58, 60, 63, 67, 80, 84, 102-104, 112, 114, 117, 118, 125, 128, 129, 132, 137, 139

1991 ..... 11, 12, 20, 26, 43, 45, 49, 50, 58, 59, 64, 68, 69, 72, 75-78, 86, 102, 104, 109, 113, 118, 120, 126, 129, 132, 138

1992 .... 8, 11-13, 19, 23, 33, 46, 55, 57, 62, 94, 98, 104, 112, 114, 118, 126, 129, 132, 137

1993 ...... 8, 21, 43, 59, 72, 77, 79, 83, 97, 99, 102, 104, 108, 112, 114, 120, 122-124, 126, 128, 132, 139

1994 .. 5, 7, 8, 11-13, 19, 22, 23, 25, 30, 31, 33, 34, 37, 39, 45, 46, 50, 51, 55-60, 68, 70, 76, 83, 85, 86, 88, 101-104, 110, 114, 115, 117, 123, 125, 127, 128, 131, 135, 139

1995 .... 7, 11-13, 20-24, 30, 32, 36, 37, 39, 40, 43, 46, 57, 59, 61-63, 66, 70, 72, 74, 78-80, 82-84, 86, 87, 98, 103, 104, 107, 110, 112, 114, 117, 120, 125, 126, 132, 135, 137, 139

1996 .. 4, 6, 8-12, 14, 17, 18, 20, 23, 26, 31, 33, 36, 40, 44, 46, 48, 49, 51-53, 55, 56, 58, 62, 63, 67, 69-72, 79, 84-88, 96, 111, 125, 139, 140

1997 .... 23, 31, 48, 60, 62, 68

※※※※※※※※※※※※※※※※※※

143

- Club Index -

Arsenal 10, 15, 17, 18, 21, 22, 25, 26, 30, 31, 36, 37, 44, 46, 47, 51, 55,58, 59, 61, 63,71, 75, 79, 82, 83, 87-89, 91, 108-110, 112-114, 125, 127-129, 131

Aston Villa 4, 7, 8, 10, 12, 14, 18, 21, 25, 26, 32, 35-37, 39, 44, 52, 53,55, 57, 59, 68, 69, 86, 87, 89, 96, 101, 104, 111, 112, 115, 120, 121, 132, 134, 135, 137, 138

Barnsley 11, 14, 30, 44, 68, 96, 97, 110, 111

Birmingham 7, 26, 53, 66, 67, 69-71, 82, 87, 88, 90, 94, 102, 109, 114,125, 129, 140

Blackburn 11, 12, 22, 24-26, 32, 33, 42, 47, 52, 55, 70, 71, 75, 77, 86,94, 96, 108, 113, 121, 122, 132, 139

Blackpool 9, 23, 25, 26, 36, 40, 43-45, 50, 99, 102, 104, 107, 109, 111,121, 127, 131,135, 138

Bolton 4, 5, 9, 10, 26, 30, 34-38, 55, 64, 71, 78, 89, 94, 95, 107, 108,117, 123, 125

Bournemouth 6, 30, 62, 69, 88, 104, 109

Bradford City 4, 20, 68, 92, 94, 103, 116, 117, 120, 121

Brentford 5, 8, 24, 87, 90, 132

Brighton 8, 24, 34, 35, 52, 57, 60, 61, 63, 66, 71, 75, 82, 91, 98, 124, 139

Bristol City 4, 5, 10, 12, 35, 50, 52, 89, 94, 95, 104, 110, 112, 127, 134

Bristol Rovers 12

Burnley 4, 6, 21-24, 26, 31, 33, 34, 38, 44, 46-49, 77, 78, 84, 90, 94, 97,102-104, 107,109, 110, 112, 120, 136

Bury 8, 12, 24, 32, 39, 52, 57, 69, 77, 82, 86, 98, 101

Cambridge United 35, 80

Cardiff 43, 67, 75, 77, 79, 99, 107, 110, 129, 136

Carlisle 6

Charlton Athletic 23, 31, 39, 91, 94, 99, 109, 111, 129, 135

Chelsea 39, 40, 43, 52, 55, 59, 69, 70, 74, 75, 80, 85, 87, 89, 95, 97, 98,100, 112, 120, 121, 129, 138

Chester 8, 48, 110, 113, 136

Chesterfield 34, 53, 57, 117, 124

Colchester 87

Coventry 12, 18, 20, 27, 35, 44, 45, 53, 55, 57, 80, 82, 89, 104, 135, 137

Crewe 14, 36, 69, 104, 108, 116, 127

Crystal Palace 4, 11, 19, 21, 36, 47, 50, 58, 60, 62, 63, 72, 75, 79, 94, 102, 104, 117, 139

Darlington 7, 31, 68, 90

Derby 7, 10, 17, 22, 33, 37, 42, 49, 52, 53, 56, 57, 75, 83, 91, 95,100-102, 108, 109, 111, 112, 115, 117, 121-123, 132, 139

Doncaster 42, 53, 116, 129, 135

Everton 7, 11, 12, 20-22, 25, 37, 52, 53, 57, 60, 61, 64, 66, 75, 78, 83, 85-88, 90, 95, 97,100, 110, 114, 122, 124, 129, 131

Exeter 67, 113, 116, 134

Fulham 10, 12, 24, 36-38, 43, 49, 52, 62, 70, 87, 112, 115

Gillingham 140

Grimsby 4, 8, 9, 19, 38, 42, 46, 47, 49, 79, 90, 92, 99, 138

Hartlepool 99, 124

Huddersfield 10, 25, 30, 32, 34, 67, 68, 75, 99, 116, 122

Hull 31, 39, 52, 70, 83, 90, 102, 124

Ipswich 25, 30, 37, 44, 66, 82, 84, 95, 96, 112, 121, 125

Leeds 5, 6, 9, 13, 20, 24, 26, 32, 36, 37, 39, 48, 50, 52, 59, 62-64, 68, 69, 71, 75, 79, 95-97, 110, 116, 118, 122, 127, 128, 132, 134, 136, 137

Leicester 6, 23, 25, 39, 44, 47, 56, 62, 67, 71, 89, 90, 98, 108, 109, 120, 122-124, 127, 134, 135, 137, 139

Leyton Orient 25, 104, 124

Lincoln 50, 95, 104, 110, 125, 127, 135

Liverpool 5, 7, 12, 17, 22, 23, 30, 31, 34, 36, 38, 42-44, 46-48, 52, 56-59, 61, 63, 67, 69- 71, 75, 76, 82, 84, 85, 87, 88, 94, 96,

(Liverpool contd.) 97, 102, 107, 109, 111, 117, 120, 124, 125, 135, 137

Luton 6, 21, 25, 31, 38, 71, 82, 98, 104, 108, 124, 135, 138

Macclesfield 69, 82

Manchester City 4, 6, 7, 9, 10, 12, 17, 19, 23, 25, 34, 36, 37, 44, 46, 48-52, 55, 56, 59, 63,74, 75, 79, 82, 86, 94, 97, 100, 102, 104, 108, 110, 112, 115-117, 121-124, 131, 132, 135, 136, 138

Mansfield 10, 31, 71, 110

Middlesbrough 6, 8, 23, 30, 33, 36, 37, 52, 55, 56, 60, 72, 88, 91, 97, 98, 101, 102, 117, 128, 133, 139

Millwall 27, 42, 56, 89, 90, 95, 99, 100, 115, 117, 138

Newcastle 4, 7, 8, 15, 24, 26, 31, 34, 35, 38, 39, 45, 68, 74, 75, 77, 82, 83, 85, 89, 90, 95, 97-99, 101-103, 110-112, 117, 134, 135

Northampton 19, 24, 90, 103

Norwich 9, 17, 102, 127, 137, 140

Nottingham Forest 10, 15, 24, 25, 37, 40, 46, 47, 52, 61, 62, 77-80, 84, 91, 98, 102, 118,126, 127, 135, 138

Notts County 18, 21, 69, 79, 115, 138

Oldham 11, 14, 17, 31, 38, 44-46, 50, 58, 84, 86, 88, 100, 109, 110, 116, 118, 122, 124, 127, 138

Oxford 5, 26, 35, 55, 120

Peterborough 27, 68, 75

Plymouth Argyle 4, 5, 34, 39, 90, 95, 109

Port Vale 20, 44, 50, 69, 90, 101, 109, 115, 117, 125, 128, 136

Portsmouth 38, 47, 69, 76, 80, 113, 122, 140

Preston 5, 13, 14, 18, 21, 24, 34, 38, 60, 67, 75, 82, 89, 91, 101, 111, 113, 115, 116, 118, 121, 136

Queen's Park Rangers 35, 42, 43, 51, 66, 87-90, 98, 99, 107, 131

Reading 8, 10, 14, 27, 80, 89

Rochdale 44, 69, 84, 96, 122

Rotherham 67, 75, 89, 111

Scunthorpe 71, 122

Sheffield United 4, 63, 87, 95, 112, 115, 132

Sheffield Wednesday 12, 17, 22, 24, 35, 37, 44, 45, 49, 56, 84, 88, 91, 102, 109, 110, 116, 123, 125, 127, 134, 135, 138

Shrewsbury 34, 45, 53, 75, 116

Southampton 5, 9, 12, 19, 24, 27, 31, 34, 37, 43, 44, 46, 51, 52, 55-57, 66, 75, 82, 87, 94, 101, 102, 110, 113, 117, 121, 126, 128, 134

Southend 39, 138

Stockport 18, 30, 36, 37, 46, 56, 62, 84, 91, 95, 98, 101, 129, 133

Stoke 6, 7, 12, 32, 34, 47, 49, 53, 57, 59, 67, 69, 75, 82, 88, 96, 99, 101, 102, 113, 116,132, 134, 135

Sunderland 9, 10, 13, 23, 27, 32, 37, 43, 45-50, 52, 58, 101, 122, 123, 128, 129, 134

Swansea 13, 21, 61, 70, 77, 109, 116, 121, 131

Swindon 18, 53, 66, 67, 103, 116, 127

Torquay 63, 67, 115

Tottenham 4, 6, 9, 13, 17, 18, 31, 42, 46, 55, 59, 63, 75, 85, 95, 101, 108, 112, 123, 125,129, 131, 133, 135

Tranmere 75, 98, 123, 126

Walsall 26, 32, 42, 128

Watford 36, 44, 45, 56, 77, 89, 96, 124, 126

West Bromwich 6, 8, 24, 27, 35, 36, 44, 51, 53, 55, 60, 61, 75-77, 87, 88, 90, 98, 102, 108,109, 119, 122, 134-138

West Ham 11, 12, 17, 27, 45, 56, 57, 63, 66, 67, 69, 70, 98, 100, 104, 110, 112-114, 117, 133

Wigan 36, 104, 111

Wimbledon 18, 58, 67, 86, 137

Wolverhampton 8, 38, 42, 50, 51, 55, 57, 96, 108, 109, 112, 117, 137, 138

Wrexham 10, 35, 74, 108, 109, 121, 132, 133

York 40, 71, 116

144